Advancing the Witches' Craft

ALIGNING YOUR MAGICKAL SPIRIT
THROUGH MEDITATION, EXPLORATION,
AND INITIATION OF THE SELF

by Lord Foxglove

NEW PAGE BOOKS
A division of The Career Press, Inc.
Franklin Lakes, NJ

ADVANCING THE WITCHES' CRAFT
EDITED BY JODI BRANDON
TYPESET BY EILEEN DOW MUNSON
Cover design by Cheryl Cohan Finbow
Printed in the U.S.A. by Book-mart Press

To order this title, please call toll-free 1-800-CAREER-1 (NJ and Canada: 201-848-0310) to order using VISA or MasterCard, or for further information on books from Career Press.

The Career Press, Inc., 3 Tice Road, PO Box 687,
Franklin Lakes, NJ 07417
www.careerpress.com
www.newpagebooks.com

Library of Congress Cataloging-in-Publication Data

Foxglove, Lord.
    Advancing the witches craft : aligning your magickal spirit through meditation, exploration, and initiation of the self / by Lord Foxglove.
        p. cm.
    Includes bibliographical references and index.
    ISBN 1-56414-811-4 (pbk.)
    1. Witchcraft. 2. Magic. I. Title.

BF1566.F69 2005
133.4'3--dc22

2004065576

I dedicate this work

to the same person
to whom I have dedicated every breath
that remains of my life on our beautiful mother earth:
my patient and loving wife,

Lady Becca,

whose endless and unquenchable thirst for knowledge
was the muse for the teachings that I humbly
offer within the covers of this book.

An artist has a palette of colors from which to choose to create his work.

Much in the same way as the artist, an author also chooses from their palette of words to write about that which has yet to be described. An artist mixes the colors of red and blue together on his palette and creates the perfect shade of purple; an author mixes red and blue in his mind and suddenly the word *claret* materializes on the page to describe the color that he wants the reader to envision. Both the artist and the author begin with a blank canvas. Both must somehow find a way to re-create the vision in their mind and render it onto the white sea of nothingness that is the blank canvas or the empty sheet of paper.

At one point or another in the creation of this book, many people rolled up their sleeves and went to work with me to bring "dimension to the dimensionless idea." I would like to take this opportunity to thank and bless each and every one of them.

First and foremost, blessings and thanks to Barbara Ardinger, without whose unwavering (although sometimes stubborn) guidance and support, my true author's voice might never have been found. Just as I tell my students what they need to hear, she has never told me what I *wanted* to hear but what I *needed* to hear, and that has made all of the difference in the world.

To my best friends, Tim and Tina Fiducci, who believed in me and my hopes for this book and from the very beginning reassured me that it was never a question of *if,* it was only a question of *when*. To the beautiful and talented artist Carol Rosinski, endless thanks for honoring me with the wonderful drawings you created for the pages of this book. Special thanks go out to Gavin Bone and Janet Farrar for their priceless insights and suggestions. To Stanley Modrzyk, for deciphering all of the legal mumbo-jumbo and for accepting a bottle of mead in payment for his services. To Lori Nyx, Denise Dumars, and the grey wizard himself, Oberon Zell-Ravenheart, for their amazingly powerful words of insight and inspiration. Finally, to Ron Fry, Michael Lewis, Kirsten Beucler, and everyone else both seen and unseen at New Page Books for all of their hard work and inspiration.

Most of all, my greatest thanks go to acquisitions editor Michael Pye for his unwavering support and belief in me and in this project from the very beginning. Your help, patience, time, and dedication will never be forgotten.

I thank you all for your priceless additions to my work.

Lord Foxglove

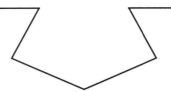

Contents

Section IV: The Book of Shadow, 283

Section V: The Conclusion, 315

The Shadow's Edge

Between the covers of this book you will find no chapters on reading the tarot or how to construct a magick wand. No history of Witchcraft, no retracing of pagan roots, nor how to live life as a Witch. No degree systems, no handholding, no Wicca 101 fluff. This book is about *the power of advanced and eclectic Witchcraft*. This book is about the discovery and development of your inner strength and how, through the development of your inner strength, you can make contact with your true magickal self and obtain a flow of power and balance far beyond anything you have ever imagined.

I am sure that I would be preaching not only to the choir but to the entire magickal congregation if I were to point out that the Wiccan/pagan community as a whole is made up of a group of very strong-willed, opinionated, and diverse individuals. We all come from different backgrounds, traditions, and learning experiences. For every thousand readers of this book (or, for that matter, *any* book on the subject of Witchcraft), there will be a thousand differing opinions as to what the book meant to them and how they felt about the views that were expressed by the book's author. Keeping this in mind, there are probably a few things that I should discuss with you before you begin doing the work in this book.

You will most likely find words, phrases, and symbolisms in the text of this book that could be interpreted in a number of different ways. For example, many have pointed out to me that much of my work appears to be very shamanic in nature and that many of my references and comparisons could easily be related to Jungian psychology. I will say the following to you as plainly as I can. If you want to learn about shamanic magick, then read a book about shamanism by Michael Harner or Mircea Eliade. If you want to study Jungian psychology, then study Carl Jung. I am by no means a scholar or an expert in either of these areas, and I would be doing you a great disservice and disrespecting you by claiming that I was. As I understand it, any magickal work in which you delve into your own underworld and explore the realms of shadow is by its very nature shamanistic. At the end of the day, widely used and believed in or not, Jungian psychology is still just a theory.

As I went about the process of writing this book, the labor of love that you are this very moment holding in your hands, I found myself wearing many different faces, speaking with many different voices, and taking on many different forms. This became necessary when I made the decision to throw the "textbook" approach to writing a book about Witchcraft out the window and by taking a decidedly more intimate approach. As together we walk the path that lies before us, I will be wearing the face of the guide and the guardian, the companion and the friend. I will be speaking to you with the voice of both the teacher and the student. I will be taking on the form of the sage and the mystic, the psychologist and the shaman.

Over the centuries, magick has worn many different faces and taken on many different forms. As each new magician adds his or her own unique face and form to the cauldron of magick, what is in the cauldron becomes more and more diverse. The cauldron must therefore expand to accommodate these new faces and forms. If we could see into the mind of a modern Witch and look into his or her magickal spirit, we would see the shamans and druids of old chanting their mystic spells to the earth and to their gods in hopes of revealing the very mysteries of life itself. We would see the secret meetings of the Golden Dawn and the first assemblages of Gardnerian covens reviving the old ways and writing the liturgies of a new religion. We would see the divinatory magick of the ancient mystics and the eclectic practices of contemporary conjurers blending together to create a new breed of magicians.

Every step in the magickal timeline has influenced and impacted each of our spiritual lives. Each of us carries within us the sum, both the old and the new, of the magickal spirit itself. Just as those who have come before me have, and as will all who come after, I add my own unique face and form to the cauldron of magick. I have absorbed the very essence of Witchcraft, and so shall you see its magickal spirit in me and in my writings.

Each of us sees in anything what it is we wish to see. Each of us believes in the things in which we choose to believe. If seeing is truly believing, then magick is something that must be believed to truly be seen....

—Lord Foxglove

The Shadow and the Flame, or Who Is Your Shadow Spirit?

You have been asleep for far too long and now you
must awake,
For the day has already begun and there is much to do.
Return now, gentle dreamer, to your reality, and I'll return
to mine.

—Anonymous

The following definitions from the American Heritage Dictionary point to my use of two very important words:

Shadow. n. A mirrored image or reflection.

Spirit. n. A supernatural being.

What would you do if I told you that one of the most powerful magickal forces imaginable was out there right now, waiting for you to make contact, and that I could show you how to do so? And how would you feel if I told you that, not only were you its creator, but that it was, in fact, a facet of yourself that you never knew existed? To discover the true form of your shadow spirit, we must travel back in time to a very special day in your life: the day you took your first small steps onto the path of Witchcraft.

At the very moment you knew without question that you were a Witch, you felt the power of realization flowing through your spirit, and something quite amazing and unexpected happened. Not only had you performed your very first act of true magick, and perhaps the most powerful act of Witchcraft you will ever know, but also, without realizing it, you had projected the sum of your desire onto the astral plane and created an entity of unimaginable power and potential. Your longing for what lies beyond the veil gave birth to your counterpart in the astral world. This astral counterpart is your shadow spirit, your *other*.

Explaining the mechanics of this creation to you would be nearly impossible. How do you put into words the feeling of receiving the call to magick or the sound of the Goddess's voice inside your mind? How do you relate to someone the feeling of that one perfect moment in time, when you knew that your life had changed and was never going to be the same again? *I* cannot put your magick into words, but *you* can. I want you to think back and try to recall the very moment that you felt magick flowing through you for the very first time…. Do you remember? That moment was a spell. The very first spell you cast, and a very powerful spell of creation it was. At that moment, you focused the intense energy of a brand new Witch being born into the Craft. You projected that energy beyond the veil and your magickal twin was born. Your shadow spirit sprung into being.

It was your fascination with magick and yearning for the unknown that created your shadow spirit, and it is with those very same ambitions that you can unlock its secrets and join with it in a union of power and balance unlike anything you have ever known before.

I will be your companion on your journey to meet your *other*. Together we will walk the path of the shadow spirit and discover the whole of your power and potential. You will watch walls that you never knew existed crumble and become dust at your feet. You will know for the first time the real truth behind what you thought was balance. For all of your efforts, you will be rewarded at the end of the long and arduous journey that lies ahead with a magickal companion who holds all the keys to all the doors you could never before open on your own.

Are you ready? Then let us begin....

Your shadow spirit is not contained in, nor limited to, the physical boundaries that we experience as humans. Our bodies, the vessels through which we make our way through our earthbound experience, have as many weaknesses as strengths, and as many demands, too. Our bodies require such things as food, water, and rest to retain life and function properly. Our muscles hurt when we overuse them. Our skin grows thin and our eyes dim with age. A simple microscopic organism that we cannot even see with the naked eye can render us all but useless for a time and, in some cases, even end our lives.

Our shadow spirit on the astral faces none of these weaknesses or limitations. You will discover, however, that your physical and magickal well-being can have a direct impact on your shadow spirit. Your shadow spirit is as much a reflection of you as you are of it, and you can affect each other directly. Who exactly your shadow spirit is, I cannot say for I am not you, and *only you* can make this discovery and unlock its secrets. As you will see, the possibilities are endless, but the veils, some small and some deeply entangled in mystery, that hang between you and your shadow spirit must first be lifted one by one. My job, as the author of this book and the guide on this adventure, is to simply light a candle that will illuminate a small part of the path that lies ahead. This little light will also allow you to step outside yourself for a time and see things from a different vantage. Your *other*, a word I will frequently use to refer to your shadow spirit, has probably only been as aware of you as you have been aware of it: a fleeting shadow, an intuitive guess, a powerful flow of energy that washed over you that felt all too familiar, but then vanished as quickly as it arrived. You have only felt echoes from the other side of the mirror. The reality of the shadow spirit was so simple that it was in front of you the whole time, and yet you never saw it. You looked beyond it, beckoning to the gods and goddesses to hear your pleas and unlock the secrets of the mysterious unknown, when the whole time you should have been looking a little bit closer to home for the answers. As Doreen Valiente put it so eloquently in her Charge of the Goddess: "If that which you seek you find not within you shall never find without." Your shadow spirit is a reflection of *your* inner power, not someone or some *thing* else's.

As a Witch, you have been intuitively drawn to the forces and realms that lie beyond this world. It is as if something in your life has been incomplete without these forces and realms. You have not been wrong, only limited by your earthbound needs and existence. Your *other* has never known the earthly pleasures you have experienced. Love and hate. Life and the value that death brings to it. The juice of an apple as it flows through your mouth and down your chin. The warmth of a loved one's embrace and the feeling of loneliness when that loved one is away from your side.

On the other side of the veil, your shadow spirit holds the magickal balance. It doesn't have to try to access the Akashic Records; it simply walks through the doors of the library, pulls the books of mystery from the shelves, and absorbs the knowledge it finds.

Your *other* dwells in its reality of endless time, space, and possibility. It feels no need to be apologetic for who it is or what it does. It exists knowingly within the balance of light and dark the universe holds. It has no time for, or understanding of, "can't," "won't," "don't," "couldn't," or "shouldn't." It is a being of pure magickal energy that you have created.

Because you are its creator, and it is your magickal twin on the spirit plane, the possibilities are endless. Imagine a guide in the Akasha that in its most basic form is an astral projection of your magickal self. Have you ever wanted to look beyond the veil between the worlds unimpeded by your physical form? Ride the spiral of time to any point you desire? Join with the energies of the gods and goddesses in their realm rather than always have to invite them to yours? Possess the deepest spiritual intuition combined with the most effortless magickal flow you can possibly conceive? *Your shadow spirit is the key.* Though it has had some small role to play in every act of magick you have ever performed, it is also one of the most elusive and deeply veiled entities you will ever encounter. Unlock the mystery of the shadow spirit and your only limitation will be what *it* reflects in the mirror: you.

The path of the shadow spirit is not a simple one. It is potentially not devoid of peril. To walk this path, you will have to erase and relearn many things. It will take an iron will and steadfast conviction along with patience, time, effort, and, above all, courage. In the end, if your motives are corrupt or wavering, there may be a hefty price to pay. But if you are successful, you may become one of the most balanced, most powerful Witches who have ever existed. Going forward from here means leaving limitation and impossibility at the threshold. Lock the door behind you as you leave. You're going to be gone awhile.

Before we go any further, I offer this one warning: *Manifestation in its entirety of your shadow spirit into this world or you into its world is unacceptable and dangerous.* Although aligning with your shadow spirit can (and will) erase many of the boundaries between the worlds, removing these boundaries completely would be catastrophic. The work in this book should only be attempted by those who are already well trained in the arts of Witchcraft or who have an extremely competent teacher and guide.

Just as we change the lives of everyone we meet, know, love, and, hate, and just as we bring change into the world with everything we touch and every breath we take, so also do we affect our shadow spirit. Working with your shadow spirit will affect and change you forever.

The Journey of Self

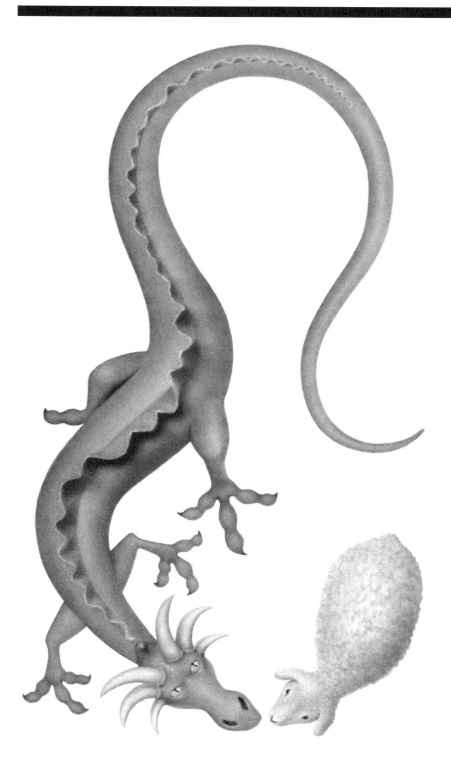

Hanging in the Balance

*A*ll things being equal, we need to take steps to ensure that the meeting between you and your *other* and the changes that will inevitably occur are as positive and mutually beneficial as they can be. Do not, however, deceive yourself with the notion that all of these changes will be good. You and I and every living person or creature on earth and force on the astral hold an element of balance within. To everything we touch and everyone we know, we bring as much light as darkness, as much life as death, as much harmony as discord. This is the way of the universe, of both the macrocosm and the microcosm. But this is not something to fear.

Instead, let us embrace this balance. As seekers on the path and travelers through the veils of mystery, we should strive to understand this balance and become one with it. To do otherwise would be to reject the natural order of things and deny others and ourselves the true beauty of the gift that's known as our existence. Your shadow spirit, your reflection on the astral, is as much a part of your magickal balance as you are a part of its magickal balance. Together, you can become the perfect mixture of light and dark, yin and yang, flame and shadow, widdershins and deosil. You cannot do anything without using these energies as they naturally exist together in balance, and any attempt to separate them would be futile and bring about dysfunction and inertia.

Try taking the battery out of your car and trying to start it, and you will see what I mean. Negative and positive flows of energy working together in harmony within a single cell (the battery) means you get to work on time. Protons and neutrons being orbited by electrons within an atom means you get to experience this thing called life. Energy flowing and counter-flowing through the cosmos means you get to practice Witchcraft. These balanced energies flow through every living and magickal thing. Accept this and move forward. Deny it and stagnate. The choice is yours and yours alone.

So much emphasis has been placed upon the separation of these energies as "good" or "evil" that it has become second nature to view them as such. It is now up to you to erase the dogma that Hollywood, society, and the religions of jealous gods have forced down our throats where these energies are concerned. It is time to purge yourself of this deception once and for all. Lose *their* concept of these energies, realize your own concept, and the truth will stand naked before you.

Do dark forces and evil people exist? Of course they do. Can they harm you physically, emotionally, or spiritually? Of course they can. Am I asking you to open yourself to these energies? To gain total understanding of them and then align yourself with them?

Of course I am.

I can read your mind. "Yikes! He wants me to do what? Why would I ever want to do that? What could I possibly have to gain by opening myself to dark or negative energies? I am a good person and a good Witch. I would never have any use for such powers or energies."

Wrong. Way wrong.

First, calm yourself. Second, I would never suggest to any of you that you use dark or negative energies or powers against anyone or anything, and that includes against yourself. Only you can truly understand your concept of right and wrong, and it is not my purpose to change that. I suggest, however, that these energies that flow in opposite directions—light and dark, negative and positive, call them what you will—are neither inherently good nor evil.

They are subject to the same rules and laws that everything else is. They are simply streams of energy that flow and exist in balance. It is all how we use and bend them that makes them what they are.

Let's break this down a bit further, shall we? We need to view both of these opposing streams of energy as colorless. Not black or white, not good or evil. Get it? *Either* of these streams is capable of causing great harm or generating a fantastic outcome. As a Witch, you have learned how to use and bend energy to your will. That being so, you need to drop the notion that, by using an opposing stream of energy, you are using some "dark power." I am not suggesting that there are not pockets or pools of energy, entities both earthbound and on the astral, that are out of balance. To us, these energies or entities might feel dark or even evil in some way. But we must come to the realization that these are separate and different from the natural flows of energy I am referring to. Just imagine how much easier it would be for you to recognize and disperse unbalanced energies once you have attained perfect balance and alignment with them yourself.

I'm reading your mind again. You're a pretty darned balanced individual, right? And because you are balanced, none of your magickal workings have ever caused harm to anyone or brought about an undesirable outcome. Correct?

Wrong again.

How many times in your life have you learned that someone has inflicted some sort of emotional, spiritual, or physical harm that fell under the umbrella of what they called their "best intentions"? How many times has this happened to you? Ah, yes, I thought so. Are you beginning to understand? Every action has an opposite and equal reaction. The goal here is not to use opposing energies to inflict harm or practice black magick, but to gain complete understanding of them and eventually control over them.

Let us now take a deeper look at the word *align*.

The American Heritage Dictionary gives the following definitions of this word: (1) to adjust to produce a proper relationship or orientation, and (2) to arrange in a line or so as to be parallel. These are our goals: to adjust ourselves to these energies and form the correct relationship with them. To learn to manipulate, interact with, or deflect them. To discover how they affect our physical and spiritual personas and inner selves. Finally, to learn how to hang in perfect balance between these two parallel flows of energy.

Let us begin by removing once and for all the negative connotations associated with these energies. We will no longer be using words and phrases such as *good and evil, light and dark, negative and positive,* or *widdershins and deosil.*

We must also learn to view these streams for what they really are: opposite flows of energy that already contain perfect balance within themselves. It is now our mission to detect the patterns and signatures within these energies and discover how they relate to us, to themselves, and to the universe that contains them. We must learn to reprogram our subconscious to erase fear, doubt, and bigotry that we associate with these dynamics. To describe these energies we will use new words: *flow* (to push or stream out) and *counter-flow* (to spiral or draw within), *reflect* (to manifest or create) and *deflect* (to prevent or redirect).

Understanding this concept of balance is imperative to your growth as a person and as a Witch. It is what you must learn to accept and accomplish before you join with your *other*. As far as these energies are concerned, ignorance is *not* bliss. Just because you didn't know that your next-door neighbor was a murderer doesn't change the fact that he is. Just because it was not your intention to cause harm by your action, inaction, or reaction to something does not change the fact that the unintentional harm did happen.

Although most of us (myself included) will perhaps never become so aware of the reality of energy that we never harm anything or anyone, or become able to psychically sniff out the killer next door, by aligning ourselves with the flows and counter-flows of energy within all things we *can* become more powerful and better attuned than we ever thought possible. We can evolve into higher, more responsible practitioners of the magickal arts. One day, one of us may sense and prevent a tragic act before it occurs. That possibility alone is worth the effort of rediscovering balance and aligning with our shadow spirit.

The time is now to reconsider and relearn what balance is. The expanse between you and your *other* is wide. It is time to close the gap.

The exercises that follow are the first labyrinths that you must navigate to be able to join with your shadow spirit. Beyond that, however, these exercises can enrich you in many other ways. Though the ultimate goal of this first series of exercises is to help you rediscover balance and rejoin it with the proper alignment, walking these paths will also allow you to experience wonderful new journeys that can give you deep insight as to who you really are and show you how to ascend to who you truly want to be. They will also allow you the first glimpse of your shadow spirit, although without direct interaction for now.

At the beginning of each exercise is a keyword that embodies the essence and spirit of what it is you need to learn before moving on. Every step brings you closer to the time of joining with your *other*.

Flow: The Twilight Pool

In each of the journeys you will be taking to rediscover balance, you will need to attain a deep meditative state. I will assume that if you are reading a book on advanced Witchcraft you already know how to do this. For this reason, you will not find a chapter explaining how to meditate. As you work through these exercises, you will establish a method to gain quick access to the realm you are about to create. Yes, I said *realm*. The first thing you need to accomplish is to build a world within a void. This is where you will perform the following exercises in balance. It is also where you will, piece by piece, create a place of power that you will use to commune with your shadow spirit from this time forward.

We cannot read from an earthly book while in a meditative state, so you have some choices. You can have these exercises read to you by someone you trust. You can commit each exercise to memory before you begin it. Or use the audio CD included with this book. I highly recommend using the CD.

I will be traveling with you into this unknown realm. Before we begin our journey, let us recite the following Invocation for protection and strength in our travels.

I call to the Goddess of Magick and of the Night! I call to the God of Power and of the Sun! Hear me and grant me your protection and strength as I embark on this quest for knowledge and balance with you and within all things. Shield me from all harm, but gift me with an open mind and spirit so that I may grow and learn, and rise ever closer to you.

Let us begin. Assume a comfortable position and we will set out on our journey into a state of deep meditation and begin construction of your shadow realm. Using your normal method for meditation, begin now, but do not try to envision any particular thing or place. Just achieve a deeply relaxed state of being.

You are not traveling to a time or to a place, but into nothingness. A complete and absolute void surrounds you. Even my voice is the sound of the void itself. There is nothing to touch or see. You do not feel hot or cold. You can feel no sensation of any kind, only the peace and solitude of emptiness. There is no ground beneath you, no sky above you. Free from ties of any kind, you float in the vastness of the void. Your mind is barren of concern or thought. You are only aware of floating inside of nothingness. You are calm, relaxed, and completely free. You are more at peace with yourself and your surroundings than you have ever been before. Drift here for a time until you become one with this emptiness.

Now you hear a sound that does not startle you. Instead, it draws your interest to an area of space directly below you. As you look down, you see that somehow a pile of stones has appeared within the void. They are the manifested symbols of the first building blocks. You envisioned them the moment you learned you would be constructing a shadow realm. Without physically touching these stones, examine them carefully. Take note of their size, shape, and color.

Now that you are familiar with these stones, you realize that it is now up to you to use them to construct something. But what? You notice that lying next to the pile of stones is a perfectly rolled parchment. It is bound by a simple black ribbon. You pick up this scroll and run your fingers over it, feeling the roughness of the paper and the smoothness of the ribbon. As you untie it, the ribbon vanishes into the void, and the scroll floats out of your hands and unrolls itself before you. On the parchment, in what appears to have been written by a very artistic and ancient hand, appear five words:

Blueprint for a Mirror Frame.

This, and nothing more.

It appears that the architect neglected to finish the plans. You are puzzled by this, but only for a moment. Soon you are astonished to see that very faint lines and words are beginning to form on the parchment. As their vagueness slowly begins to give way to crisp clean lines, you suddenly realize that *you* are the draftsman. This is a drawing of the mirror frame you envisioned the very moment you read the title on the parchment. You must now decide where construction of the stone frame will begin. But do not begin building it just yet.

Carefully choose a place in the void that feels right. This is where you will be able to work readily.

You are now satisfied with your decision. Using only magick and your will, move the stones to the spot you have chosen. Do not physically touch them.

You are eager to begin work. So you mentally lift the first stone, marveling at its beauty. Suddenly you realize that something is needed to bond the stones together.

Without warning, to your left, a small shimmering pool of energy appears. If pressed to describe it, you might liken it to moonlight reflecting off the ripples in a slowly moving stream. As you examine this pool more closely, you see that it is slowly spinning in reverse. It is a counter-flow of energy. You have the perception that all time is rotating within its vortex. Gazing upon it makes you feel as if you could draw the very breath of magick itself from its center and manifest it inside of you.

Before you can contemplate this wonder any further, to your right another pool of energy appears. It comes as quickly and deliberately as the first. It does not shimmer in quite the same way as the other, however. The rays shining off of this pool are brighter and more intense. They look like unobstructed sunlight reflecting off the points on a mighty ocean wave. Between its bright flashes of light, you see that the energies in this pool are advancing in a forward flow. As you look deeper, you can see all life circling within this pool in perfect harmony.

These two pools of energy fascinate you, and you open yourself completely to them. You focus your mind to gain deeper concentration, and you raise an open hand to the pool of counter-flow energy. You tug at it just enough to feel its tingle, but not enough to draw it to you. You lift your other hand to the pool of flow energy to your right, and experience it in the same way.

Like a dream within a dream, still yourself for a time. Using only your third eye, experience the sensations of these two energy pools. Become acquainted with the differences between them and how the flow and counter-flow behave.

Now that you feel you have gained a good understanding of the flow and counter-flow within these pools, you bring your attention back to the void. Far off in the distance, to your left, you can see an unmistakable vision of moonlight. But you cannot see the moon from which it beams.

To your right, you see the light of the sun, just as if it has barely broken the horizon. But you cannot see the sun itself, as it has not yet fully risen. The lights from both sources grow stronger and more intense, each threatening to overcome the other, when suddenly a great surge of power pervades the void. Sunlight and moonlight intermingle and become one. Sun and moon now hang together in perfect balance. Twilight illuminates your realm and shall from this time forward. The very first recognizable symbols now exist within your realm. A ghostly crescent floats above the pool of counter-flow, and a softly glowing golden orb hangs over the pool of flow. From these pools of the sun and the moon, of flow and counter-flow, you will be able to draw power and create anything you need within your realm. You realize that equal parts from each pool must be used to maintain a balance within these energies.

Now that you have experienced these two flows without prejudice, it is time to bring your magickal self to full attention within the void.

It is time to mix some mortar.

Once again, you extend your hand toward the moon pool and draw from it a ball of counter-flow energy. As you feel its power pulse and revolve around your hand and wrist, you are charged with anticipation. You beckon to the sun pool with your other hand and pull from it an equal amount of flow energy. You hold it tightly in your grasp. You draw in a deep breath and feel the ball of counter-flow energy as it builds in strength and its spiral gains in momentum. You breathe out and the ball of flow energy balloons and pulses with unbelievable power.

The two forces are attracted to each other like the opposite poles of a magnet. It takes all of your effort to keep them apart. You find the strength to keep them separated for a few more moments, but they are growing stronger. You feel their energies enveloping your arms and flowing down your sides and around your legs. They stream back toward your hands.

Now they are moving faster with each pass. They are building to a blur of speed and power. Faster and faster, they flow around you. Faster and faster. You quickly envision the mirror. With all of your will, you spread your arms as far apart as you can. You push and hold. You see the image of the mirror frame in your mind. It is the goal. You stop resisting and release the energies!

The streams join together with the force of a super-collider and blast forward into the pile of stones. Creation explodes before you in a plume of power. A shockwave of magickal energy races outward toward you. But you are not afraid. You open yourself completely to the surging flood of power and energy. As it reaches you, you extend your entire being toward it in wonder and anticipation, and you merge with it like water into water, and you flow with it through the void. It washes you up, higher and higher. The void fills with energy, and you feel as though you are spinning perfectly within it, flowing forward and spiraling inward at the same time. Now you feel a tremendous thrust of speed. You are being propelled around the perimeter of a gigantic circle. You see that the energy flood is creating a massive wall of stone that is encircling the void. You realize that the boundaries of your realm are being created. The protective walls of energy that will guard it are being formed. Faster and faster you fly, higher and higher in a cone of power, until at last the flood of energy fills the circle.

At last, you feel yourself slowly becoming solid again. You are returning to your self as you separate from the flood. The flowing tides of energy have lost their momentum. You feel all movement stop within the void.

And now there is nothing.

You hang in the absolute center of your realm, in perfect balance, feeling cleansed and renewed by the tides of energy. You have been bathed in energy, and now the bath begins to trickle off and drain away. As it flows down and away, you see that it is returning to the moon pool. As the last of this stream glides into the pool, you notice that a single drop of energy from the diminishing stream splashes into the pool of the sun. The golden orb floating above the sun pool flashes and a brilliant spinning prism of crystalline energy floats gracefully up from the pool. The colors are unlike anything you have ever seen before.

Glints of light sparkle and dance over each facet of the prism as the light pulses in and out. It dangles for a moment over the sun pool, as if held by a single gossamer thread, then it gently rises and glides toward the mirror frame constructed of stone and magick. In a final flash, as if the light itself sees that there is no looking glass inside the frame, the energy crystal enters the stone frame and floats in its center.

The colors in the crystal begin to blur. The crystal melts and flows forth like liquid metal and fills the frame, creating a mirror that reflects from either side of the frame. You see that one side of the mirror cascades downward like living water and churns and bubbles at the base of the frame. Gazing upon the mirror, you feel peaceful and pleasant. It stirs your memory and you recall the very first sunrise you ever beheld.

As you move around and look at the frame from the other side, you observe that the mirror on this side is flowing upward toward the top of the frame. The edges of the mirror ripple and stir in a subtle awakening of promise and magick. A distant, almost phosphorescent light pervades its surface. You feel as if you are witnessing the genesis of moonlight itself.

Entranced, you move towards this new curiosity with fascination and hope. You reach towards the mirror, eager to touch it. But you don't touch it yet.

It is now time for you to leave.

The awakening world beckons to you and you must answer its summons. You have accomplished much this day. Now it is time to find reverence within yourself for this fact. You instantly find yourself very relaxed and untroubled by concern or desire. You empty your mind and begin to float upwards towards your earthly self. Slowly, softly, you are floating toward the reality of the world.

You are very near the edge now, between your shadow realm and the mundane. Very close, but just before you cross over, without longing or anticipation, you focus your eyes for one last glimpse of your new domain.

You see the pools of flow and counter-flow, sun and moon, still powerful, but growing distant and vague. You see mighty walls of stone, a symbolic barrier that now encircles what was a void only moments ago. A strange sight suddenly catches your attention. A simple orb of glass appears before you, almost within your reach. Floating inside it is an ornate silver key with a glistening golden tip. You start to reach for it, but you are suddenly distracted by movement from below. A shadowy figure appears within the cascade of the mirror. It raises a hand as if to touch the looking glass from the other side.

You are coming back now. You are waking up in *three, two,* and *one.*

You have piqued someone's interest.

Chapter 2

Reflections in the Stream

$\mathcal{I}$f you have not already done so, now is the time for deep reflection upon what you have accomplished and what you have created. You need to examine all aspects of your first experience, carefully and without delusion. You may very well be excited and eager to move on, but take some time to look back upon your first journey and dig below the surface to find its deeper meaning. Reflect on all aspects of your expedition into the void and ask yourself some hard questions.

What, if anything, have you learned or rediscovered? Do you feel any different about yourself and your limitations than you did before? Is the concept of the shadow spirit still deeply perplexing to you, or have the veils begun to thin? Has the experience changed your outlook in any way, or are you still uncomfortable with the concept of flow and counter-flow that I introduced? If your answer to that last question was yes, then I suggest that you spend more time in meditation. Find out why you feel uncomfortable before you move to the next exercise. You can do this in any way you desire, but I press you not to return to the shadow realm for any reason until you are ready to navigate the next labyrinth. There will come a time when you will be able to access and develop your new world at will, and I am not trying to prevent you from doing so. You must, however, understand that the guidelines and exercises in this book are very important first steps and must be completed one by one to reach the goal. Your safety and development must come before anything else.

The spirit of the first exercise was *flow,* or the movement of universal energies and how we interact with them and how they relate to us. I suspect that you felt comfortable with the use of flow energy before you began the first exercise but were probably uneasy about using the counter-flow. By now hopefully you have abandoned at least some of the negative connotations and fears associated with counter-flow. Some uncertainty will, of course, remain for a time, but this will eventually be erased by your realignment and relearning of balance. Our use of this energy stream is entirely natural. You should begin to feel this more and more as you continue to clean the pipes that have been clogged with fear and mistrust.

Until you gain a complete understanding of the counter-flow and begin to feel at ease with using it, however, you will continue to filter out a great deal of its power and potential. Because you have been taught that the counter-flow is something dark and negative and should never be used for any reason, you have pushed away much of the power and potential that was at your fingertips all along. You have been disturbing the natural balance of the flows and have denied yourself your full potential as a human being and a Witch. You have also been draining power away from the flowing energy you have been using and weakening that stream as well. How? I will tell you.

To be able hang in perfect balance with flowing and counter-flowing energies and bring them to the height of their power, you need to become what I call an *omnidirectional practitioner of the magickal arts.* This is a magician who has the ability to send and receive energy to and from all directions at the same time. To this point, you have been primarily using only flow energies and have, in essence, been looking at the universe through a one-way magickal mirror. In basic terms, because you have been denying the power of the counter-flow, most of its energy has had to try and sneak in the back door when you weren't looking. You have placed so many roadblocks in its way that, by the time it got to where it needed to be, the right moment had passed and its purpose had been denied.

You have also been attempting to draw everything you need from a single source. You have been dissecting the stream of flow energy to the point of near ineffectiveness. You have been draining and returning energy to the same pool in an endless loop that has forced the energy to feed off of itself to survive. You have unintentionally broken the perfect ring of the two energy flows.

Right now, you are a *unidirectional Witch,* and this simply will not do. Opening yourself completely to both energy streams can turn you into the perfect magickal transmitter and receiver, and restore the natural balance and harmony in everything you do.

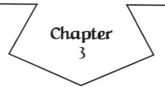

Chapter 3

The Currents at Work

*A*s a Witch who has traveled the path for some time now, you probably manipulate energies constantly in your day-to-day life. This has most likely become so commonplace and natural that you don't even realize you are doing it most of the time. We push and pull, banish and invoke, protect and open things constantly using our magickal will. I have observed this in myself and many of my fellow travelers, and I am sure I would also see it in you.

When you draw something toward you, or inside of you, you are tapping the counter-flow. When you release or push out you are using the flow. When you create or bring something into being, you are reflecting from within yourself (flowing). When you have prevented something or someone from approaching, or redirected energy to banish or protect, you have been deflecting (counter-flowing).

To gain a deeper understanding of just how your magickal clock ticks, spend one day closely observing yourself. Pay attention to precisely how you have been using energy flows in your day-to-day existence. Take mental or written notes on all aspects of your observations, and after you have completed this task spend some time in reflection or meditation. Make a fair but strong evaluation of your findings. The goals are to judge just how open or closed you have truly been to the energy streams around you and to see if there tends to be a common thread that motivates most of your minor workings.

After you have done this, spend another day concentrating on opening yourself as much as possible to the counter-flow. Before you can do this, however, there is a process that you must learn that will allow you to feel the counter-flow energies much more clearly.

Here is an advanced technique that you can use to gain a better understanding of what you have been using and what you have been rejecting from the energy streams. Most Witches use one hand to draw energy to them and the other hand to send it off to manifest their goal or desire. Beyond the physical aspect, you have also been dividing up your mind and spirit to these energies in the very same way. Half of your self has been concentrating on drawing from the energy flows, and the other half of you has been focused on sending them on their way. For us to truly understand the nature of anything, all aspects of it must be experienced without bias or prejudice, and that goes for the flow and the counter-flow as well. What you need to do is switch the cables on your magickal battery. Yes, all of you southpaws should switch sides, and that goes for you right-handed Witches as well.

You will need to find a nice quiet spot where you can relax and focus without being interrupted, as doing this exercise effectively will require your full attention and concentration. When the time and place is right, assume a comfortable position, ground and center yourself, and open your third eye. Using the mental, physical, and spiritual parts of yourself that you use for sending energy, reverse gears and concentrate on receiving with those parts. To do this, cross your arms in front of you and open your hands. Position the hand that you normally use to *send* energy with the palm facing up. Position the hand that you normally use to *receive* energy with that palm facing down. Your sending and receiving hands should now be reversed and opposite of what you are used to. To get the energy stream flowing, give a little push of energy with your *normal* sending hand (the hand that is now palm-up). This should deflect the stream of energy that naturally flows towards you because you are used to sending with that hand and not receiving with it. You should be able to feel a disturbance in the stream rather quickly, but, if you can't, keep pushing and concentrate on sensing the energy stream. Once you can sense the effect you are having on the energy stream, it should feel as if you have put a dam in its path. Now, instead of pushing with your sending hand, start pulling the energy towards you. It may take some time to lift the dam and get the flow started back up again, so don't give up. Keep pulling until you can feel the energy stream enter you. Keep allowing the energy to enter you and let it pass through you until you can feel it exiting through your *normal receiving* (palm-down) hand. Keep doing this until the flow feels natural and unblocked. Now concentrate on sensing how the energy stream feels different than usual. You may have to practice this technique many times until it feels natural and you can read the energy patterns easily. You may have to experiment by changing which hand is palm-up and which is palm-down for this to work. Because magick flows through all of us differently, the standard technique may not work for everyone.

This practice will probably seem strange and quite difficult at first, but with practice and effort you will be able to begin reading energy patterns and their signatures in a whole new way. How will this help you? Basically, this technique is the magickal equivalent of getting a second opinion from an unbiased source. It will give you a fresh, new perspective to consider. As with many things in our lives, when we get too close to something or its use becomes second nature, we tend to simply accept it and carry on with business as usual. We don't examine the finer details. But this is where mistakes and missed opportunities find fertile soil and grow. Learning to switch your battery cables will also help greatly with your examination of the counter-flow. It will help you discover what energies you have been using and what you have been filtering out.

We inhale to gather life, and we exhale to release what is no longer useful. We draw energy in to prepare it for departure, and we send it out to manifest into our desire. Breathe in and feel the counter-flow enter you, carrying with it what you need. Breathe out and feel the energy flowing to its goal. Breathe in and breathe out. One breath enters and the other departs. One is the beginning and one is the end. One is the flow and one is the counter-flow. One gazes into the mirror wondering *why* as the other gazes back, wondering *why not.*

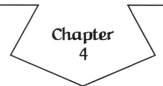

A Circle Within a Circle

Close the circle and open a door.

—L'Mat

Jf you've been taught not to move widdershins in a circle, raise your hand. That's what I thought. Not to worry. My hand is in the air right next to yours. As most of us have, you have simply accepted this as law and never looked back. After all, you've been reading this in almost every book that has ever been published on Witchcraft. Or your priest and priestess told you that it was a bad thing and should never be done for any reason except in highly specialized rituals or to close down the circle. You didn't want to invite negativity into the circle or prematurely close it down, so you've always been very careful not to do this horrible thing.

Think back for a minute. Have you ever been so caught up in the moment that you went widdershins by accident? Have you ever been in such a hurry to grab your wand or athame off the other side of the altar that you moved widdershins without thinking? I'm going to guess that you probably have. Other than the scared look on the face of a coven mate, or the raised eyebrow and redirection from the priest or priestess, what actually happened?

If you're reading this book, you are apparently still here. The banishing energy didn't grab you up and spirit you away into some deep, dark place.

Did your mistake cause the circle to collapse around you? No. Did it tear a rift in the energy field allowing dark and negative entities and powers to enter and muck the whole thing up? No. Did you get even the slightest sensation of negativity or foreboding until you realized what you were doing? If you are being honest with yourself, I'm going to guess probably not.

So, then, tell me why moving widdershins in a circle, let alone casting one in that direction, is one of the biggest taboos and most frowned-upon acts in the practice of Witchcraft that you or I have ever heard of.

I don't have the real answer either, but I hypothesize that at some point in the history of circle casting this rule was written as if in stone. Whether or not the genesis of what would become a major law in the practice of Witchcraft came from a solid foundation or from an irrational fear, we may never know, and I'm not going to debunk these methods as they pertain to casting and moving within a magickal circle. After all, following this law has been ingrained into us as a fundamental practice of Witchcraft, and I'm not going to tell you that it is wrong. I am, however, going to point out that it is part of the systematic approach to circle casting that you and I have been taught. Are these circles flawed or incorrect? Well, of course not. They are, plain and simply, *weak*.

Okay, now that I've raised a few eyebrows and perhaps even a few tempers, give me the benefit of the doubt and hear me out. There will be points in this book where you may very well feel that I am being harsh, that I'm even beating up on what you believe in and what you have been taught. In reality, I am merely trying to get you sparked up enough to take some daring leaps on the path of discovery. I want to give you a boost into outer—or inner—space, to allow you the opportunity to consider a new point of view. What I tell you comes from my own experience. Everyone who knows me, and every student to whom I have ever taught magick, will tell you the same thing. I do not believe that there is any right or wrong way to practice Witchcraft.

I hope that you don't, either. The techniques you use to practice Witchcraft or ritual are your own, and nobody should tell you that they are wrong, but I would not be doing you justice as guide on this adventure if I didn't open up a few new doors. I will only *show* you the new doors. It is up to you to walk through them or to turn back. The choice is yours, and yours alone. That being said, and hopefully understood, let us get back to the business at hand.

Do you recall ever hearing the saying "a circle within a circle, or a wheel within a wheel"? This image appears most famously in the Judeo-Christian Bible as Ezekiel's so-called spaceship. Let us open up a few possibilities and "what ifs." What did you envision the very first time you read in a book or heard someone say the word *circle* as it pertains to Witchcraft? If you're anything like me, you didn't envision a bubble of intense energy and power separating you from the mundane and protecting you while you did your magickal deeds between the worlds. The first image that popped into my head was simply that: a circle. A two-dimensional chalk outline on the floor. For some reason, it represented something magickal. Whatever our first vision of a circle was, we eventually learned that it was much more than what we originally imagined. But we also had to rethink the concept and deprogram our subconscious. Now I am comfortable with the notion that if I say the word *circle* to you, an experienced Witch, that the first thing you envision isn't going to be a chalk outline on the floor or a geometrical shape. No. You probably imagine a sphere of pure magickal energy and get a tingle or two just thinking about it.

From the time when you were sitting at your desk in first grade learning what a circle was and eagerly drawing one on a sheet of paper until now, what has happened to you? You grew. You no longer look at neat little circles drawn on the chalkboard and say to yourself, "That's a circle. There is nothing more." No. You took a step up the staircase of possibility. You took yourself to the next level by being dissatisfied with the concept of "there is nothing more." There was more, and you knew it. Much more. Just as you know it now. Do you really think you have reached the top of the staircase? Can you just rest on the landing, full of satisfaction that you know all there is to know? Do you think you already know all there is to learn about a circle of power and magick? Are you assured that the Hooded God and Dark Goddess will manifest before you and erase you from existence for daring to move forward on the path of discovery? I certainly hope you don't. As far as you have come on your journey, as strong as you have grown to be—are you sure that you are not still seeing your circle as an outline of chalk on the floor?

I said that your circles were weak. Why? There are gears missing in your machinery. What do I mean? I will show you.

Envision yourself as you walk the perimeter of the circle deosil three times. What are you doing? You are conjuring a circle of power to be a boundary between the worlds and protect your sacred space, or at least something similar to that. Correct? Fine. No harm done. But every time you have manifested a circle *you have simultaneously created a second circle* without even realizing it. Whether you like it or not, this second circle exists. It's there for you to use or to ignore. Again, the choice is yours and yours alone. In the simplest terms, you cannot do anything without also doing its opposite. You cannot light a fire to illuminate the darkness without also creating shadows. You cannot throw a coin into a wishing well with the hope of gain without depriving yourself of the coin. You cannot create a circle of flow without also creating a circle of counter-flow. Period.

A very long time ago, I became aware that every time a circle was being cast, a secondary circle was also being created outside the primary circle. I became aware that their flows of power and energy were opposite and equal to each other. I discovered, however, that, although the outer circle was indeed present, it was also going unnoticed by everyone else and therefore not being used to its full advantage. Our ignorance of the outer circle was also creating a great weakness to the inner circle. This aside, both circles were both still doing their jobs, though not even close to the extent that they could be. The Witches were not using a great deflective force of energy, perhaps the stronger of the two circles, in fending off unwanted forces. They were missing gears in their machinery.

Try to visualize it this way. Imagine a great wheel spinning in space, as in the indelible image of the revolving spacecraft in the 1968 movie *2001: A Space Odyssey.* As it rotates, it creates a flow of energy in much the same way that a gear turning in a machine creates energy. On their own, gears serve their purpose, but are they really efficient? Now, in your imagination, bolt a second gear to the first, or interlock two space wheels together. What happens? Bingo! Twice the energy with half the effort. As they work together in harmony to produce this energy, what are they doing? They are pushing each other in *opposite directions* and *generating maximum results.* They are creating a flow and a counter-flow of power. Your first circle has served its purpose, but to tap its full potential it must join with its counterpart. Buckle your seat belts. You're about to go on a little ride.

Exercise
2

Balance: The Circle of Possibilities

Before we begin this exercise, let's do our invocation, but this time let's put a slightly different spin on it. Let's look to the Egyptian culture and call upon Anubis and Ma'at for the needed protection and balance for the next leg of our journey.

> *Great and ancient Goddess Ma'at, as seekers of the balance that pervades all things, we call to you not for judgment, but for guidance. We ask you not to grant us entrance to the underworld, but for power so that we may grow ever stronger on the plane in which we now exist. Great and powerful God Anubis, protector of Isis, guard us with your fearsome might as we ascend to new levels of enlightenment so that when the time comes we may be prepared for our next level of existence. Keep our path safe and defend us from all that would bring us harm.*

Assume a comfortable position and begin your process of attaining a state of deep meditation. As before, we start in emptiness, floating free and completely at ease. The mundane world is melting away into nothingness, and your concerns for the day are washing away with it. Be still for a time and enjoy this moment.

You feel yourself slowly floating downward. Softly slowly floating towards your domain.

You feel a sensation of power flow over you like a warm bath, soothing and protecting you as you pass through it. You are crossing over into the shadow realm. Nothingness slowly gives way to twilight, and you float downward past a simple orb of glass that contains within it a key. You pay little attention to this orb, as you know that it is not yet time to discover its purpose and its meaning.

You see the mighty walls of stone that encircle your realm. You are comforted by their presence. You float ever downward, further and further, until finally you come to rest between two pools of power and a great mirror of promise and magick.

You can hear the subtle bubbling and churning of the unknowable waters that make up the mirror, and you gaze upon it with hope and anticipation. But you see nothing in the glass.

Suddenly you get the familiar feeling of having left something undone. What could it be? All at once, a fierce torrent of wind blasts by you, pushing you sideways with its force. You stand and try to brace yourself against this mighty wind, but its course changes direction and the winds begin to encircle you. Within the swirling flow of the mighty winds you can hear voices, some loud and some but a whisper. These voices see-saw back and forth, as if they were phasing in and out of reality. The sound of the circling winds is thunderous as it whips around you and throughout your realm. You feel as if you are standing in the center of a tornado. You move towards its spinning mass, feeling as though you could pluck knowledge of anything you wished to learn from inside this tornado. But as you begin to move, a powerful blast of heat stays you in your path. A jet of flame passes over you. And yet you are not burned by it! Instead, you begin to feel an amazing courage and desire growing within your breast.

The stream of flame intensifies and its warmth impassions your spirit. The flame quickly grows into a massive wall of fire, and it merges with the swirling circle of winds in a vast eruption of power. The feeling of something approaching from behind distracts you. As you turn to face it, a wave of blue-green water washes all around you. Your breath halts in your throat and you begin to tremble as every emotion you have ever known fills you all at once. A thousand voices resound in your mind, and you can understand what every one of them is saying. As the peace of understanding flows through your entire being, you become steady.

The last of the mighty wave of water flows around you and washes against the wall of fire and wind, joining with it seamlessly. You are held in wonder at the unimaginable sight before you. Fingerlike cyclones of energy are beginning to pulse in and out from the spinning wall as it wheels ever faster around you. Its pull is intense and commanding. You begin to wonder if you are going to be pulled into the energy storm.

You hear a tremendous crunching and cracking all around you. It is as if a huge tree is about to crash to the ground. Leaves and branches seem to come from nowhere and bombard the walls of the tempest, only to be drawn into its spinning mass. An ever-increasing deluge of debris is now flying past you. Pieces of stone and earth join the frenzied current of branches and leaves smashing into the wall. They are increasing in size and are passing dangerously close to you. You start to question your safety. Your concern is heightened as the monstrous rumbling of what could only be an avalanche swells throughout the realm. Huge boulders and entire trees are now being sucked into the vortex of the wall. It is as if an entire mountain is being ripped apart around you. Feelings of panic threaten to overtake you.

But you are strong. You still yourself. Now you begin to listen more carefully to what is within the mighty noise all around you. From deep within the destructive deluge of the avalanche you hear the unmistakable sounds of a peaceful meadow. The song of a breeze gently blowing through tall grass surrounds you. The soft chirping of birds and the smell of fertile green earth envelop you. All at once you feel grounded and at one with all life within the meadow. You lie down in the soft grass of this peaceful place, and you begin to dream.

Something stirs you. You awaken in the shadow realm, but the sight before your eyes makes you wonder if you are not still dreaming. The tornado of energy has vanished completely! You can see that it has left behind a few gifts. You find yourself surrounded by four huge statues arranged evenly around you in a circle. They have been sculpted to represent the magickal elements of earth, air, fire, and water. In the center of each of these elemental statues is a slowly spinning portal to the domain from which it came, and each glows with a different color of ghostly spectral light. "Have you learned the lessons of the elements?" a fragile yet familiar voice asks you. As you turn towards this voice, you find a curious sight. An old woman is rising up and out of the pool of the moon. As she steps from it, she looks at you with a pleasing smile and twinkling eyes. You recognize her as one of the people who have touched you most deeply in your life.

"Balance!" a gruff yet somehow very gentle voice bellows. You have heard this voice many times before. You turn again and greet the elderly gentleman rising from the pool of the sun. You give him a gracious nod, and you can feel in your heart just how much he means to you. You are comforted, yet very confused, by the presence of these two in the shadow realm. You gesture toward them as if to ask a wordless question, but suddenly they are no longer the only ones there. One by one, you see other beings rise from the two pools. Some are human, some are not. Some you have known for your entire life. Some you have never seen before. Some are creatures of myth and fantasy. Some you can't quite make out at all.

As they rise from the two pools, each being gives you a knowing glance. Now they begin to encircle you from two different directions. They pass by and through each other until at last they have formed two perfect rings around you. You see that the beings making up the external ring are facing outward toward the boundaries of your realm. Those of the internal ring are facing inward toward you. One by one, each being in each ring touches the creature beside him. Now the beings begin to rise into the air. The two rings of beings revolve around you in opposite directions.

This bizarre dance of mismatched creatures slowly spinning around you is the most curious thing you have ever witnessed. You can't help it, but an amused grin comes over your face. Your grin lasts only a moment, however, as you see that the entities that make up the two rings do not share in your humor. Their eyes seem troubled and lifeless. They look upon you with great need and desire. They are looking for something that only you can give them: *power.* As you read the patterns of energy emanating from the two circles, you are stunned by how weak they are. "Help us.... Help us," they cry out to you. One by one their voices are raised, louder and louder in a desperate call for assistance. You know that you must act quickly, for the momentum of the rings is slowing.

You move to the pools of flow and counter-flow and draw from each of them a ball of energy. You join these balls of energy together. The power they create is mighty, and you hurl it into the two rings of calling beings to supercharge them. Nothing happens. You draw from the pools again and again. Faster and faster, you bombard the rings with intense balls of energy. But they are still becoming slower. In desperation, you turn to the mirror. You hope for an answer, and you receive one.

In the glass you can see only your own reflection. Now you realize what must be done.

With powerful purpose and intent you soar high above the two diminishing circles within your realm and look down upon them. There—you see it! The empty space between the two rings. You know that you must fill this empty space. Wild energy races through you, but you know that you must remain steady and open yourself completely to the opposite flows of the two rings. You feel the balanced energies within these two rings, the flame and the shadow, the breeze and the storm, the balance that the elemental portals and the two rings contain. In a blinding burst of speed, you wing toward your goal. You enter the gap between the two rings and release your energy. Your power unites the two rings and accelerates their pace. You feel the power of the flow and the counter-flow as they speed around you. The two circles are gaining in strength and meaning, and now you know that your work between them is complete. You separate yourself from the energy that you have created between the two rings. You float away from this energy, and enter into the exact center of the inner ring. There you hover and watch and wait.

The rings have now reached an incredible speed. They seem to be tilting back and forth on some unseen axis. Suddenly both rings are not only encircling you. They are also revolving around you in opposite directions. One passes overhead as the other passes below you. It is like being in the center of a gigantic gyroscope. The strength and power being generated by the spinning rings is unlike anything you have ever felt before, and your spirit tingles with excitement. You feel the balance the rings contain, and you know that the secrets of these rings are yours for the taking. You extend your arms and open yourself to the balance and the power of the rings flying around you. Streams of flow and counter-flow energy begin to enter and move through you. As each one passes, you feel more and more attuned to them and to yourself. Each wave of energy washes away doubt. Each wave of energy infuses you with possibility.

You float inside of the two rings with perfect trust and perfect understanding. The rings are yours. It is time to seal them and cast the most powerful circle you have ever known.

With great will, you call for the elements and the elementals. A gale of wind blasts forth from the portal of the east and swirls about the base of the statue of air. A mighty flame shoots forth from the portal of the south like the breath of a great dragon and dances about the statue of fire. A great wave of water and emotion washes forth from the portal of the west and flows freely around the statue of water. The smell of green leaves and fresh dirt surrounds you as energy pours forth form the portal of the north and green magick grows on the statue of the earth.

You breathe deeply of the elemental energies and ready yourself to call for deity. But the gods and goddesses are already here. A spectral crescent moon floats before you. It is steeped in magick and the ancient mystery of the Goddess. It lunges toward you and pierces you just below your heart. But you feel no pain. You know that your very soul has been impaled by the crescent moon, and that a piece of it has been taken from you by the tip of this holy horn. Your courage has been rewarded and the spirit of the Goddess Herself has blessed you. The crescent moon slowly raises you upward, and you are filled with the pleasure of being held by the Great Mother. The crescent moon slides through your soul and out of your body and rises high above you.

In a blinding flash, a great glowing ball appears before you and hangs in the air. The power and light that radiates from it is like the power of a billion suns compressed into a single sphere. A stream of flame bursts from this sphere and burns across your chest. You know that the very spirit of the God has touched you. The glowing ball expands and sweeps upwards towards the crescent moon and joins with the moon in a brilliant flash of power and light.

You can feel the piece of your soul in the center of their union. You know that this part your soul is being remade into something new. Something powerful. It is as if a part of you is being reborn for a reason you do not yet understand. Billowing vapors begin to swell from this place of creation. They slowly build into a storm of energy and magick. Monstrous crashes of thunder and bright flashes of light and color emanate from the ever-growing mass of clouds.

You look hard into the center of the energy storm. What do you see? You see that the hands of deity have forged the piece of your soul into the most beautiful and commanding sword you have ever seen. You extend your hand toward this sword, and it spins and races toward you in a blur of speed. It pierces the two rings, crystallizing and shattering them into a billion shards of glass. They explode around you at the exact moment the sword reaches your hand, and you drive the sword down to seal the circle. You feel the sword penetrate and hold inside some unseen force. The shattered pieces of the rings fly outward and melt together, and they form two gigantic spheres of crystalline energy around you. You stand in the center of your realm and the two spheres. You are feeling more magickal and more powerful than you ever imagined you could.

You reach down and wrap your hand around the hilt of the soul sword. You are eager to reclaim it. But the sword won't budge. You can see that the blade of the sword is half buried in the center of a huge circle of white marble that has somehow formed beneath you. Looking out toward the edge of this new addition to your realm, you see that a ring of jet-black stone encompasses the inner circle of white marble. It is slowly spinning around it in a counter-clockwise direction.

Again, you reach for the soul sword and pull at it with all of your physical and magickal might. Still it refuses to move. "You do not yet possess the strength to claim that sword," a brusque voice says to you.

You look up in time to see the elderly gentleman slowly sinking back into the pool of the sun. Now you hear the gentle voice of the old woman. "Don't despair, dear," she says. "Your time will come." She disappears completely into the pool of the moon. A soft, calming breeze brushes your forehead, relaxing and refreshing your spirit.

You look around at the vastness of the shadow realm and are awed by its power and its beauty. You know that you have learned much this day, and any feelings of lack or disappointment flow away from you and vanish completely. You know it is time to rest now, so you sit down on the circle of white marble at your feet and open your third eye. You feel the great circles of power you have cast, intact, but still and quiet around you. All is calm and at peace within the realm. You are satisfied with its balance.

You begin to float up toward the reality of the waking world. Softly, slowly, you float up. Small doorways melt and form in the walls of the two spheres, and as you pass through them you are returning to your human body and mind. Softly, slowly you rise farther and farther away from the shadow realm. You feel yourself becoming solid again. You are aware of your breath as it enters your lungs and exits again. You take in a deep cleansing breath, and as you exhale you open your eyes and return to the earthly plane.

Chapter 5

The Chains of the Scale

My good friend and onetime mentor, L'Mat, had a favorite saying: "Close the circle and open a door." What he meant by this is that once something has ceased to be of use or need, or a particular path we have been traveling has been completed or has reached an impasse, it is time to bring closure to it and thereby open ourselves to new ways of thinking or new adventures to embark upon.

Have you ever considered how many things in your life you have never brought to closure? How many remnants are still floating around inside your spirit and your subconscious? If you're human, I'm going to guess that it's quite a few. What effect do you think those leftovers are having on your inner balance? How many circles do you think your magickal self has left open? Are there things you still do that no longer feel right? Do you keep doing them just because that's the way you were taught to do them? Are there any paths that have led you nowhere that you are still traveling because you're afraid of what change might bring? Have you practiced Witchcraft the same way for so long that it no longer feels magickal to you?

Close the circle and open a door.

When we leave these old circles open, they create an imbalance within us because they have never become balanced in themselves. They have been left one-sided with no real answers. They have nothing to feed off of except more questions. We have never given these circles completeness because they represent some great pain or fear we have never faced, or an inner weakness that we just won't admit to. A parent who wouldn't accept us or a former lover who hurt us by turning us away. A bad habit we couldn't kick or a defeat we have never accepted. Something inside that haunts us that we have never dealt with because it hurts too much or we are afraid to face.

Without closure, these are only ghosts that we cannot deal with because they have not been made tangible or real to us. If once these circles are closed, they become a wound or a scar, then that is what they become. If they change into a source of great power or a well of inspiration from which we can drink, that's all the better. The point is that, once these circles are allowed to close and become whole, their counterbalance will eventually manifest inside of us and the scales will once again be allowed to even out.

Close the circle and open a door.

Finding true balance within ourselves can be one of the most difficult, yet rewarding, paths we can travel. Our faults and flaws are part of what creates balance within us. Our faults only become problematic when their counterparts are not allowed to grow at the same rate or if this imbalance manifests itself in the form of destructive behavior or a physical and mental addiction that grows beyond our control. That is not to say that we should not all be in a constant state of self-improvement and enlightenment, but that completely ridding ourselves of our imperfections is impossible. Even if we could accomplish this feat, it would turn us into a monster of horrific proportions. Imagine that you could locate either the dark or light half of yourself and remove it completely. Imagine what you would become if you plucked out every part of yourself that you didn't like. The scales would tip so severely that they would come crashing down and cause your immediate destruction.

Even the most peaceful person on earth or the greatest Zen mind never reaches a state of tranquility by ridding him or herself of his dark half. On the contrary, he recognized the shadows inside of himself, gained deep understanding of them and how they affect inner balance, and then made his peace with who and what they are.

So what do your rethinking and realignment of balance have to do with your shadow spirit? In a word, *everything*. What do you think it would be like to join with an entity that is an exact reflection of your magickal self? What you fear, it claims for its own. What you think is impossible, it does without trying. Where you cannot go, it travels to on a whim. What you don't know, it has stored in its memory.

Can you imagine the consequences of this kind of change if you are unprepared or are unable to understand what is happening to you? This magickal reflection of yourself, which is your shadow spirit, has none of your earthly weaknesses to contend with, and you have none of its ethereal attributes.

So what does this mean in the big picture? If and when the two of you join, any circles you have left open or any disharmony you are still harboring can cross over and infect your shadow spirit, creating areas of imbalance between you. Eventually the scales would naturally even themselves out, but if you are well balanced beforehand the gaps between you and your *other* will be inconsequential. The goal of the exercises and tasks I am leading you through is to leave you well prepared when the time comes for you to meet your shadow spirit. If you are well equipped with the right tools when this time comes, you will be able to bring an instant completion to each other that otherwise would take you centuries to acquire on your own.

The purpose of Exercise 2 was to open you up further to the many aspects of balance and to reveal some of the changes that will occur by joining with your *other*. Step by step, we are creating patterns of thought that will serve you well when that time comes. If you think you are already prepared to reunite with your shadow spirit, guess again.

Imagine sending and receiving the whole of who you are and who you want to be and joining with your equal opposite at the very same moment, all the while trying to keep your sanity and identity intact.

I will leave you to ponder that one for a time. We will delve ever deeper into the secrets of the shadow spirit with each chapter, but the path is still dark before us, and there is still much work to be done.

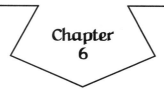

Chapter 6

The Balance at Work

In the previous chapter, I asked you to consider how many magickal and mundane circles you have left open in your lifetime. If you haven't begun the process of figuring this out yet, start counting, because I'm about to ask you to deal with them. I am unfortunately unable to give you clear and concise advice as to how you might go about this, as you are an individual and, through the written word, I can speak only to the masses. Through my own experiences, however, I may indeed be able to give you a few pointers.

Most often, if something is not functioning correctly, it is a small problem, not a catastrophic situation. I will start you on your quest for the open circles by simply jogging your memory. Sit down and reflect on all the things that you have experienced that brought you pain or disharmony and ask yourself if you have ever brought closure to that pain. Ask yourself if you have ever truly forgiven the person(s) who gave you that pain or if you are still harboring unforgiveness. Think about the pain *you* have inflicted on others either purposely or unintentionally. Have you forgiven yourself for those mistakes, or are there still demons hiding in the dark corridors of your mind?

Consider all the experiences that you have gone through that were disturbing to you in some way and try and recognize what you have or have not brought to closure. Begin with the larger issues that have occurred over the course of your lifetime. Make sure that you haven't left any big circles open. Being completely honest with yourself is paramount to success on this mission, so trust your intuitions at all times and don't second-guess yourself. If any large circles are still left open, trust me—you will know them when you see them.

Once the big ones have been dealt with, methodically seek out the smaller ones and close them down one by one. You may be surprised to find that some of these smaller circles are even bigger thorns in your side than the larger ones were. As you go about your task, however, remember the major rule: *If it ain't broke, don't fix it.* This is not the time to be digging through old garbage. If you still feel there may be open circles still locked deep inside of you, try the tried-and-true method of deep meditation to locate them and shut them down. You will be amazed by just how clean and renewed your spirit will feel after these circles have been dealt with. You'll be equally amazed at all the new paths and possibilities that will open up before you.

Close the circle and open a door.

What was your second trip into the shadow realm like? Hopefully, you like what we've done with the place. If not, you can redecorate after I leave, and I will not be offended. It is your realm. By now, if you and I have both done our jobs correctly, you are starting to feel pretty much at ease with using the counter-flow to your advantage. It is a powerful tool to add to your bag of tricks, and your skill at using it will be vital when the time comes for you to meet with your *other.* At this very moment, two perfectly balanced circles of power are still intact and slowly spinning opposite of each other in your shadow realm. Before you can partake in the next exercise, however, there is a major puzzle you must somehow solve: *how to get back inside.*

In Exercise 2, you cast what is known as a bipolar circle. When properly executed, this circle can be one of the most powerful and yet natural circles you will ever create. The earth itself has bipolar regions, and everything natural and supernatural contains these opposite and contradictory charges. It is only when we start messing with these flows and try to separate them that they become dysfunctional and dangerous.

Casting the bipolar circle in meditation is fine, but the time has come for you to experience it in person. As I said earlier, the secondary or outer circle is naturally created whenever *any* circle is being cast. You simply may not have recognized it before. For starters, therefore, I want you to cast a circle in your usual fashion and see if you can detect the outer circle. See if you can feel its properties and movement. After you have done this, whether you were able to feel the second circle or not, cast the two circles separately, one at a time, and see what you can learn in the process. Finally, cast both circles at the same time. The outer circle is cast widdershins, and the inner circle, deosil. To be successful in its creation and bring it up to full strength, you need to open yourself completely to this new method and put a little heart and soul into it.

I think you will be surprised and impressed by the power and balance of the bipolar circle and by what you can learn and feel in its casting. At least, have *some* fun with it. There is nothing to fear, and there's a mountain of experience to gain.

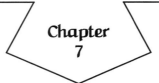

The Dragon and the Lamb

"You fool!" croaked the frog. "Now we shall both die!
Why on earth did you sting me?"

    The scorpion shrugged and did a little jig on the
drowning frog's back. "I could not help myself," he said.
"It is my nature."

—A Fable

In the eighth-century Irish manuscript, *The Book of Lismore,* there is a brief mention of a board game that was played by the Romans every year at Imbolc. The game pitted a crone and a dragon against a maiden and a lamb. The object of the game was for the lamb to conquer the dragon, thus turning the crone back into her aspect as a virgin goddess, thereby turning the wheel of the year to spring. Each of us contains within ourselves the equivalent of the dragon and the lamb, and they are in constant battle to win supremacy over each other. This contention between these two facets of ourselves is in itself not so much the problem as it is the answer to our dilemma of discovering true balance.

Both the dragon and the lamb have a tendency to reveal their greatest weakness and most profound influence over us at the most inopportune moments in our lives, sending us headlong into conflicts that manifest inside of us or, even more regrettably, in our relationships or life situations. Years of hard work or building trust can be destroyed in a single moment of failure by either of these aspects of ourselves and weaken our resolve to move forward on our chosen paths. The voice of the dragon is smooth and compelling. It speaks to us of great power and influence, majesty and pride, accomplishment and success. It also speaks of jealousy and suspicion, of anger and deceit, of hunger for what does not belong to us, and of the treasures that await us if we take advantage of people and their situations. The voice of the lamb is also constant and persuasive. It speaks of kindness and comfort, of gentleness and love, of peace and oneness. It also whispers of fear and panic, of stagnation and ineptness, and of the safety of just staying home and not taking chances.

We owe our most monumental triumphs and greatest moments of cowardice to the dragon and the lamb. Both of them must exist inside us to keep the other in check. Too often, however, they are engaged in a battle to gain prominence and claim the throne that rules our inner selves and our public personas. These conflicts arise because we have not given them a basic language with which to communicate. We have not taught them the value of cooperation. To gain the balance and strength we need to continue on our quest, we must find a way to resolve the conflicts between the dragon and the lamb. We must bring about a new level of balance and harmony between them.

We have all experienced it: that perfect day of peace and happiness. A day when our inner light was shining at its brightest and we were a joy to be around. A day we thought nothing could possibly ruin. But that day was suddenly destroyed in a single moment of interference that surfaced in us as anger or apathy. The dragon saw its chance to strike and took it. Our lamb had spent this day methodically trotting through the sweet green pastures in our mind, basking in the sunshine, and grazing among the sweet grasses of peace and enjoyment that we had grown for it. The dragon had spent this day observing the lamb with indignity and contempt. No one had asked the dragon's opinion of how this day should proceed. No one had thrown it so much as a bone or a scrap on which to feed. All it needed was the smallest opening, a wrong word from a child or coworker, a demand on our time that we saw as an interruption of our perfect day, to topple the lamb and regain dominance. The lamb, in turn, is capable of infusing our greatest moments of strength and accomplishment with doubt and indecision, undermining our self-worth, and denying our dragon the use of its claws and teeth for a time.

To bring an end to this war being waged inside us, we must become both counselor and student of the dragon and the lamb. We must discover a way to hear both of their voices at the same time and give them what they need so they will be content and at peace in each other's presence. If a treaty can be reached and an alliance formed between the two, they will be able to reason things out between themselves and offer us the best possible advice or a solution to any given problem or situation without conflict. Their union and cooperation can manifest a balance within us unlike anything we have ever experienced. It can allow us to truly understand ourselves and accept who and what we are. The internal roller coaster we have been riding will eventually begin to slow down and give us time to appreciate our needs and accomplishments without guilt or self-doubt. We will be able to understand our fears and weaknesses and learn how to overcome them without taking them to extremes or beating ourselves up over them. We can know the power of the dragon and the lamb being presented in a united front against our most challenging and formidable roadblocks and adversaries. No longer will their contention become the instrument of our undoing.

I have given you a lot to consider thus far in this chapter, as well as in this chapter of your life, but we must press on to the next logical question: What has become of your *magickal* dragon and lamb? I want you to put down this book right now and run outside and shout to the heavens that you are a Witch and that you are not afraid.

Okay, one of two things just happened. Either you have just picked this book back up again, having done what I asked you to do, or you are sitting there saying to yourself, "He's got to be kidding me, right?" Who won the battle, the dragon or the lamb? More important, was doing *either* of these things a good idea? Sure, proclaiming your Witchiness to the powers that be and not giving a damn about who else heard you may have felt wonderful and filled you with satisfaction, but what does your lamb have to say about it? Did you weigh all the possible benefits and downfalls that doing this could bring? And what if you just sat there doing nothing? You certainly have the satisfaction of heeding the warnings of the lamb to stay put and not make waves, but you may also have one pissed-off dragon you are going to have to answer to.

As a Witch, you have taken on a most daunting responsibility. That is the responsibility of power. You are responsible for how and when you use it. Sometimes you are responsible for *not* having used it when you probably should have. The meaning of the word *responsibility* is "the ability to respond." To be able to respond to the needs of the dragon and the lamb at the same time while keeping your spontaneity and safety intact may sound similar to a superhuman feat, but isn't becoming more than human what you had hoped to accomplish by practicing Witchcraft in the first place? To be able to hook your willpower up to a nuclear reactor instead of a nine-volt battery and do what most "humans" cannot do? To be able to affect universal change without having to throw money at something or make it so afraid of you that it has little choice but to do your bidding?

As it has been said so many times and in so many ways, if it is indeed the destiny of the human race to be destroyed by its own hand, then we as Witches must strive as never before to become more than human. To become a race of magickal entities that will not accept destruction by our own hand. To become so attuned to the harmonics and balance of the universe that we become an example of how all intelligent life on this planet should behave. To accept our power and the responsibility that comes with it and take ourselves to the next level of humanity. We must find a way to become a great and powerful dragon with the temperance of a wise and gentle lamb.

In the following exercise, you will have the opportunity to meet the ambassadors of the dragon and the lamb in your shadow realm and, hopefully, gain some deeper insights into how they affect your human and magickal selves. Remember: The ultimate goal of both the dragon and the lamb is to gain your favor and dominate the other. They are both tricky and very clever when it comes to getting their way, and they will say just about anything to convince you that their point of view is the one you should trust. I advise you to listen carefully to what each of them has to say and figure out how to turn the tables on them and become their master instead of their slave.

Oh, by the way, I'm also tricky and very clever. Fair warning!

Strength: Through the Looking Glass

Let's pretend there's a way of getting through into it,
somehow, Kitty. Let's pretend the glass has got all soft like
gauze, so that we can get through. Why, it's turning into a
sort of mist now, I declare! It'll be easy enough to get
through—

—Lewis Carroll, *Through the Looking Glass*

As we look for the deities who are best suited as guides and protectors on this leg of our journey, we find the Roman god Janus awaiting us. It is often stated that Janus, the dual-faced god of beginnings and doorways, has no feminine counterpart, but this is untrue. A counterpart for this god is readily found in the Goddess Cardea, who is the goddess of the hinges on the door. Cardea, who looks both forward and backward in time and is the keeper of the four winds, is said to live in a starry castle at the hinge of the universe behind the north wind. It is the opening of a new doorway we seek, and so we now approach this pair.

Great God Janus. Give me the strength to leave what has
already passed behind and guide my steps well as I travel
through the new doorway that lies before me. Protect me
and fill me with the skill of foresight, that I may see any

*dangers that would stand in my way or bring to me harm.
Ancient and wise Cardea, keeper of the four winds, fill me
with the power to see the things that I must now leave behind
so that a new path will open before me. Guide me with your
ancient wisdom, so that I may see the truth in all things that
are masked and hidden from me.*

Find a comfortable place where you can relax easily. We will now
begin our third journey into the shadow realm. Using your normal method
of meditation, drift just below the surface of this world and hang between
the boundaries of the earthly plane and the shadow realm.

You feel the edge of the earthy plane becoming distant and vague as
you slowly drift downward, ever closer to the edge of the shadow realm.
You are softly, slowly descending toward your domain. Your spirit is
strong and grows ever stronger as you near the border of your place of
power.

You feel the sensation of an intense force of magickal energy emanating from below. As you look down, you see the two gigantic circles of
energy you created on your last visit into the shadow realm. You can
almost make out the center of your domain deep within these circles, but
it is blurred by the powerful energies of the two circles.

As you drift closer to these circles, you begin to feel the repelling
energies of the outer ring. You are being pushed away by its force. You
build your own energy and try to move closer to it, but the power of the
outer circle matches your own. You find you cannot move any closer to it
than you already are.

Something suddenly flies past your head like a bullet. You see a key
imprisoned within an orb of glass as it passes through the boundary of the
outer circle. It stops and hovers in the empty space between the two
circles. You realize that the only way you are going to be able to get back

inside of the shadow realm is by obtaining this key. You extend an open hand toward the key and will it to come to you, but it remains frozen between the boundaries of the two circles.

A small pulse of energy suddenly flows from the outer circle. It rises, as if to touch you, and when it does touch your hand, it stings like a bee! "Why have you come to this place?" a thunderous voice asks. You realize that the outer circle is somehow speaking to you in your mind. You know that if you hope to gain entrance to the shadow realm you must answer its questions. As each question is asked, you must answer it, either aloud or in your mind. "I asked you why you have come to this place!" the voice thunders again. You answer this question. "What," it asks, "what do you intend to do with the knowledge and power you will gain by your experiences in the shadow realm?" You answer this question. "Why should I grant *you* entrance to the shadow realm, and not someone else?" You answer this question. "You have left the old path behind you. What will you do if you fail on this new path?" You answer this question.

As you ponder these questions and the answers you have given, you see that your answers have somehow already been etched onto the crystalline surface of the inner circle. They are also etched now into your memory.

For good or bad, your answers have revealed how powerful the protective walls of the circles will be. They show how much influence you currently have within the shadow realm.

Now as you watch, the orb of glass around the key begins to crack and separate. As the pieces of glass float away from the key, they rejoin and transform themselves into a gold and silver necklace that slides itself through the hole in the key, creating a necklace for you, surety that you will not lose this precious key.

The necklace and the key rise and pass through the outer circle, floating toward you, and soon they are hanging in the air directly in front of you.

You reach for the necklace and take it in your hands. As you clasp it around your neck, you are instantly transported to the center of the shadow realm. Now you find yourself standing before a great mirror of magick.

You gaze into the mirror and reflect for a moment on the answers you have given to obtain the key and enter again into the shadow realm. A symbol of either your strength or your weakness flashes across the surface of the mirror. As you look down at the key hanging over your heart, you see that this very same symbol is carved in its shaft.

A dense fog begins to flow from the mirror, and the symbol in the looking glass begins to fade and slowly disappears. The fog fills the shadow realm with a heavy blanket of mist. It envelops everything so completely that you can barely make out anything within the realm.

The air around you suddenly becomes cold and icy. A shiver runs down your spine as you sense that something is circling you within the veil of the fog. You feel as if you are being hunted.

You carefully begin to move toward the only thing you can still see in the shadow realm. This is the soul sword. You slowly reach for the hilt of the sword as you peer through the fog for any sign of your would-be attacker. Suddenly the rustle of flapping wings startles you. You jump backwards.

As you glance down at the soul sword, you witness a most curious sight. A black raven has perched on the cross-guard of the soul sword within biting distance of your hand. The raven also appears to be searching through the fog for signs of movement.

"You can leave any time you want to, don't you know," the raven says as he looks up at you and twitches his head. "That key around your neck?" he continues. "All you have to do is hold it in your hand and wish your way out of this terrible place. But if you go, take me with you."

"Coward!" something roars from deep within the mists, and a huge shape comes bounding through the fog toward you. "If you listen to him," the roaring voice continues, "we will never accomplish anything!" It is a lioness. She paces up to the raven and swipes at him with her paw. The raven lets out a loud caw, flies up, and perches on your shoulder. "I think," says the raven, "that I will stay here for awhile. That is," he looks you in the eye, "if you don't mind. She wants to eat me, don't you know." The lioness shakes her head. "You're hardly worth the effort!" she says, glaring at the raven with contempt. She shifts her attention and looks more closely at you. "Now *you* on the other hand…." She chuckles as she studies you. If a lioness can shrug, she does so, and then she turns to face the heart of the fog. "It's going to be difficult finding our way through the fog," she says. "I do believe it's getting thicker by the minute." The lioness paces back and forth at the edge of the mist.

"We aren't going in there!" the raven shrieks as he hops about on your shoulder. You can feel the grip of his claws in your flesh. "We most certainly are," the lioness replies. She walks closer to you again and looks you in the eye. "You have to listen to me," she says, "because this is very important. Forget about the dangers. We *have* to find the mirror. It is a portal, a gateway to anywhere you want to go. If we don't find it right away, it may be lost forever in the fog." "It's a gateway all right," the raven shrieks, rising into the air above your head. "It's a gateway to death and torture at the hands of gods know what! You don't know what kind of evil is waiting on the other side." The lioness begins to walk in a circle around you. The raven begins to fly around you in a circle from overhead.

You feel very uneasy about being in the presence of a raven and a lioness that have human-like personalities and have somehow developed the power of speech. Something about the way they are acting is wrong. *Very wrong.* Ravens are normally curious, fearless birds, but this one seems to be afraid of his own reflection. For some reason he seems desperate to get you to leave the shadow realm with him. Lionesses are normally only aggressive while they are hunting or when they are threatened. This one is acting like she is going out of her way to pick a fight with anything that crosses her path. She seems anxious to get you alone in the fog with her. You are very suspicious about this strange pair of creatures.

You can see that the lioness is becoming increasingly annoyed by the raven's presence in the shadow realm. The lioness is taking on a very aggressive posture and her contempt for the raven shows clearly in her eyes. It is quickly turning to hatred. The raven notices this, and he seems to get a boost of courage from the fact that he is able to annoy the lioness. The raven begins to swoop down toward the lioness from the air, and he is getting closer and closer to her with every pass. He seems to be taunting the lioness by his ability to fly past her and her inability to do anything about it.

The raven's growing confidence gets the better of him, and he flies too close to the lioness. With one swing of her mighty paw, she smacks the raven to the ground. As you see the raven hit the ground, something very strange happens. The shape of the raven seems to flux and change for a few seconds. It is as if some unseen energy field surrounding the raven has been momentarily disrupted. Badly shaken, the raven tries to right himself, but the lioness is upon him immediately. She begins to thrash the helpless raven again and again with her massive paws.

The energy being released by the struggle between the raven and the lioness is intense, and it soon begins to take its toll on the shadow realm. Every shriek from the raven tears the energy field that surrounds the shadow realm. You can feel the raven's fear and pain manifesting as dark creatures crawling around inside the fog. Every powerful blow being struck by the lioness is violently shaking the entire realm. You can feel things beginning to crack and crumble.

The raven somehow manages to peck the lioness on the paw and, as she rears back, roaring in pain, you see that her shape and form also seem to flux with disrupted energy. Just for a moment, you can see the scales of a reptile where her fur should be. There is magick at work here. The magick of glamoury! And you know that you are going to have to unmask it quickly, before the shadow realm is completely destroyed.

You open up your third eye. You focus your concentration on the raven and the lioness. The glamoury burns away and their true forms are revealed to you. The raven and the lioness were the dragon and the lamb in disguise, and you are fed up with their destruction and trickery.

You raise your arms and open your hands. You discover that you are able to sense and locate the pools of flow and counter-flow within the veil of the fog. You call to these two pools with your mind and your will. You now see two glowing and powerful streams of energy as they move through the fog towards the dragon and the lamb. As the energy streams reach the dragon and the lamb, one of the streams weaves itself about the dragon's throat like a chain and pulls the mighty beast to the ground. The second stream of energy encircles the lamb, creating a protective bubble of energy around it. You move toward the dragon and the lamb and sit down between them. You raise an open hand to the dragon. You can feel the dragon's anger still raging.

You open your other hand to the lamb and immediately sense the pain and isolation it is feeling. The lamb is badly injured. Its spirit is drawing deeper and deeper inside of itself for protection. You know that you must somehow try to heal the fallen creature before its purpose and meaning are lost forever. The lamb is too weak, the dragon, too powerful. You know that you must somehow restore the balance between the dragon and the lamb.

You focus your mind and concentrate on establishing a mental link between the dragon and the lamb. You feel the link take hold. As it does, the dragon begins to thrash madly about. The dragon can feel the lamb's pain and hopelessness. The dragon slowly begins to calm down, as the realization of the damage it has caused overtakes it. Shame replaces the dragon's contempt. Empathy replaces the dragon's anger. You feel the energy patterns surrounding the dragon beginning to change. They are changing into healing energies, and you can feel these healing powers as they pass through you and enter the lamb. You add your own healing energies into the stream. The lamb begins to respond to the healing energies almost immediately. It rises, steadies itself, and stands and looks into the dragon's eyes. The feeling of shame for taunting and teasing the dragon shines in the eyes of the lamb, and the dragon and the lamb seem to be silently acknowledging the harm they have caused each other. An unspoken apology resonates between them.

The dense fog within the shadow realm begins to thin and soon disappears altogether. Now you see that you are sitting directly in front of the mirror and the pools of flow and counter-flow. You see the energy streams that were protecting the lamb and holding the dragon at bay are slowly returning to the pools. As you gaze into the living waters of the mirror, you are astonished by what you see. The mirror reveals the dragon in the guise of the lioness, but she is changing, aging rapidly and changing in gender as well. Her reflection in the mirror reveals her now as a lion, but not just any lion. He is ancient, but still powerful. The light of life is fading within his eyes, but the light of wisdom cuts through the haze of his years. "You have done well," the lion says to you as he shakes his massive mane. "You have brought strength to us all."

You now see that the lamb's reflection in the mirror once again reveals it as the raven. You see the raven fly up and perch on the lion's shoulder. "You have changed us forever," the raven says to you, "and for that I thank you." The raven gives you a nod. As you look upon his reflection, you see that he is changing as well. The raven transforms into the most beautiful female eagle you have ever seen. Her feathers shine and shimmer with the energy and strength of youth.

She spreads her massive wings, and you are humbled by her grace and power. Her eyes seem to be speaking to you, and you can hear her voice in your mind. "Go where you will and I will follow," she says. "I will protect you with all my skill and all my strength, for you have united us and made us stronger than we ever could have been on our own." You see that the forms of the eagle and the lion are slowly beginning to melt together and merge with each other, as if they were meant to be together all along. Huge wings and feathers begin to sprout from within the shapeless mass that the eagle and lion have become. Beak and claws, tail and fur, feathers and mane emerge from the shape-shifting form, until at last you see what has become of the eagle and the lion. You are facing a griffon.

The griffon regards you with anticipation and hunger for adventure. "Claim the heart of the sword!" the powerful beast roars, and its cry echoes throughout the shadow realm. "Never mind the sword itself. It is a piece of your soul that must remain here in the shadow world. It is your anchor, your foundation. Draw the fiery spirit of the sword itself from the blade."

You stand and begin to move towards the soul sword, but suddenly you hesitate for a moment to gaze at your own reflection in the mirror. You are amazed at how much your reflection has changed since you last saw it. Your aura glows with confidence and strength. You also see the spirits of the ancient ones swirling around you and you know that you are not alone. The spirits of all those who have walked the path before you are now gathered around you and are at your side. You know that these spirits will be with you for all time. They will guide and protect you on your every journey. You are charged by the powers of the spirits. You are eager to continue on your quest for balance. You move to the soul sword and grab onto the hilt of the sword. You open your third eye and concentrate on the sword. You find that you can feel the difference between the metal of the sword and the energy of the sword's spirit. You relax your hand and slowly draw the energy spirit from the blade of the soul sword.

Now that the spirit of the sword is yours to command, you go to the mirror and plunge the sword into the center of the looking glass. The waters of the mirror begin to bubble and churn. A ring of energy erupts from the mirror's surface, and the living waters of the looking glass separate and part before you. You have opened a gateway to the astral plane. You can feel the unimaginable energies that exist on the other side of the mirror as they pulse through the spirit of the soul sword and through your entire being.

You may now travel through the gateway and enter the astral world. But before you do so, listen carefully to my words. *The griffon is yours to command.* You can take it with you, or leave it behind to guard the shadow realm. The protective circles in the shadow realm also exist in the astral world that lies beyond the portal of the mirror. *Do not pass beyond the boundaries of these astral circles for now.*

The energy spirit of the soul sword you hold is fearsome and powerful. It will protect you in the astral world. The sword itself was forged from a piece of your soul. It must remain here, fixed in the shadow realm. It is tied to you at all times and binds your astral body to your human self.

The necklace is still clasped around your throat; the key hangs over your heart. If at any time you need to leave the astral plane quickly, take the key in your hand and you will be transported back to your physical body.

I cannot travel with you through the portal of the mirror. The path that lies ahead is for you, and you alone, to experience. What is revealed to you on the other side of the mirror is meant for you and no one else. After a time, however, I will call to you, and you will hear my voice either aloud or in your mind. When you hear my voice beckon to you, *you must return to the shadow realm.* Go now. Pass through the gateway of the mirror. Enter the astral plane.

You must now return to the shadow realm. Follow the sound of my voice and return to the gateway of the mirror. Pass through the gateway. *Return to the shadow realm now!*

You are now back within the protective walls of your domain. You feel safe and at home. What you have experienced in the astral world is stored in your memory. You will never forget. You are calm and at peace, refreshed and renewed. You feel the energy spirit of the soul sword leave your hand and return to the blade from which it came.

The griffon jumps up and perches atop the frame of the mirror. Its eyes show its weariness, and you see that it is badly in need of sleep. It closes its eyes and slowly turns to stone. The griffon will sleep here until you are in need of it once again.

You see that the waters of the looking glass are flowing back into themselves, sealing the gateway. You begin to float upward toward your earthy self. Softly, slowly floating away from your domain. You drift up through the boundaries of the twin circles. You are nearing the edge of the shadow realm. You pass beyond the boundaries of your domain and cross over to the earthly plane. You are aware of the sounds of the world and the breath within your chest.

You open your eyes and your mind to your earthly reality.

The Mouth of the Lion

If you were to look through the major arcana in many decks of tarot cards, you will find the familiar picture of a maiden holding open (or, in some cases, shut) the mouth of a lion. You may already know this card as Strength. The symbolism of the Strength card, as with *any* card in the tarot, can be interpreted in a number of different ways, depending upon who you talk to or which book you read. But the undeniable message of this card—that inner strength is more powerful than raw, physical strength—shows through clearly. The deeper psychological meaning of the Strength card may be interpreted as doing battle with the beast(s) inside of you, wherein your stronger "higher" self overcomes your weaker "lower" self. I like to say that this symbolizes your ability to *command and silence the dragon and the lamb.*

Once you have attained the goal of overcoming the dragon and the lamb, the Strength card will become the perfect icon for your victory over your "lower selves." When you have learned how to control and unite the dragon and the lamb, I want you to honor this victory by searching through your tarot deck for the Strength card. Better yet, try to *feel* the Strength card in the deck and see if you can pull it without looking. Place the card on your altar or a prominent place in your home or sanctuary so you can see the card every time you walk by. If you don't own a tarot deck, you certainly don't have to run out a buy one. Instead, consider taking a nature walk through the woods (or a local park, if there are no wooded areas nearby) and see if you can find a symbol of strength as you walk. Place what you find on your altar in place of the Strength card. Even if you already own a tarot deck, you may want to consider going on a nature walk and finding a natural symbol of strength. Doing this will also give you a chance to contemplate your victory in peaceful and relaxing surroundings.

Visual aids and symbols such as the Strength card can be very powerful representations of our goals, our magick, and our strength. They can show us what we have achieved, or perhaps *what we wish to achieve.*

However, as we learned from the raven and the lioness in Exercise 3, symbols are not always what they seem to be. A very good friend of mine used to wear a skeleton key on a silver chain around his neck as a symbol of his control over a dark and powerful magickal force that he felt he had accidentally unleashed. As is the case with any Witch with half a brain, he didn't believe that the key itself held any real power over this magickal force. It was simply a symbol of his mistake and his eventual correction of (and control over) his mistake. A skeleton key, after all, is just a piece of metal that has been transformed into a tool to lock and unlock a door, just as our wands, staffs, and athames (even though they may be magickally charged) are simply tools that are used by the Witch to gather or direct energy. Any experienced Witch already knows (or *should* know) that the *real* power is in the mind and internal energy of the Witch, and not in the tool itself. Or even in what the tool symbolizes.

I am reminded here of a scene from the movie *Braveheart,* in which a young William Wallace is standing beside his uncle, Argyle. As bagpipers play solemn tunes in homage to William's dead father, Argyle notices William's interest in the sword he is holding. Argyle hands his sword to young William. Looking down at the boy, Argyle says to him, "First learn to use *this,*" and he taps William on the forehead. "Then," he says as he takes the sword from William's hand and brandishes it in the air, "then I'll teach you to use this." The symbolism being shown here, I believe, is that all the power in the world will not do you one bit of good if you have not first learned how to use your wits and your willpower instead of brute force to win in battle. How do you think the movie *Braveheart* would have ended if William Wallace had been taught to rely on his sword alone? What if he had lost his weapon in the middle of combat? Although I am fully aware that power can be manifested by the use of symbols and visual aids, far too many teachers of Witchcraft seem to place much more emphasis on the use of these tools and symbols than I am comfortable with. As in the case of the raven and the lioness, symbols and tools are usually not seen by (or taught to) the new student of Witchcraft for what they truly are: window dressing. Though I myself greatly enjoy the power of the symbol, there is a *far greater power* that should be considered, taught, and learned by the new Witch before anything else: This is the *power of intent.*

The magic behind the power of intent is easy for me to explain, and hopefully even easier for you to understand. It is not the color of the candle, the phase of the moon, the magickal circle, the wand, the athame, or even the gods and goddesses that give us the power to practice Witchcraft. It is what *we believe* about these things that gives them (and us) power. If *we believe* that we cannot perform magick without them, then we have just erased any power we may have had to begin with. The American Heritage Dictionary gives us the following definition of the word *intent*: the state of one's mind at the time one carries out an action. So if new Witches have been taught (and believe) that they cannot successfully cast a spell without the "correct" color of candle and the "correct" magickal herb during the "correct" phase of the moon, or that they cannot successfully draw down that moon without using the "correct" gestures and the "correct" athame, what do you think would be the state of their mind if I took their tools away? Would they still be able work their magick without them? I have had to do this very exercise—taking the tools away—many times with my students. Believe me, their initial response wasn't pretty. Their behavior wasn't magickal. It is *all about intent,* but no one had told them.

It is my belief that far too many "newbie" Witches have been taught early on to rely on the trappings of magick, on the tools and symbols instead of on their own creative imagination. As with anything else, once ingrained, the falsity of this reliance will have to be exorcised (usually quite painfully) before the Witch will be able to grow in his or her Craft. I have heard all of the arguments on why these symbolic facets of the Craft should be taught before anything else. One of the most common arguments I have heard for emphasizing tools and symbols is that these new Witches come from a Christian or Catholic background and that the teachings of the new student's former belief system must be purged before the student can understand and accept the lessons of Witchcraft. That is, you can't teach new students too much too soon about the "inner" workings of Witchcraft while they are trying to "unlearn" Christianity or they might freak out on you. Teachers who work this way seem to feel that the Craft must be watered down so the new students aren't "overburdened" with too much new information while they are trying to change over from their former religion. Through the best of their *intentions,* however, these teachers of Witchcraft are doing to their students exactly what they have accused the Christian Church of doing: They are telling their students only what they want them to hear, not what these students really *need to hear,* which is the truth. As one of my older, wiser students so said just the other day during a discussion on this topic: "If you baby your students, you will end up with a coven full of babies." This was a profound insight. Anyone who teaches Witchcraft should seriously think about it.

Now don't get me wrong. I am not suggesting that you should gather up all of your herbs, oils, candles, and magickal tools and throw them in the trash. I love my magickal goodies just as much as you probably do. That isn't the point I'm trying to make here. Nor am I suggesting that anyone should teach their students how to cast a bipolar circle or advanced theories on Witchcraft before they teach the basics. What I would like for you, the reader, to do is to strongly consider what I am saying. Then make up your own mind as to whether or not you think what I'm saying is valid. Brand new Witches, whether they come from a Christian background or not, are usually not the fragile little vessels that they are often made out to be. They are as well equipped as any of us to discern between what's a load of crap and what's not. That awareness probably played a large role in why they left their old path and started seeking a new one.

If we water down the lessons of Witchcraft, the students will most likely catch on at some point. Then they may feel that they have been misguided, and they won't be too happy about that. They decided *for themselves* to answer the call to magick and service to the Lord and Lady, who, by the way, will teach them more than any of us ever could. I don't think that very many of them tripped and fell onto the path of Witchcraft by mistake. It took trust in themselves and courage to take that first small step, so we should give them that much credit and honor that first step *by teaching them to be self-reliant before we teach them anything else.* Then (if we must) we can spoon-feed them some fairy dust. What these new students of the Craft learn from us, or read in books, will determine the future of Witchcraft and the destiny of our kind. We must be mindful of this fact when we decide to share the mysteries with them. We should not be attempting to mold these new Witches into what *we* would like to see them become until we have first taught them how to discover what *they* want to become. We must show them how to rely on their own inner strength before we teach them anything else. New Witches' understanding of the sabbats, the quarters, deity, herbs, oils, candle colors, and the symbolism of a Witch's broom won't do them a damn bit of good if they have not first been (metaphorically) tied up, gagged, blindfolded, spun around until they're dizzy, locked in a dark closet, and succeeded in casting a circle without using anything except their mind and their willpower.

If you don't believe this is possible, then you need to retrace your footsteps back to the beginning of your path and figure out exactly where you went wrong. Some of the most powerful Witches in the world may very well be those who are physically challenged and bound to a wheelchair. These Witches' inability to dance in a circle, or use a magickal tool, makes them no less of a Witch than you or I. In fact, many of these physically challenged Witches have probably far surpassed most of us by their ability to use their minds to raise energy, instead of relying on magickal apparatus to do the job for them. It is all about *intent*.

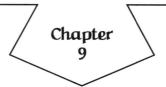

Chapter 9

The Power at Work

Hopefully, by now you have seen how the dragon and the lamb are simply aspects of the duality that exists in deity, in nature, and within each and every one of us. They are the inner voices of emotion that speak to us constantly about every facet of our mundane and magickal lives. The dragon and the lamb dictate how we react to any given situation. They tell us how to interact with ourselves and others. What follows is a true story about how the dragon and the lamb spoke to me one day and how I recognized their existence inside me. This is how, for the first time, I was able to give them faces and names that allowed me to see the battle they had been waging with each other. These insights set me on the path to become a general in their conflict instead of a private under their command.

One day I drove my son to a video game store so he could spend some money he had earned by doing some yard work for his grandmother. I had never been to this particular store before, and the parking lot was small and not laid out well. After my son's money was safely stashed in the store's cash register and it was time to leave, I noticed that two very large trucks were parked very close on both sides of our car. I somehow managed to get into the car, started it, and began the process of trying to back out without hitting anything. I was almost clear of the trucks when the car suddenly came to an abrupt halt, accompanied by a loud crunching sound. I jumped out. I looked around. I had somehow managed to back into a huge steel pole in the middle of the parking lot. The back of the car was smashed. *My wife's car.*

My heart sank into my stomach; I felt like a complete idiot. "How could this have happened?" I asked myself. "My wife is going to be *so* upset!" I checked my son to make sure he was okay, then went back to asking myself questions such as: "Why didn't I drive the van instead of her new car? What did I do to deserve this?"

After living with the woman for many years, I really knew better than to behave like such an idiot. I knew that when I got home and told her what had happened, she would say things including, "At least nobody was hurt," "It's just a car, after all," and "Everything happens for a reason. You're safe, and that's all that really matters."

Yes, *I* knew what she was going to say. But my *inner lamb* didn't know or care, and he was out in full force today. Well, yes, at least he was out for a minute or two until my anger took over. "What a stupid-ass place to stick a steel pole!" I shouted at the front of the store. "If you're going to start a business, then why don't you give people enough room to park? If those goddam trucks hadn't been parked so close, I would have been paying more attention to what was behind me!"

Aaah, yes, my *inner dragon* had lifted its head. The lamb went running for cover as my dragon rose up, spread its wings, and started breathing fire.

And at that very moment the Goddess grabbed me by the shoulders, gave me a good shaking, and asked me just what the hell I thought I was doing.

Three days later, I hopped into my van and drove down to the corner store for a cola. A *big* cola was in order this day. "A *super* big cola with ice and a straw and its very own plastic lid," I said to myself. I had some pretty good thoughts and observations going on in my head about the dragon and the lamb, so after buying my giant cola I hopped back into the van, threw it in reverse, and put my foot on the gas. I was eager to get back home and get my thoughts into the computer before they disappeared forever into my caffeine buzz from the cola.

What happened next? You guessed it. I backed the van into a nice sturdy steel pole. My van was dented and crushed *in the exact same place* that I'd dented and crushed the back of my wife's car. As I sat dumbfounded in a puddle of ice and cola, the dragon stirred. He raised his head, looked sleepily around, shook his head, snorted at me…and went back to sleep. The lamb looked up briefly and went right back to grazing in its meadow. I rolled down the window, let out a loud sigh, and said, "I'm learning."

Walking with the dragon and the lamb can be a very powerful learning experience. Once you understand them, you will attain a balance within you unlike anything you have ever known. Your task for this chapter is this: start listening to your own dragon and lamb when they speak to you. I want you to observe them in others. I want you to do this every minute of every day until it becomes second nature for you to recognize which one is speaking. Pay attention to what affect their voices are having on your emotions and your actions. I want you to question their motives, their reasoning, and the control they hold over you and over each other. I want you to learn how to hear both of their voices at the same time, to discover how to unite their best attributes into a single voice that surfaces in you as a whole new language. *This is the language of balance.*

I would also like you to take some time to ponder all the symbolic elements of your third trip into the shadow realm. See what buried insights and lessons you can unearth.

More than anything else, remember this: True strength is not always about winning. It is not always about coming out on top, being a leader, or proving that you are tougher than everyone else. True strength is defined by how well we handle life's situations, how we take other people's needs into consideration before feeding our own need for power. True strength is holding back and suggesting that someone with low self-esteem lead a ritual, even though you know you could do a much better job. True strength is going back a few steps and helping someone less capable than yourself climb the ladder of life, even though it impedes your own progress. Some of the strongest people I have ever known were the gentlest souls. They brought out the strength in everyone else, and in doing so are revered as examples of what true strength really is. Now *that* is strength worth having!

Chapter 10

The 2-Way Mirror

First Witch: *But in a sieve I'll thither sail,*
and, like a rat without a tail,
I'll do, I'll do, and I'll do.

Second Witch: *I'll give thee a wind.*

First Witch: *Th'art kind.*

Third Witch: *And I another.*

First Witch: *I myself have all the other,*
And the very ports they blow,
All the quarters that they know....

—William Shakespeare, *Macbeth*

As practitioners of Witchcraft, we have developed our own unique belief system and culture that differs from any other found in civilization. Because we are Witches, we are often viewed by society as being odd and very different from everyone else. Sure, most of us try our best to fit in and demonstrate to the public that underneath it all we are pretty much the same as they are. Why should we be viewed as different? We work, play, and raise our families side by side with the rest of our communities. We have the same physical needs and in many cases the same desires. We all shop at the same grocery stores, receive bills in the mail from the same utility companies, and pay the mortgages on our homes to the same banks. Is it right for society to make us feel as outcasts simply because we practice an eclectic religion? Should we be viewed as freaks because we don robes and gather together under full moons, whereas most people play card games with friends or watch sitcoms on cable television? Are we really so different from everyone else?

Of course we are.

Not only are we different from every*one* else, but we are also different from every*thing* else in one very fundamental way: We are the only creatures on this planet that intentionally distort the universe and disturb the natural order of things.

I imagine I just gave the cauldron a good stirring, but, if you consider my point for a moment, I think you will see that it makes perfect sense. Envision the universe and its energy streams before the human race ever existed. Serene scene, isn't it? Now along comes humanity with sentient thought and conscious action, exerting its will over the environment and everything else it comes into contact with. However, as destructive as our species can be, the human race was (I believe) still an act of nature, so we must consider that any effect that humanity is having on the universe and the earth as a *natural process.*

Now introduce the practice of Witchcraft into the picture, and the entire macrocosm suddenly becomes the equivalent of a magickal shooting gallery. Witches and their Craft are still a part of the natural process, you say? *I don't think so.* The basis of magick may indeed originate in the natural world, but it is transformed by the Witch into the *super*-natural, and that, my friends, is a whole new animal that nature never intended to create. Now, though most of this particular theory of mine will probably be debated until doomsday without any mutual conclusion being reached, its basis remains in the realm of possibility and therefore demands a closer look.

Natural or otherwise, the practice of Witchcraft has an astounding effect on the universe. On that I think most of us can agree. Whereas most of the human race can only implement change on a global level, or pray that their will be done through the hand of their god, Witches can take it upon themselves to manipulate the energies of the cosmos at will—oftentimes without discretion. Although most of these injudicious acts of magick are being performed by those new to the Craft or by those who lack proper guidance or self-discipline, they *are* being performed none-theless and must be considered when we look at the bigger picture of magickal cause and effect.

Magickal cause and effect differs from mundane cause and effect only because the supernatural element has been added into the equation. The addition of the metaphysical "x-factor" can, however, lead to an extremely complex chain of events and outcomes. An example of mundane cause and effect could be as simple as this:

> Cause: You are out of gas.
>
> Effect: Your car won't start.

Magickal cause and effect could start out just as simply:

> Cause: You are out of money.
>
> Effect: You cast a prosperity spell.

But exactly what happens after you have cast the spell? Do you know for certain where that spell is going? Do you know what might be affecting your magick along the way? Do you know what effect your spell may be having on other people or even on another Witch's spell? This is where the chain of events becomes more complicated. The work in this chapter is about to become very intense, but before it does let's have a bit of fun and set the stage for a little drama to get a better hold on our understanding of magickal cause and effect. Let's try to clarify the role Witches play in the chain of events.

If you have ever attended a Pagan festival or gathering, then you have probably seen Witches who constantly watch the skies for any sign of inclement weather. No sun-loving pagan likes rain on their ritual, after all, so these Witches take it upon themselves to use magick to try and push even the most innocent storm cloud away from the festivities. Most of you already know those who perform this form of magick as "weather-witches." These meteorological manipulators of the forces of nature are prime examples of the point that I am trying to make about the effect that Witchcraft is having on the universe.

Let's envision a fictitious character whom we shall call Stormraven the Weather-Witch, who is this day attending the Festival of the Frisky Pagans. On her way to ritual, Stormraven happens to spot an approaching rain cloud that she feels could be a threat to the festivities. So she gathers up some energy and starts pushing the rain cloud away from the festival. Unbeknownst to her, however, she just happens to be pushing this rain cloud directly towards Wendy the Wiccan, who has just spent the morning painting her porch. Now it just so happens that Wendy has had a little experience with weather-witching herself, so when she spies the approaching rain cloud, she decides that she doesn't want an entire morning's worth of work and a gallon of paint wasted. So Wendy gathers up some energy and goes to work on the rain cloud. She just happens to push it right over the head of Malkavien the All-Powerful, who is attending a meeting of the Brotherhood of the Golden Stag about a mile away. Malkavien takes one look at the rain cloud and decides that he doesn't want the fires he has just lit for the sweat lodge to be prematurely extinguished, so he raises his staff to the heavens and wills the rain cloud away…pushing it right back over the head of Stormraven the Weather Witch, who now feels the first few drops of rain land on her brand new ritual cloak.

Exactly what do you think is happening here (or is going to happen)? Well, for one thing, if I were the rain cloud, I would probably give everyone involved a good zapping with a few well-placed bolts of lightning. We now have three magicians locked in combat with an innocent little rain cloud, and each of these magicians is ignorant to the others who are magickally involved. This example is admittedly a bit silly, but it makes my point—and, besides, every time I see a storm front passing through my area, I grin at the thought of all the Witches out there who might be trying to manipulate the storm. I can't help being amused by wondering just whose lap the storm is going to end up in.

So for the sake of argument, let us say that on any given day, ten thousand different spells are being cast by as many Witches. How many of these spells do you think are canceling each other out? How many of the energy streams being produced or manipulated by these Witches are interfering with each other? How many undesirable outcomes are being manufactured because of this interference?

Do you understand now what I meant by the chain of magickal cause and affect becoming so complex? Without knowledge and understanding of exactly where your energy or spell-work is going, or what may or may not be affecting or interfering with it along the way, for all of your efforts you might as well be shooting a BB gun at the moon. How, then, do we solve this magickal dilemma and raise the odds of successful spell-casting and energy manipulation in our favor? Once the *cause* has been determined, how do we gain better understanding and control over the *effect*? I will show you.

In Chapter 2, we discussed your learning to become what I referred to as an *omnidirectional practitioner of the magickal arts*. You began this process when you learned how to switch your magickal battery cables. That's when you began to get an unbiased understanding of the universal flows and counter-flows of energy. I explained to you that an integral aspect of being an omnidirectional magician is having the ability to send and receive energy to and from all points at the same time.

You cannot accomplish this feat, however, unless you have first developed the ability to *be* at all of these points at the same time. Learning and understanding how to do so will not only bring you one step closer to your shadow spirit and take you well on your way to becoming an omnidirectional magician, but it can also give you power over the effects in the process of cause and effect. How will learning how to be everywhere at once help you with energy manipulation? How will it help you become an omnidirectional Witch? In essence, once you have learned this lesson, you will have the ability to equip your spells and willpower with an advanced magickal guidance system and be able to paint a laser target, so to speak, for your energy streams and "magickal missiles" to follow. Do I have your attention now? Good. Let's get started.

On page 104 you can see a symbol that most of us see repeatedly in our day-to-day lives. I want you to look at this symbol and tell me what it is.

I am going to assume that you said, "It's a stop sign." You're correct. Well, *almost* correct. You have been forced to look at this symbol over and over again, so many times, that you probably only see it with your mundane eyes, not through your magickal eyes. So what could possibly be so magickal about a silly old stop sign, you ask. In the stop sign itself, absolutely nothing is magickal. It is when we discover where this mundane symbol can *lead* us that its magick is revealed.

Imagine that you are driving down an old country road in the middle of nowhere, and you happen to come across our magickal stop sign. Now imagine yourself doing exactly what the word on the sign tells you to do: You stop. Now, in your mind, look down any roads that might intersect at this crossing and try to imagine where they might lead you if you were to follow them. At this point, you are looking forward in time to possible future events. Now look back at the stop sign. Work your way backwards through time, and imagine what the stop sign might have looked like on the very first day it was planted in the ground here. Imagine the road worker who installed this very stop sign. What might they have been thinking while they were at work installing the stop sign? Imagine that at one point in time there were no stop signs or roads here at all. What might this place have looked like at that long-ago time?

By understanding what the magickal stop sign is *really* telling to you to do, from this lonely little corner of the world, from this one moment in time, you are able to connect with everything, everywhere, and also be everywhere at the same time. All you need to do is Stop. *Stop and think....* Let us try the following technique in visualization to get your wheels turning in the right direction and give your mind a boost into how it should be looking at things so you attain a more universal mindset.

Picture the stop sign in your mind. Now imagine all of the cars and all of the people that at one time or another may have stopped here. Without losing this vision, imagine all of the houses that these people live in. Now imagine these people's families, their neighbors, and all of their families. Imagine all of the trees that grow in their yards and all of the trees that grow in the yards of the families and neighbors. Now imagine the peoples' lives, and their friends' lives, and what all these people know, and where they have been. Imagine all the leaves on all the trees, all the branches on the trees, and all the birds sitting on all the branches looking at all the yards of all the people. Suddenly you see—you're seeing everything in the world. You can even see the tree directly behind you without having to turn around to look at it.

Do you understand what I am trying to get you to do? Do you see how one thing can build on the next until the very fabric of what they are intermingles to the point of becoming indiscernible from anything else?

This visualization technique is merely the proverbial tip of the iceberg. You are going to have to take it much further before you can truly understand what it is I am trying to get you to learn. When you can learn to view the entire microcosm and the entire macrocosm and all of their individual pieces, and then follow them to the ultimate end of being able to experience any part of the universe you desire from the comfort of your living room couch, then you will know for the first time what it really means to achieve "oneness" with everything. When you can *literally see and feel* the interconnectedness of all things, when you can *be* all of these things and *be* all of these places and still *be yourself* at the same time, then you will have come to the very definition of an omnidirectional practitioner of the magickal arts. You will become an omnidirectional practitioner, and the power of your magickal skills will increase without measure.

This way of thinking and experiencing the universe is available to *anyone* who cares to take the time to learn to use it. It isn't some great mystery that only the most magickal mind or advanced intellectual genius can grasp. You don't have to find some secret place of power or undiscovered beauty to attain it.

You can begin the process by starting with a spoon, a blade of grass, or a painting by Renoir, and achieve the same outcome. For example, you could look at a spoon and then imagine all of the spoons in all of the houses in your town. Then take the process to the next logical step of imagining all of the spoons in all of the houses in the world. Then imagine all of the people who eat with these spoons, and imagine the food they're eating. Imagine the farmers who grew the food, imagine the seeds in the ground, imagine the harvest and the preparation of all that food—on and on until you can feel everything, everywhere. You can start by envisioning anything you have ever seen or anything you can possibly imagine in any form. In your imagination, the spoon can be the metal in the ground before it was mined and forged and shaped into a spoon. The Renoir painting can be the paint, the painter, the brush, or—my personal favorite—the blank canvas. You can start with anything. The most important thing is that you *begin the process of practicing this technique* over and over again until you master it. Trust me: This technique will come in very handy when you undertake the final exercise in balance (Exercise 4). It may very well be vital in your ability to successfully complete the meditation. Again, try to have some fun with it. You don't have to be intense and mysterious all of the time.

Let me show you one final approach to achieving the goal of this chapter, which is attaining universal oneness. I call this technique the "harmonic trance." If you don't already understand it, there are a number of differences between a trance state and a meditative state. If you searched hard enough, you could probably find as many differing definitions of the word *trance* as there are opinions about what it truly means. For the sake of this lesson, we will consider a trance to be *an altered state of consciousness where our subconscious is being guided by an unseen force to attain a state of heightened awareness.* In other words, a harmonic trance is a state in which our outer, "perceptive" mind is unaware and unconcerned with our surroundings and with what is going on around us, and our "inner" free-flowing mind is brought to the forefront, thus putting us into a dreamlike state while we are still awake.

So exactly how do we get there? Lucky for you, I have developed a method that is much easier to explain and (hopefully) understand than the many different definitions of what a trance is. To achieve a harmonic trance, we will look once again to our trusty old friend, the tree, for help.

Preparing to enter a harmonic trance is very similar to preparing for meditation. You will need to find a comfortable spot where you will not be interrupted and where there are few distractions. There is, however, one fundamental requirement for this exercise. You will need to be in a place where you can see a tree. If you cannot, or do not wish to be outside, then find a window through which you can see a tree. If it is winter where you are, try to find a place where you can see an evergreen tree. If you are in the desert, you'll have to make do with whatever you can see that is treelike. In a pinch, you could use just about anything, but I prefer that you use a tree if at all possible, because a tree is a part of nature and, even in a dead-calm, there is usually some kind of movement in the leaves.

Once you are in a comfortable spot, start to relax and clear your mind of thoughts or concerns, just as you do when you prepare to meditate. Do *not,* however, close your eyes at any point in the exercise. Unlike meditation, you are not trying to focus or center on the core of your being. Instead, you are allowing your spiritual essence to float freeform away from your mental control, to become distant from your conscious mind and from your awareness of self. To do this, pick out a tree as far off in the distance as you can see clearly. Now, pick out a single leaf or a spot on the tree's trunk. Without thinking about the *tree,* the *leaf,* or *anything at all,* stare at the leaf. Do not look away from the leaf for any reason (other than for reasons of personal safety).

Looking away from the leaf before you have reached the trance state will break the connection, and you will have to start over from the beginning. Yes, you can blink. Blinking is a normal physical function and will not interfere with the process. As you continue to stare at the leaf, the three-dimensional world as your eyes perceive it should begin to distort. The space closest to you will feel strangely spread out. Do not let this distract you. *Keep staring at the leaf.* You will eventually feel as though you are leaving your body, that your entire being is floating toward that leaf. Do not let this sensation alarm you. It is completely normal, and your safety is not in jeopardy.

As the trance deepens, you will literally feel as though you are in the tree, right next to the leaf. You will then feel as though you are merging with the leaf and the energies that it is made of. At this point, you will feel very small and that you are swirling around inside a swarm of insects. You may even hear a vague buzzing noise. You may be able to feel the sensation of gentle vibration. When you reach this point in the trance, you will lose all awareness of your self. You will feel as though you are a tiny speck of energy flowing within the stream of the life force itself. You will feel an utter and complete connectedness to everything, everywhere, in the universe. You are now harmonically resonating with the very fabric of existence.

At this point, any number of things can happen. I have known people who have done automatic writing, created works of art, and even written down or spoken aloud complex formulas and mathematical equations that they could not possibly have been able to know outside of the trance. None of these people were aware of what they were doing at the time.

I have been told that while I was in a harmonic trance I have spoken in other languages and explained advanced theories on topics of which I have no knowledge or expertise whatsoever. In my very first experience of journeying into the harmonic trance, I was given the first part of the key that would eventually unlock the mystery of the shadow spirit…but that is a tale we will get to later.

You should be fully prepared for the fact that anything and everything can and will happen while you are in the state of harmonic trance, but, in my opinion and experience, the harmonic trance is perfectly safe for you to attempt. In fact, it may be the single most important key to your realization of your full potential as a Witch. Remember, however, what I have said to you repeatedly throughout this book: *The choice is yours and yours alone.* The exercise of the harmonic trance is *not required for you to continue walking the path of the shadow spirit.*

One last thing: If you decide to attempt this exercise, before you do so, make sure that there is not someplace you need to be or anything that you have to do in the immediate future. Time has no meaning while you are in the harmonic trance, and what you may perceive as mere seconds having passed may actually be hours. So please make sure that you haven't left the stove on or left a candle or cigarette burning somewhere in the house. Make perfectly sure that the physical world will get along safely and smoothly without you for a time.

I want you to strongly consider all the things we have discussed so far in this chapter. Before you return to the shadow realm and undertake the fourth and final exercise in balance, ask yourself if you truly understood the work we have done so far. In Exercise 4, you will be challenged far beyond anything you have experienced thus far in any of the other meditations. I promise that even if you are well prepared, you may be tested to your absolute limits. I have, however, to the best of my ability, given you the option to make your own choices and decisions as we have traveled the path of the shadow spirit together, even while trying to preserve the spirit of what I feel you need to learn by walking this path.

Reflection: The Hall of Mirrors

This final exercise in balance will be split into two separate paths, and you will have to *decide for yourself* which one you will follow. Exercise 4 is split into the right-hand path and the left-hand path. (I'm reading your mind again. Get those dark, nasty, fairy tale ideas about the left-hand path out of your head.) The right-hand path contains all of the key elements needed to complete your realignment with balance, but it will be far less mentally and spiritually challenging than the left-hand path. If you wish to test your mettle, or desire a more intense and challenging learning experience, you should choose to follow the left-hand path. But if you do, heed well my words and be prepared for what you are about to face.

The left-hand path will not be a lighthearted little game by any stretch of the imagination. You will be facing the blackest, most hidden parts of your mind and soul. You will have to learn the final lessons in balance while you are being ripped apart and reborn, tormented and metaphysically beaten, psychically drained, and left all alone to find your way out of the dark abyss of your weaknesses.

Why would I want to put *anyone* through such an awful experience, you may be asking. The answer is that anybody who can successfully make it through such a meditation will have faced the very heart of his or her darkest self. That person will emerge transformed and cleansed of his or her inner demons, deepest fears, and darkest nightmares. He or she will have a refreshed mind and a reborn spirit that has been cleansed by the hand of the Goddess Herself. *That's why…*

There will be quite a few Pagans and Witches who will probably scold and criticize me, and perhaps even be angry with me for devising such a meditation as the left-hand path. To them I say that they should just stay at home in the relative safety of their closed doors and closed minds. They should shut their windows and their mouths and leave the future and its promise to the *real* adventurers and explorers. They should leave the pioneering to those of us who do not fear what lies beyond the veil. Remember the *dare* part in "to know, to will, to dare, and to remain silent"? As for *this* Witch, I never did agree with the "to remain silent" part, anyway.

And from the darkness, the light shall be reborn….

No matter which path you decide to follow, take a mental picture of the "old you" so you can remember who you used to be. You're leaving that old you behind. You can look forward to the person and the Witch you are about to become. Consider all of the options before you make your final decision as to which path you are going to take. Keep in mind that no matter what you decide, I am most proud of you for having made it this far. I wish you safety and well-placed footsteps on your next journey.

The Right-Hand Path

You will now be undertaking the final exercise in your realignment with balance. Because you have chosen to take the right-hand path of Exercise 4, your final journey in balance will take place in the light instead of in the darkness. However, even though you have chosen to walk the path of light, to successfully complete your realignment with balance, you will need to remember all of the lessons you have learned by doing the work in this book. You will also need to tap into your inner strength and use that strength to your full advantage while you navigate this final exercise. Use your inner strength as an anchor to steady your mind and concentration as you add this final piece of the puzzle to the picture of balance.

Up to this point, we have always done an invocation to a particular god and goddess to protect, guide, and watch over you as you have navigated the labyrinths of balance. This time, however, we will forego the invocation. Everything you need to complete Exercise 4 you will find either within yourself or within the shadow realm. As always, however, the choice is yours alone to make, so if you feel you need extra support and guidance for this final exercise, feel free to call upon the deities of your choosing in any way you see fit before you begin this final meditation in your realignment with balance.

Find a place where you will be comfortable. Relax your body, your mind, and your spirit, and we will begin your fourth journey into the shadow realm. You close your eyes and empty your mind. You imagine that the gold and silver chain is clasped around your neck, and that the key is hanging over your heart. You imagine yourself grasping the key and holding it tightly in your hand. You feel the power of the key's energy growing stronger as you hold it. As the power of the key's energy increases, it is pulling you away from the earthly plane. You feel yourself drifting slowly downward, away from the mundane world. With every beat of your heart, you drift ever closer to the borders of the shadow realm.

You can now see the twilight of the shadow realm growing more intense as you approach your domain. The twilight's magickal luminescence begins to surround you, and you feel the power of the shadow realm grow stronger as you pass through the protective energies of its boundaries. You see the massive walls of stone that encircle the shadow realm, and the two slowly spinning circles of power below you. You slow your descent, and you hover directly over the two crystalline circles of energy and magick.

The shadow realm looks exactly the same as it did the last time you saw it, but somehow, it *feels* very different. Wild energies seem to be flowing freely throughout every corner of the shadow realm. Your presence here is somehow supercharging these energies, and you can feel an intense and powerful magickal force emanating from the center of your domain.

As you look down toward the center of the shadow realm, you see that the heart of this intense energy seems to be focused around the frame of the mirror. You also see that, once again, you have visitors. The gruff-voiced old gentleman and the kindhearted elderly woman are sitting on the white marble floor next to the soul sword. They seem to be playing some kind of a board game.

Intrigued, you float down and pass through the crystalline circles to get a closer look. You now see that they are playing a game of chess. There are only two pieces left on the board: a white king and a black king. The elderly gentleman looks up at you and sighs. "Neither one of us can win this game," he says, sounding almost exasperated, "but she makes me keep playing it with her anyway." "My dear Sir!" the elderly woman exclaims. "You are very well aware of the reasons why we can't stop playing this game." She moves the white king to an open square on the chessboard. "She's right," he says as he moves the black king randomly to another square on the chessboard. He looks up and catches your eye. "Life is not a game that can be either won or lost," he says to you, "only played."

The elderly woman smiles at the old man, takes his arm to brace herself, and gingerly rises to her feet. You see that she is wearing an old, white apron that is very badly stained, its edges tattered and worn. You find yourself feeling sorry for her for having to wear such an old rag of an apron. As if she had read your mind, the old woman looks at you and says, "Don't feel sorry for me, dear. These are the stains of life. We all have them, you know. I just wear this old thing to remind me. Besides, not all of these stains are bad ones. Yes, quite a few of them make me sad when I remember, but just as many are pleasant to recall." An amused smile crosses your face as you realize the truth and wisdom within the old woman's words. She now motions for you to come closer. You go to her side and she takes you by the arm. "Be a dear and walk me to the mirror," she begs. "I need to check my hair and makeup." Her grasp on your arm is warm and comforting. You reach over and wrap your hand over hers. Her skin is as thin as tissue paper. It feels soft and pleasing in the palm of your hand. You slowly walk with her to the mirror.

As you approach the mirror, arm in arm with the old woman, you are mindful of where she is stepping. "Just as I thought," the old woman exclaims, "I'm *quite* the mess!" You glance up at the looking glass and your breath stutters in your chest. The elderly woman's reflection reveals her to be the most beautiful, most imperious woman you have ever seen. A blazing crescent burns upon her forehead.

"I am known by ten thousand names, and I have worn ten thousand faces." It is now the Goddess who speaks to you. "Each and every person sees the facet of me that they need to see. There are many facets to you, also, and you, too, bear the stains of life," she says, as she takes the key hanging over your heart into her hand. The key starts glowing with powerful energies, and tiny beams of light begin to shine and dance across the shaft of the key.

The elderly gentleman now walks over to you and stands at your other side. He begins to speak. "You must embrace every aspect of yourself," he says, "both the good and the bad. You must accept the stains of your life, be they light or dark." He reaches past you and takes the hand of the Goddess, so that they are both holding the key, and, as he does so the rays of light surrounding it grow brighter and more intense. When you look up and see the old man's reflection in the mirror, you are not surprised. He is the God. He is powerful yet inviting. Wisdom and light shine in his eyes. A symbol of the sun burns upon his chest.

The God and the Goddess slowly open their hands. The key has been transformed into a large gemstone with thousands of facets cut into its surface. Each facet shines with its own unique ray of light. "Open your hands, my dear," the Goddess says. You cup your hands and hold them open in front of you. The God and Goddess place the gemstone in your palms and fold your fingers around the sparkling jewel.

The gemstone feels very warm in your hands. You can feel the energies within the stone begin to move through your fingers. Your hands and arms begin to tingle with a sensation that you have never felt before.

Suddenly you notice that the tips of your fingers are beginning to crystallize, to sparkle with facets just like the gemstone you hold in your hands. You look to the God and the Goddess, as if asking them what is happening to you. "It's nothing to worry about," the Goddess assures you. "You are merely taking on a different form for now." The voice of the God also sounds. "She is right," he says. "You are changing, but this is nothing for you to fear. But you should probably get going before the transformation is complete." The God and the Goddess take you by the arms and lead you into the living waters of the looking glass of the mirror. They release their hold on your arms, and you float away from them and enter the portal of the mirror.

The waters of the mirror flow around you like thick, warm honey, soothing you as you pass into them. You feel as if you are floating inside the womb of the Goddess herself. The glow emanating from the gemstone in your hands begins to grow brighter, and the stone rises up until it is hovering inches above the palms of your hands. The gemstone slowly begins to spin in a prism of color and light. The shafts of light bouncing off the thousands of facets sparkle and glitter, becoming more intense with every revolution of the gemstone. You also see shafts of light are bouncing off of the crystal facets that your fingertips have become. You can now feel that you are somehow absorbing the thick warm waters of the looking glass into your body through your crystal fingertips. As the living waters enter your fingers and begin to flow inside you, you see that your hands and arms are now also becoming crystalline. You raise your arms and hands before you in wonder. Even though you are transforming into a human gemstone, you are still able to move your body with the fluidity of the living water itself.

You feel the crystallizing waters flow up into your shoulders and through your chest. They cascade down through your hips and legs, transforming every inch of your body. The waters now well up and wash into your throat and over your face. They flow over your temples and fore-head, and, at last, the living waters stream through your eyes like re-versed tears. You are suddenly seeing through the kaleidoscopes of the faceted crystal lenses of your new eyes.

For the first time in your life, you know what it might be like to see through the eyes of deity. With your crystalline vision, you see a comet as it races past a dying star into the deepest recesses of space. You see a child as it is being born into the world, another child as it dies in its mother's arms. You see a gray-bearded old man tending a fire deep in the wilderness. You see an ocean of people as they walk the streets of a large city. You feel the loneliness and desperation of an old woman as she stares out of her window, watching life passing her by on the streets be-low. You see through the eyes of a young man as he gazes down upon the world from the top of a mountain. You feel the unity of life on earth, and you feel humble to be part of the oneness of the world.

The images and the emotions of a thousand lives and a thousand deaths flash before your crystalline eyes, pass through your crystalline mind. The images and emotions combine into visions that are coming to you faster than you can grasp them. The emotions you feel wash over you like a mighty waterfall.

To try to slow the momentum of feelings and visions, you focus your eyes and your mind on the gemstone, which is still slowly spinning and floating a few inches above your hands. But the visions keep coming, faster and faster, pouring into your crystalline eyes, filling your crystalline mind.

You see that the rays of light beaming from the slowly spinning gem-stone are generating the visions. You see that the visions are also being reflected onto the countless facets that cover your crystalline body.

You know that you must quickly figure out some way to gain control over the visions before you are completely overwhelmed by them. You intensify your focus and concentration on the slowly spinning crystal. The crystal stops spinning, and you look deeply into a single facet on the surface of the crystal floating just above your hands. The vision in this facet seems to freeze and hold still in time. But something else happens as well. The countless other visions also seem to be slowing down. But you can feel them building into an unstoppable deluge behind the single frozen vision on the surface of the crystal. You know that it could be very dangerous to hold back these visions for long. You know that you have only a few seconds of clear thought before you have to release the visions. You can feel that the energies within the facet are somehow sending the vision into your body and your mind through the beams of light emanating from the gemstone.

The energies within the facet feel very familiar to you, and you quickly recognize them as being the same energies that make up the sun side of the looking glass of the mirror. You know that the looking glass of the sun side of the mirror is made up of flow energy and that it is capable of either sending or deflecting energy. You trace the beam of light emanating from the frozen facet on the gemstone to a single crystalline facet on your arm. As you look deeply into the facet on your arm, you see that the vision is frozen within this facet as well, but the energies within the facet on your arm feel very different from the energies of the gemstone. You recognize these energies as being the same as those that make up the moon side of the looking glass of the mirror. You know that the moon side of the looking glass is made up of counter-flow energy and that it is capable of drawing energies into it. You now know that it is the counter-flow energies within the facets of your crystalline body that are drawing the visions inside of you.

Now you remember that you have learned how to reverse the flows of energy around you by switching your sending and receiving hands. This gives you an idea. You slowly uncup your hands, and the crystal floats away into the air above you. You cross your crystalline arms. You concentrate on the counter-flow energy within the single frozen facet on your arm. Using your will and the magickal skills that you have learned, you concentrate on reversing the counter-flow of energy within this single crystalline facet on your arm.

The reverse flow slowly begins to work, and you can see and feel that the vision in the facet is being deflected. It is moving away from you. You now see that the deflected vision is still caught up in the beam of light emanating from the gemstone. The energies within the facet on the gemstone and the reversed energies within the facet on your arm are now trying to send the vision in opposite directions. This causes the gemstone to resume spinning.

You can now feel the countless other visions swelling up within the facets of your crystalline body and mind. The dam is about to break! You ignore them for now as you keep the deflective energy stream of the reversed counter-flow concentrated on the single vision that is caught up in the gemstones beam of light.

You can see and feel that the powerful controlling force of the flow energy is now combining with the deflective force of the reversed counter-flow of energy. You release your hold on the reversed counter-flow of energy, and the counter-flow returns to normal. It is now working in perfect harmony with the flow energy. You can now use the power of the combined flows to guide the vision to anywhere you desire. You quickly use the force of the combined energy streams to move the vision away from the beams of light being generated by the spinning gemstone.

You look at the single vision being held at bay by the combined streams of flow and counter-flow. You are arrested by the wonder of what you are seeing. The single vision is no longer frozen in time! It is playing out as normal within the looking glass of a small mirror that has somehow been created within the stream of flow and counter-flow energy. Not only is the vision carrying on as it should, but you can now look upon the vision without it being overwhelming to you. *You have gained control over the vision.* You can now use and manipulate the vision in any way you see fit.

You can feel that the countless other visions are quickly building again behind the dam of your crystalline mind, so you concentrate on tapping the sum of the power within the stream of flow and counter-flow energy around you. The stream quickly builds into a powerful flood and washes over the countless facets that cover your crystalline body.

As the controlling power of the combined energy streams flows over each crystal facet of your body, each vision is caught up in the flood of flow and counter-flow, and one by one they begin moving away from your mind and body. You now see a very strange sight. There are now hundreds of small looking glasses floating within the powerful combined streams of flow and counter-flow energy all around you. Each of these small looking glasses is reflecting a different vision.

The number of looking glass visions quickly grows. There are now countless thousands of reflected visions surrounding you. Thousands more are being washed away from your crystalline body by the energy tides of the flow and counter-flow. One by one, they are being adding to the ever-growing ocean of looking glass visions.

There seems to be no organization as to where the looking glass visions are appearing. How are you ever going to be able to keep track of them all?

As if in silent response to your concern, the gemstone slowly floats up and into the stream of flow and counter-flow energy. It hovers in the center of the ever-increasing ocean of visions. You are astonished to see that the beams of light emanating from the spinning gemstone are somehow locking onto each of the looking glass visions. The beams are connecting them together and locking them into place next to each other. The looking glass visions are being organized into a monstrously huge sphere that resembles the faceted gemstone itself.

The few remaining visions are now flowing away from you and are being drawn up and locked into place by the light beams of the gemstone. You gaze upon the gigantic faceted sphere made up of the looking glass visions. As before, you are held in wonder by the power and beauty you behold. You focus on a single vision on the sphere, and the vision within the looking glass is projected directly in front of you like a hologram. Fascinated by the possibilities, you take a few moments to learn what you can see and feel within the vision that is being projected in front of you.

You now know that you can use the looking glass facets of the vision sphere to see, feel, and experience anything, anywhere within the universe, at any time you desire.

Something suddenly calls to you in your mind. It is time for you to return to the shadow realm. The living waters of the looking glass portal begin to drain away from your body. As the living waters leave your body and form a pool beside you, the crystal facets of your body begin transforming back to flesh and blood. The last few droplets of the waters drain away from your fingertips. The looking glass portal has been restored.

As you begin to move toward the shimmering pool of the looking glass portal, something suddenly distracts you. The gigantic sphere of the countless visions is growing smaller. The spinning gemstone floats towards you and, as it comes closer, you see that it is returning to its former shape. It is turning back into the necklace and the key.

The silver and gold necklace slides over your head, and now the key is once again hanging over your heart. The vision sphere has now grown so small that you can barley make it out in the distance. There is a sudden flash of bright light, and the vision sphere disappears altogether almost like an UFO vanishing into the night sky.

A second smaller flash of light near your chest draws your attention back to the key resting over your heart. You see that the vision sphere has shrunk down to the size of a small stone. It has embedded itself into the shaft of the key. As you take the key into the palm of your hand, you are instantly transported through the looking glass portal and back into the shadow realm.

The first thing you see in the shadow realm is the old woman. She is sitting on a large wooden trunk next to the moon pool. She appears to be sewing something together with silver thread that is rising from the pool. You also see that the griffon is not only awake, but that it is resting next to the sun pool as it plays a game of chess with the elderly gentleman. Looking more closely at the board, you can see that the elderly gentleman is losing quite badly to the griffon. "I never win at this stupid game," the old man grumbles as he lays his king on its side and concedes the game. He looks the griffon sourly in the eye, and says, "Good boy. Now lie down and go back to sleep." The griffon chuckles, jumps back up on top of the mirror frame, closes its eyes, and slowly turns to stone.

You now see that the old woman has hidden whatever it was she was sewing inside the chest. She closes the lid, turns the latch, then turns and looks you in the eye. "Never mind that for now," she says. "It will be safe in there until you need it." The elderly gentleman has also risen to his feet, and he and the old woman give each other a kind and loving glance. The old woman walks behind the moon pool and stands there quietly. The elderly gentleman walks behind the sun pool and does the same. He now speaks one more time. "Never forget how far you have come on your journey," he says. "Never forget what you have learned. Use your knowledge and skills wisely and humbly. Know that I will always be there for you when you need me." He closes his eyes, and his skin begins to turn gray. He is transformed into a statue of a wise and powerful god.

The old woman also speaks one more time: "Guard well the powerful key that hangs over your heart, my dear. The vision sphere embedded into its shaft is there for you to use whenever you need it. Use it to learn the ways of all peoples and of all magicks. Pass on your teachings. Share what you have learned with all who would know the ways of power." She too closes her eyes and is transformed into a statue of a wise and powerful goddess.

A gentle wind begins to blow in the shadow realm. Its breeze touches your forehead, and you are calmed by its presence. You are at peace within yourself. You sit down before the great mirror of promise and magick. Within the living waters of the looking glass you can see only your own reflection, and this comforts you. You have accomplished a great deal this day. It is now time for you to leave the shadow realm. You grasp the key in the palm of your hand. As the key grows warm, you begin your ascent toward the waking world. You slowly drift up through the crystal circles and towards the boundaries of the shadow realm.

You are very near the edge now, very close to the earthly plane. The key grows warmer in the palm of your hand. You cross over the boundaries of the shadow realm. You open your eyes and your mind to the waking world.

The Left-Hand Path

You will now be undertaking the final exercise in your realignment with balance. You have chosen to take the left-hand path of Exercise 4, and your final journey in balance will take place in the darkness instead of in the light. I offer you one final warning before you travel the left-hand path: You will be facing the blackest, most hidden, parts of yourself in this meditation. You will be confronting the dark mirror of your own soul. You will see many things that most people never want to see about themselves.

To successfully complete your realignment with balance, you will need to remember what you've learned by doing the work in this book. You will also need to tap into your inner strength and use that strength to your full advantage while you navigate this final path. Use your inner strength as an anchor to steady your mind and concentration as you add this final piece of the puzzle to the picture of balance.

Up to this point, we have always done an invocation to a god and goddess before undertaking the exercises in balance. Not this time. The path that awaits you lies deep within the darkest of places. You must walk there alone.

Find a quiet, comfortable place. Relax your body and clear your mind. Let go of your fears and your fantasies. They will deceive you if you let them. You close your eyes and imagine that the gold and silver chain is clasped around your neck, and that the key is hanging over your heart. You imagine yourself grasping the key and holding it tightly in your hand. You feel the power of the key's energy growing stronger as you hold it. As the power of the key's energy increases, you feel it pulling you away from the earthly plane. You feel yourself drifting slowly downward, away from the mundane world. With every beat of your heart, you drift ever closer to the borders of the shadow realm.

You are now nearing the borders of the shadow realm. You are very close. The key begins to grow warmer in your hand. Without warning, it suddenly becomes burning hot! You release your hold on the key, but, as you do, the clasp of the necklace breaks, and the key and the necklace fall into the shadow realm below you. You look at the palm of your hand. An imprint of the key has been burned into your flesh.

You resume your descent, and you pass over the borders and enter into the shadow realm. Instead of the usual twilight, you are greeted by a nearly pitch-black world. You hover in the air high above the darkness. Soon you are able to see an eerie glow of crimson light breaking on the horizon, and, as you watch, a blood-red crescent moon rises high into the skies of the shadow realm. But it is not the light of the sun reflecting off of the moon that is creating the shape of the crescent. The moon has been almost completely destroyed! Huge chunks of what remains of the moon float aimlessly about the jagged blood red crescent of the destroyed moon.

Now, rising into the sky far off on the horizon, you see what is creating the eerie crimson glow on what remains of the moon. The sun has become a dying red dwarf star. Its crimson light is muted and vague.

You can now hear distant screams and ghostly cries echoing from somewhere deep within the blackness of the shadow realm below you. Distant thunder rolls across the horizon, and the air of the shadow realm is charged with wild energies. Ghostly flashes of St. Elmo's Fire appear and disappear below you in the blackness of the shadow realm. You now hear a vague, but very unsettling, cracking sound far off in the distance. It is as if some huge unseen creature were slowly moving towards you in the darkness.

You notice the glow of a faint yet constant red light far below you. You are somehow being drawn towards this light. You resume your descent and slowly float down into the blackness.

As you begin to approach the center of the shadow realm, you can now see vague outlines and shapes in the glow of the blood-red moonlight. You are drifting toward the crystalline spheres of the two circles of power. The circles have been smashed to pieces! Some incredibly powerful force has destroyed the circles. Pieces of the walls of the circles remain intact, but they jut out in sharp jagged edges like two huge broken snow globes.

As you float into the center of the smashed circles, your feet touch down on the white marble floor beneath you. You can hear a subtle rustling sound all around you. You feel as though someone or something were watching you.

You can see that the constant glow of red light is now only a few yards away from you, but the source of red light is still hidden in the darkness. You take several small, cautious steps toward the red light. Small pieces of the smashed circles crunch beneath your feet. Whatever was rustling around in the darkness stops moving. The entire shadow realm becomes eerily quiet.

A haunted feeling washes over you. Slowly, carefully, you continue to move towards the glow of red light. But as you approach it, you are frozen in your tracks. You are suddenly able to see the horrors revealed in that awful crimson glow.

The griffon lies dead on the ground. The animal has been ripped to pieces from the inside out. It is as if the eagle and the lion had tried to separate themselves from each other, and that they tore themselves apart in the process. A stream of slick, black blood flows from the body of the fallen beast. It pools beneath your feet. Next to the still and silent body of the griffon, you see that someone or *something* has written the words *Welcome to the nightmare lands* in blood on the white marble floor of the shadow realm. The bloody tracks of a large bird lead off into the darkness. Your blood runs cold through your veins.

Suddenly something hisses at you. As you turn to face this new horror, your feet slip in the bloody puddle under your feet. You fall backwards into the pool of crimson gore. Frozen with fear, you see a pair of huge, glowing, red eyes staring at you out of the darkness. Now a huge Cheshire grin of sharp white teeth smiles at you from the shadows. Smoke and flame issue from flared nostrils, and a clawed and scaly hand thrusts the bloody carcass of a dead lamb at you. It shakes the carcass a few times to be sure you notice, then the thing in the shadows turns and runs away into the darkness. You can hear its laughter echoing throughout the wreckage of your domain. It was the dragon, and he has become an insane killer.

The shadow realm has become a land of nightmares and madness.

You carefully regain your feet and peer around in the darkness for any signs of movement. You see nothing. You return your attention to the red glow. It is now only a few feet away from you. Carefully, carefully, you move toward it. Now you can see that it is a glowing red crystal of many facets. The faceted crystal is lying on the white marble floor directly in front of the mirror. You see that the looking glass of the mirror has been smashed, and its pieces are also scattered on the marble floor. As you bend down and reach for the glowing red crystal, you touch a shard of the broken looking glass. It slices your fingertip open. You are bleeding! Your blood is dripping from this open wound, and the droplets of your blood fall to the ground and mix with the blood of the griffon. As the two bloods mix together, something very strange begins to happen.

The mixed blood at your feet begins to swirl. It begins to flow in a stream toward the base of the mirror frame. There's more blood than you thought. The stream of blood shimmers with the eerie light of the crystal's red glow. It surges up the side of the mirror like a crimson tide, and it fills the empty space inside the frame with *a looking glass of living blood.* You see a sudden flash of light at your feet. Something is sparkling in the pool of blood. It is the soul sword. You can just discern that its blade has been broken in half. You also see that the lost necklace and key are wrapped around the hilt of the sword.

You bend down and reach for the necklace and the key, but your wrists are suddenly seized by some powerful unseen force and you are jerked up into the air. Something holds your wrists. You are dangling above the blood-stained floor of the shadow realm. You twist your body and pull your arms in an effort to free yourself, but your strength is useless against the powerful invisible force holding you in its grasp.

A horribly painful image flashes through your mind. This same image appears on the surface of the looking glass of blood.

Your memory stirs. In your mind, you now see the worst thing that you have ever done to another person. This memory replays itself on the looking glass of living blood. You must watch it as it plays, over and over again. Unable to move, you are forced to watch your own cruelty.

Your memory stirs again, and now in your mind you see the worst thing that has ever happened to you. Like your first memory, this memory too replays itself on the looking glass of living blood. You must watch it as it plays. You feel your remembered pain, humiliation, and sadness all over again. Unable to move, you must keep watching, feeling, remembering.

Now, an image of the thing that you are most afraid of flashes through your mind. The worst possible outcome of this fear plays itself out on the looking glass of living blood. You must watch it as it plays and replays. You want to run, but the unknown force holds you motionless. You are unable to move. You cannot flee.

You look at your reflection in the looking glass of living blood. What do you see? *The deepest, darkest parts of your mind.* You look into the looking glass of living blood and see your soul reflected upon its surface. You cannot move. You are totally in the power of the unknown force that is holding you before the looking glass. You must face these awful parts of yourself. You are unable to move. You cannot turn away from yourself.

There is nothing on earth or in any other realm that you can do. You must face yourself. You must face your own cruelty, your humiliation, your fear. You have no choice. You are required to look at yourself face to face in the looking glass of living blood.

Regard your mind. Regard your soul.

You have now faced the dark mirror of self.

The broken blade of the soul sword floats up and away from the blood stained floor of the shadow realm. It rises into the air directly in front of you. You see that the necklace and the key are still dangling from the hilt of the sword.

The broken half-blade of the soul sword lunges at your chest! It pierces you through the heart. You feel no pain. What you feel is the intense heat of a purifying fire burning away inside you. There is no blood, but you feel as if your life force were draining away.

Like the shamans of old, you are now dead. Like all shamans, you must be reborn into the light and reclaim your power.

Slowly, the broken blade of the soul sword pulls itself out of your chest and returns to the blood-stained floor from which it came. It takes the necklace and the key with it.

The bloody surface of the looking glass begins to spin in a dark vortex of power and energy. Its pull is intense and undeniable. Suddenly, the unseen force that is holding you aloft releases its grip. You are instantly pulled into the dark, spinning vortex of the looking glass.

You are now gliding through a pitch-black tunnel at incredible speed. You are traveling through a dark and twisting pipeline. You are speeding through a small space without sound or light. You are totally alone in the dark. As you glide through the twists and turns of the tunnel, you somehow realize that you are leaving your old life behind.

The person that you were fades away in the darkness behind you. Now you are becoming much more than you ever were before.

You can now see a vague light in the distance far ahead of you. As you glide closer to this light, you see that it shimmers and shines in a dawning aurora of color.

You have seen this light before. It is the living waters of the sun side of the looking glass. You have entered the portal of the mirror from one side and now you are going to exit from the other side. Instead of a portal to the astral plane or to another dimension, the empty space between the two sides of the looking glass became a canal of darkness. It is taking you to your destiny.

You glide through the final turn of the tunnel. Now you plunge through the living waters of the looking glass. As you pass through the sun side of the mirror, you feel as though your body were somehow absorbing the light and the unknowable waters of the looking glass. You feel as though your entire being has become fluid. You raise a liquid hand in the air in front of your eyes, and you are amazed by what you see. The surface of your hand shimmers and shines with the reflective light of the living waters of the looking glass. You can see your own reflection in the palm of your hand! You see that your entire body has somehow been transformed into a living mirror.

Other than yourself, however, nothing else is being reflected onto the mirrored surface of your body.

You are now back where you began your first journey through the labyrinths of balance. You are back inside the void. You look around and you can see nothing. You can feel nothing. The mirrored surface that your body has become reflects only the nothingness of the void.

This is, you realize, your chance to start over again. You have been reborn! The void that surrounds you is the womb of a new beginning. As you think about this, you also realize that it is what you have accomplished in the past that has led you to this new beginning. The shadow realm was the symbol of your accomplishments, but the shadow realm that you left behind is under the control of dark powers and forces. It has become unbalanced. You know that you must return to the shadow realm and restore it. But how?

You look around at the vastness of the void. It is limitless and it is empty. There is only nothingness. No mirror, no exit, no way out. You know that you, yourself, have become the living waters of the looking glass. How can you pass through yourself? As you hold your mirrored hands in front of your eyes, you begin to realize that you cannot pass through yourself. But what you see in the palm of your mirrored hand sparks an idea.

The imprint of the key is still burned into the palm of your hand. You run your fingertips over the imprint and sense that, not only has the key left behind its mark, but it has also left behind some of its magick. When last you saw them, the key and the necklace were wrapped around the hilt of the soul sword. Broken or not, you know that there is also powerful magick within the soul sword. The powerful magick of creation.

Focusing your mind, you concentrate on the imprint of the key burned into the palm of your hand. You call for the key to return to you. Instantly, you feel the key and the necklace rising up through the living waters of your body. But there is also something else. The spirit of the soul sword is returning to you as well.

The key, the necklace, and the spirit of the soul sword pass through the living waters of the palm of your hand, and you grasp the hilt of the sword. Its power and magick are still intact. It feels good to be holding the spirit of the soul sword in your hand once again. Its presence and power boost your confidence even higher.

The key and the necklace float in the void directly in front of you. As if it had been given a silent command, the key pivots and turns, thrusts forward through the air, and begins turning as if it were unlocking an invisible door in front of you.

A powerful wave of magick and energy erupt in the air around the key. A rift opens up around it, within which you can see the stone frame of the mirror. Beyond it lies the blackness of the shadow realm. As the key and the necklace float toward you, you see that the broken clasp of the necklace has been repaired. The necklace fastens itself around your throat. The key once again hangs over your heart. With the powerful spirit of the soul sword in your hand, you step through the energy rift and enter the nightmare world of the shadow realm.

The shadow realm is not the same as it was when you left it. *It is much worse.* Horrible screams and strange noises are sounding everywhere. Fires burn in the distance, and the twisted shadows of unknown creatures are writhing around you in the firelight. It is like a scene from a painting of hell. Black clouds swirl about the jagged crescent of the destroyed moon, making the shadow realm even darker than it was before. The red crystal is still lying at the base of the mirror. Its dim light is your only source of illumination. Wishing that its light were brighter, you begin to reach for the crystal. As if in answer to your wish, the crystal rises into the air and slowly begins spinning. Rays of bright red light shoot out from the thousands of facets that cover the surface of the spinning crystal. The rays of light are also being reflected and intensified as they flash across your mirrored liquid body.

The light is now bright enough for you to be able to see the center of the shadow realm. The motionless bodies of hundreds of dead ravens litter the once white marble floor at the center of your domain. The elemental statues have been hacked into strange, surrealistic shapes. The statues are now defaced monuments to the nightmare world that the shadow realm has become. The sun and moon pools are dried up and empty; their powerful energies having long since vanished.

A huge shape suddenly appears at the edge of the shadows. The shape slowly moves out of the shadows and into the light of the crystals crimson glow. It is the dragon. This time he is out for your blood. The dragon lunges forward and snatches your arm in its huge pointed teeth, but as it does the living waters of your arm separate and wash through the mouth of the beast. You are uninjured! The dragon rears backwards in confusion. The living waters quickly reform and your arm is restored.

You now see that a single droplet of the living waters of your arm is hovering in the air before the dragon. The huge beast seems to be mesmerized by the shiny-mirrored droplet.

The droplet of living water begins to expand, and it transforms into a double-sided reflective disc. Just like the great mirror, one side of this disc is capable of deflecting energy, and the other side can become an open portal that absorbs energy. A single ray of light from the spinning crystal flashes over the surface of the mirrored disc. It shines directly into the eyes of the entranced dragon. The dragon cries out as if it had been injured. It quickly retreats deep into a hidden recess inside the shadow realm.

Intrigued by the power of this disc, you focus your mind on its surface. You are amazed by what you can see and feel. You find that not only can you mentally command the disc's movements, but that you can also see in your mind what is being reflected onto the mirrored surface of the disc. You now know how to restore the shadow realm….

You quickly move back to the stone frame of the mirror and step into the frame of the looking glass. You mentally will the spirit of the soul sword to move to the other side of the mirror and wait for your command. Obediently, the spirit of the soul sword leaves your hand and moves to the opposite side of the mirror. It poises itself over the empty frame as if ready to strike. You now extend your arms, and you shake and wave your hands, releasing thousands of droplets of the living waters into the air. Each droplet quickly transforms into a mirrored disc that hovers above you in the shadow realm. As if in response to what you are doing, the slowly spinning red crystal grows brighter and brighter. It begins to spin faster and faster. Its bright beams of light are reflecting off of surfaces of the mirrored discs, and the rays of light are penetrating deep into the shadow realm.

Like the dragon, you can feel that the dark energies in the shadow realm are retreating from the bright beams of light. You release thousands more droplets of living water into air. As you release the droplets of the living waters from your hands, you see that the tips of your fingers are returning to human flesh. You know that you must act quickly before your body changes back to ordinary flesh and blood. There are now thousands upon thousands of mirrored discs scattered throughout the shadow realm. You can see and feel that not only are the dark energies within your domain retreating from the bright beams of light, but that the deflective energies of the discs are pressing the dark energies back toward the massive walls of stone that surround the shadow realm. The dark energies and forces are in retreat.

You deepen your concentration on the mirrored discs, and, as you do, the rays of light emanating from the spinning crystal begin locking onto the mirrored discs and are holding them in place. You are now mentally connected to each and every disc in the shadow realm. You command the discs to turn in unison. The surfaces of the discs are now reversed. The living waters of the discs begin to churn and flow like the ebbing tides, opening thousands and thousands of portals within the shadow realm. But you hold back the energies of the portals for just a moment. You know that whatever is pulled through these portals will also have to pass through the living waters of your body as they are drawn through the mirror frame. You brace yourself for what is about to come.

You release your hold on the energy of the portals. The dark forces and energies within the shadow realm are drawn into the powerful vacuum of the mirrored discs. The dark energies enter your liquid body, and, as they do, the horrible images of the dark energies flash through your mind. But you are strong. Stronger then you have ever been before. The purity of your reborn spirit empowers you. You face the horrible images in your mind, and by facing them you are removing their power. One by one, the defeated energies disappear into the astral world that lies beyond the stone frame of the mirror. As each piece of dark energy passes through you, you can feel the living waters of your body washing it, restoring the balance to each of these forces as they pass. Drop by drop, the living waters are returning to the mirror, and the sun side of the looking glass is being restored. The last dark energies are now passing through your body. You feel the very last trace of them disappear beyond the portal of the mirror. You have defeated the dark energies, and you are empowered by your victory. Now it's time to command the spirit of the soul sword to strike. It is still hovering on the opposite side of the mirror frame. You command the sword to strike, and the sword thrusts forward and pierces the waters of the restored looking glass. The powerful energies of creation within the spirit of the soul sword spread over the surface of the looking glass. The charged waters explode from the frame, filling the shadow realm with their creative energies.

You look up to the skies of the shadow realm high above you. The dying red star that was once the sun begins to grow brighter and brighter. Its powerful rays wash over the surface of the jagged crescent of the moon. As you watch, the sun and the moon are slowly restored. The lights of the restored sun and moon intermingle and spread throughout the shadow realm. You watch with satisfaction as the sun and the moon slowly disappear below the horizon. The entire shadow realm has now been restored. You are finally able to relax in the twilight of your world. You see that the spirit of the soul sword has returned to the restored blade, which is once again frozen in the white marble floor at the center the shadow realm. You step out of the mirror frame, and, as you do, the living waters of the moon side of the looking glass are also restored.

Now you notice a small red gemstone lying on the white marble floor at your feet. You pick up this small stone and hold it in the palm of your hand. As you look closely at this stone, you see that thousands of facets are cut into its surface. Within each facet you can see and feel all life within the universe. A bright light flashes over the stone, and you see that the imprint of the key that was burned into the palm of your hand has been healed. The stone floats up and away from your healed palm and embeds itself into the shaft of the key hanging over your heart. You know that you have a powerful new tool, but its use will have to wait for another day. Although your mind is now at ease, you are very tired. You slump, then sit on the white marble floor of the shadow realm; you can still feel the power of your rebirth flowing through your mind and body.

You grasp the key hanging over your heart with your hand. It is cool and soothing. You slowly begin to float up and away from the shadow realm. You float up and through the crystalline energies of the restored circles of power, and their energies recharge your body and spirit. You slowly float higher and higher in your domain. Just as you are about to leave your world, you look down into the shadow realm and notice that there are several new additions to your domain: A large wooden chest is sitting next to the moon pool, and a chalice of silver and gold is resting on the edge of the sun pool. Next to the chalice is a very old bottle. These new additions will also have to wait, however, for another day.

It is time for you to rest now. You continue your ascent. You are now crossing over the borders of the shadow realm. As you pass over the borders, you see the statue of a goddess standing behind the moon pool and the statue of a god behind the sun pool. The gods and goddesses have returned to you. You cross the boundaries of the shadow realm, and you open your eyes and your mind to the waking world.

Chapter 11

See Thy Self

Well, now, here you are at last. Let me take a good look at what has become of you....

Impressive, I believe, most impressive. Let's take a moment to reflect back on the first leg of your journey and recount all the things that you have managed to accomplish.

- ➡ You have built a world within a void.

- ➡ You have tapped the power of the counter-flow.

- ➡ You have defeated your fear of widdershins energies.

- ➡ You have learned how to cast a bipolar circle.

- ➡ You have closed your internal circles.

- ➡ You have opened many new paths before you.

- ➡ You have recognized your dragon and your lamb and united them into a single voice.

- ➡ You have laid down your magickal tools.

- ➡ You have learned how to use your mind.

- ➡ You have opened yourself to the oneness of everything.

- ➡ You have become an omnidirectional Witch.

- You have navigated the labyrinths of balance.

- You have successfully reached the end of the journey of self.

All of this and much, much more.

What's that you say? You haven't accomplished all of this? You skipped over some of the work in this book because you felt that it was just too hard? You didn't need it because it didn't relate to your own personal quest?

You were unable to complete some of the tasks that I had laid out for you? No matter how hard you tried, it was impossible for you to see and feel the oneness of everything?

You could not attain the state of a harmonic trance? You simply don't feel that you have evened out the scales of balance?

Let's take a realistic look at the work I laid out in this book. You may be an evolving Witch, but you're still only human, aren't you? As far as I'm concerned, if in good conscience you have attempted all the work in this book and were able to complete only half of it, even then you have accomplished a great deal.

There are, however, zero excuses for skipping over any of the work or giving up because the task was difficult. But, if you have truly listened to my advice and opinions, then you have at least reconsidered many new ideas and concepts and have opened some new doors for yourself. Would I have liked for you to be able to grasp all of the work in this book? Certainly. Did I really expect that you would? Absolutely not. If the work were that easy, the world would be crawling with powerfully advanced Witches.

Whether you were able to understand all of the work or not, you have still come a very long way from the person and the Witch that you were when you began your journey of self-discovery. You have opened your mind and your spirit to new teachings and new points of view. I've always felt that, if you're able to recognize your flaws and your imperfections, then you've won half the battle. Even if you never end up being able to change those flaws and imperfections, at the very least, now you're thinking about them. Because you've recognized them within yourself, you at least consider the possibility of being able to change them one day.

It never ceases to amaze me by how many people with extreme character flaws think there's nothing at all wrong with them and that there's absolutely no reason for them to change.

Recognition is half the battle. If *you* recognize the differences between who you are and who you would like to become, then you're halfway to where I would like you to be at this point of your journey. But, ultimately, it's not where *I* would like for you to be that really matters, now is it? What really matters is if *you* are where you wanted (or hoped) to be.

So where does all of this leave you at the moment? As the title of author Jon Kabat-Zinn's famous book suggests, *wherever you go there you are*. Be mindful of where you are at this moment in time and at this stage of your progression. Reflect on what you have accomplished, but keep in mind that the past is now behind you and the future has yet to be written. *You* are the author of your life and your future. Don't let anyone else scribe it for you.

Once again, it all comes down to the choices you make for yourself. Only you can choose which paths you will or will not follow. Only you can decide between what's good enough to get by and what you aspire to become. Nobody else can (or should) live your life for you. Of course, many people will try to influence you over the course of your lifetime and possibly try to make decisions for you but, unless you're being physically oppressed, you are really under no obligation (except in the obvious cases of your livelihood or the law) to do a damn thing anybody tells you to do. If you don't like a television program, then don't watch it. If you don't like what an author is telling you in a book, then either pick up on the bits that you do like or put the book on the shelf and walk away. I'm pointing these things out to you because I want you to be mindful of outside influences. I want you to take a good look at how you are being affected by the media and by your friends and family. It is my greatest desire for you to grow as strong and wise as you possibly can be.

Even for strong-willed pagans and Witches, it is very easy to get caught up in the moment and agree to do something, or agree with someone else's opinions, just so you fit in for that given moment. The problem with these momentary surrenders is that over time they can build up and take on a life of their own. Then you may find yourself doing and saying things that you didn't really mean to say or do.

Walking the path of self and completing your journey has left you in the position of now having to become a strong (and hopefully enlightened) leader. If you were a strong leader before you began the journey, then you must now become a stronger and wiser leader than you were before. There are no longer any precut paths for you to follow. It is now up to you to decide in what direction you will lead those who would follow in your footsteps. It is now up to you to take the lead and pioneer the future of our kind.

Chapter 12

The Mirror at Work

Believe it or not, I'm reading your mind again. *More work,* I hear you saying. *I have just completed the journey of self…. Is there no rest for the weary? Will this man not be satisfied until he has worn my magickal fingers to the bone?*

Relax, my friend. At this point I'm reasonably satisfied with your progress, so we will only be discussing *possible* work that you may want to consider doing in the future. First, let's take a look at one of the magickal tools that I wrote into creation for you. It's one of the hardest (but coolest) tools to learn how to use. Whether you chose to take the right-hand or left-hand path in Exercise 4, you were introduced to a faceted crystal through which, in meditation, you were able to see, feel, and experience any person, place, thing, or event anywhere in the universe at any given point in time. This scrying crystal is *the vision stone*.

The vision stone is a powerful tool that we might consider to be the magickal equivalent of the World Wide Web. In very much the same way that you can use the Internet to access information and make contact with millions of people around the world, you can use the vision stone to access the Akashic Records, make contact with astral and earthbound entities, and look into the minds and through the eyes of these entities. You will not, however, be able to use the vision stone to literally read people's thoughts unless you become extremely adept at using it, and at that point you are getting into the ethics of going into people's personal thoughts. Your personal ethics are your own, but you will want to take the issue of privacy very seriously before you dig too deeply into other people's lives. What you can do at this point is use the stone as a psychic and/or empathic tool to be able to feel what people are feeling, see what they are seeing, or experience what they are experiencing. Or even what they have felt, seen, and experienced in the past.

You can also use the vision stone as a wonderful tool to help you develop your psychic abilities and visualization skills, as well as to further the process of your becoming an omnidirectional practitioner of the magickal arts. If, however, your psychic and visualization techniques are not already somewhat developed, then the vision stone will be very difficult for you to use at first. So how do you start the process of learning how to use the vision stone?

You can tap the power of the vision stone at the time you are in meditation, but the ultimate place to learn how to access its powers is in the shadow realm. Beyond the obvious reason that you're already familiar with the shadow realm, your personal vision stone was created within its boundaries. The shadow realm is your—and the vision stone's—place of power.

I do not, however, want you to return to the shadow realm for any reason until you are ready to undertake the fifth and final meditation in this book. The time for you to complete the final meditation has grown very close, so please bear with me for just a bit longer. I can assure you that you will not be disappointed.

The vision stone is basically a beefed-up version of a meditation technique that I have used and taught for a very long time. It's what I commonly refer to as *the hall of mirrors*. The vision stone is pretty much the same concept as the hall of mirrors, the main difference being that the vision stone uses thousands of facets to search through the universe and the astral plane instead of hundreds of mirrors in a long hallway. You're an advancing Witch. You can handle it!

To begin using the powerful magick of the vision stone, the first thing you need to do is attain a state of deep meditation. You can begin your meditations in any way you desire, but just as you did in the later guided meditations in balance, visualize the key to the shadow realm hanging on the necklace over your heart. Your personal vision stone is embedded in the shaft of your key to the shadow realm. It will be easier for you to visualize your key at the beginning of your meditations rather than trying to conjure it up later on. Wherever you want to travel to in your meditations is fine, but try not to clutter up the place (your mind) too much while you practice using the vision stone.

Start with a single facet out of the potentially thousands, or even millions of facets that will eventually be available to you. Begin by envisioning yourself taking the key into your hand and mentally stating your intent. Your initial statement of intent should be something very basic, such as; "I want to see something new," or "Show me a place that I have never seen before." Once you have become adept at using the vision stone, you will be able to pinpoint exact locations or people, but keep it simple while you are still in the learning phase.

Now visualize the key growing warmer in your hand. See a soft glow of light being generated around the key. Now envision yourself moving one of your fingers (which you have wrapped around the key) just enough to allow a small beam of the glowing light to escape from your hand. Now see this tiny beam of light growing stronger. See it projecting a crystal screen in the air a few feet in front of you. This screen should be about the size of a small computer monitor, not so small that you can't see the picture, but not so large that it takes up too much room to add other screens (facets) at a later time. Eventually, you will be able to visualize every single facet of the crystal and their images being projected in front of you, but unless you have already tried and mastered a similar technique, start small to avoid the possibility of information overload.

At this point, *you wait* for an image, possibly even a feeling or emotion associated with the image to appear on the crystal screen, and subsequently in your mind. *Do not force an image* to appear on the crystal screen. *Do not pretend* that an image is appearing on the screen just because you badly want to see something. Patience Grasshopper. Patience. Good things come to those who wait. Illusions come to those who rush.

When an image finally does appear on the screen, try to observe it without interaction with it until the image becomes more focused. In other words, don't just jump in feet first at the first sign of life and start examining what you are seeing and feeling in great detail. At this point, you simply want to allow the image to flow on its own without any intervention from you. We will refer to the combination of an image and its associated sensation, feeling, or emotion, as a *vision*.

Once the vision has become clear and focused on the screen, you can begin the process of focusing in on it with your mind. Go slow at first. Step by step, try to pick up on the vision and how it feels in greater detail. Not all visions are pleasant to see and feel, so make sure that the vision isn't something that will be disturbing to you either mentally or emotionally before immersing yourself in it. If the vision is something that you don't care to see or feel, simply turn it off by envisioning the crystal screen returning to the vision stone. In a little while, try again with a different facet of the vision stone.

Eventually, you will be able to project many facets at one time. You will be able to experience the visions either as a whole, or as a series of single visions from which you can pick and choose the ones that you want to take a closer look at. Keep in mind, however, that the universe, its inhabitants, and their associated feelings or emotions can be as pretty to look at as they can be nasty to experience. Keep this in mind when and if you decide to project and experience the vision stone in its entirety. Again, start small, and build up the number of visions that you are able to experience until you become adept at using the vision stone.

At this point, as far as any further work is concerned, take some time to reflect back over the journey of self in its entirety. Make sure that you have a pretty good handle on everything we have covered so far in this book. If there is anything you may have skipped over or have rushed through without giving it a decent effort, consider going back and giving it another try. As always, the choice is yours and yours alone.

In the end, it is only yourself that you will be facing in the mirror. It will be the decisions that you make that will determine whether of not you like what you see in your reflection. Be careful. Your reflection just may be looking back at you.

The Initiation of Self

*So said the ready-voiced daughters of great Zeus, and they
plucked and gave me a rod, a shoot of sturdy laurel, a
marvelous thing, and breathed into me a divine voice to
celebrate things that shall be and things there were
aforetime; and they bade me sing of the race of the blessed
gods that are eternally, but ever to sing of themselves both
first and last.*

—— Hesiod, *Theogony*

In honor of your successful completion of the journey of self, I thought I would whip out the old cauldron and conjure up a special treat for you. We will call this treat *"the initiation of self ritual."* The initiation of self is not a requirement, but a nicety I thought you might enjoy undertaking as an outer honoring of your inner rite of passage. Before you undertake the initiation of self, however, let's take a few moments to look at the current state of degree systems in the pagan community.

I have recently noticed an alarming trend in the pagan community. As it gets easier and easier to receive a degree in Witchcraft, there are an increasing number of freshly initiated Witches who wear their degrees on their sleeves like some kind of magickal bulletproof vest. Within the last year alone, I have personally witnessed a great increase in the intentional flaunting of degrees of initiation in an attempt to impress and establish instant status and respect without their first having been earned by the Witch. If the pagan community continues to allow degrees in Witchcraft to be handed out like milk and cookies to hungry toddlers at a day care center, the true teachings and traditions of Witchcraft are doomed to be trampled by an ever-growing mob of new Witches clamoring for instant status and the easy way in.

I hereby charge you, a Witch who has now traveled far on the path of *know thyself.* I hereby charge you with the task of keeping the respect for Witchcraft and our Craft elders alive and well. I hereby charge you to teach those new to the Craft the ways of respect above all else.

Initiations are highly personal rites of passage that are intended to honor the beginning of a new cycle in a Witch's progress. Degrees are (or should be) titles of honor and courage that symbolize years of hard work and service in the Craft. They're not mere parchment purple hearts that proclaim their wearers as the new saviors of the pagan community.

Before you undertake the ritual of the initiation of self, we should probably also take a look at some of the differences between the ritual I have written for you and a traditional Wiccan ritual, so that the initiation of self ritual will not be too perplexing.

Very early on in my solitary training in the practice of Witchcraft, I developed a very eclectic approach to writing and performing rituals. Later, as I began working with a full coven, I also had to develop the ability to instantly pull a ritual out of my head like a proverbial rabbit out of a hat. The ritual for the initiation of self, therefore, may be quite a bit different from what you're used to if you incorporate some of the more traditional Wiccan guidelines and elements into your rituals. A major element missing from the initiation of self ritual that you will probably notice right away is the casting of a traditional magickal circle. The reasons why I do not feel that a traditional circle casting is necessary in this or any other ritual could fill an entire chapter, so for that reason I will not go into great depth as to why this element is missing from the initiation of self ritual. I will, however, give you a few quick observations about my own beliefs about circle casting for your consideration.

Beyond the fact that I feel that the Witch actually *is* the circle and creates sacred space by his or her mere presence, the most common reason for casting a magickal circle is to keep all the "astral nasties" floating around out there from entering into the magickal sacred space. It is my belief that the notion that even the most powerful Witch who has ever existed could keep everything bad or negative from entering into their magickal circle is ludicrous and laughable. After all the work you have just completed in realigning yourself with balance, I hope you see some of the reasons for my belief. If you accept what I believe to be the undeniable fact that literally everyone and everything contains an element of balance, both a light side and a dark side, then the very attempt to keep anything dark or negative out of a magickal circle is an absurd gesture of futility. In my opinion, if a Witch were truly successful in keeping everything dark or negative out of their magickal circle, then their circle would be completely empty and not even the Witch who cast the circle would be allowed to remain inside it.

Another reason I did not include a circle casting in this ritual is because when I cast my own circles I do it backwards from the way most Witches have been taught. I call in the quarters and deity first, then I cast the circle. Why do I do it backwards? Well, look at it this way. If you were an astral bad guy, would you be more apt to mess with a Witch who was casting a circle all on their own or with a Witch who had deity watching over them and the powers of the elemental quarters at their command? During this ritual, a circle will be naturally cast on its own, but if you fee that it is necessary to cast a traditional circle, I will allow you the opportunity to do so at the beginning of the initiation of self ritual.

The second thing you will notice is that I have incorporated the guardians of the four elemental cross quarters into the initiation of self ritual. In case you're unfamiliar with the elemental cross quarters and have never used them in ritual, the cross quarters are the compass points that lie between the four elemental quarters of north, east, south, and west. Let's take a look into the aspects of each of the four cross quarters as I understand and work with them in the Temple of Aradia so you can gain some knowledge and understanding of the guardians of the four cross quarters and the role that each one plays. You will be using the four main elemental quarters and the four cross quarters during the first half of the initiation of self ritual.

Southeast

The Guardian of the Southeast is the mediator, the timekeeper, and the custodian of spiritual laws. In a coven, the person assigned to take on the duties of the Southeastern point administrates coven laws, if need be. This person makes sure that any workings or discussions being carried out by the coven are flowing along as smoothly as possible. The Guardian of the Southeast also serves as a mediator between coven members should any discussions or debates between coven members become heated or start to get out of hand. The color correspondence for the Guardian of the Southeast is orange.

Southwest

The Guardian of the Southwest is in charge of monitoring the doorway between the mundane world and the magickal circle. In a coven, the Guardian of the Southwest is responsible for making sure that the members of the coven are physically, mentally, and magickally prepared to enter into the sacred space of the circle. The Guardian of the Southwest may ask a covener a series of questions to ascertain his or her preparedness before granting them entrance into the magick circle. The Guardian of the Southwest is also responsible for monitoring the gateway to the mundane to keep any unwanted entities or energies from entering the circle. This Guardian is also in charge of cutting a doorway for any covener who needs to leave the sacred space of the magick circle. The color correspondence for the Guardian of the Southwest is purple.

Northwest

The Guardian of the Northwest is the record keeper or scribe. In a coven, the Guardian of the Northwest is in charge of writing down all aspects of a coven meeting and keeping the information in good order. He or she is the holder of the coven's Book of Shadows. The Guardian of the Northwest takes notes at appropriate times during a coven meeting and records their observations of the proceedings in the coven Book of Shadows at a later date. It is also the duty of the scribe to closely observe the coveners and the general atmosphere surrounding any given coven meeting and to record these observations as well. The color correspondence for the Guardian of the Northwest is brown.

Northeast

The Guardian of the Northeast is in charge of monitoring the gateway to spirit, or "the all." The Northeast Guardian is also in charge of monitoring the energies of the magickal circle itself. In a coven, it is the duty of the Northeast Guardian to keep close watch over the magickal energies being generated inside the circle by the coven members and to keep the magickal energies flowing along as smoothly as possible. The Northeast Guardian is in charge of maintaining the integrity of the magickal circle and is responsible for keeping the energies of the circle strong. Above all else, it is the duty of the Northeast Guardian to maintain an air and feeling of magick inside the circle and within the spirits of the coven members. The color correspondence for the Guardian of the Northeast is black.

This is what you need to know about the guardians of the cross quarters before you undertake the initiation of self ritual. I am aware of only a small handful of covens that incorporate the cross quarters into the main structure of their workings, and the ones that do all have their own take on what the guardians of the cross quarters represent. That being said, take my information about the cross quarters and their respective guardians as merely being possibilities for your personal use and further study, not as absolute wisdom. There are boundless seas of eclectic practices in Witchcraft upon which you can sail and discover your own truths. At some later date, if you found the concept of the cross quarters intriguing, you may want to study the beliefs of other groups and individuals.

The third thing that we should look at before you undertake the initiation of self ritual are the Titans, and the *Protogonoi* or the "first-born" primordial gods and goddesses of Greek mythology. During the initiation of self ritual you will be referring to them collectively as the "ancient ones." According to Greek mythology, the Protogonoi were the first-born immortals or elemental beings who emerged at the time of creation, and whose forms made up the very fabric of the universe itself. The first of the Protogonoi emerged from nothingness, and those that followed were their offspring. The Titans, also known as the elder gods, ruled the earth before the Olympians overthrew them. The ruler of the Titans was Cronus, who was later dethroned by his son, Zeus.

When looking into Greek mythology, it is important to keep in mind that it abounds with conflicting information, gods, goddesses, myths, and legends. The information about the Titans and the Protogonoi that I use, like almost everything else in Greek mythology, has been interpreted and will continue to be interpreted in many different ways by various authors and translators. As you have (hopefully) been taught to do in the Craft, pick and choose the parts of Greek mythology that you like and take nothing as gospel.

In the second half of the initiation of self ritual you will be invoking the favors of the Titans and the Protogonoi, so we should take a close look at each of the Titans and Protogonoi that you will be working with during the initiation of self ritual. You will be invoking the aid of the Titans and Protogonoi that I have chosen to represent the quarters, the cross-quarters, and the main feminine and masculine aspects of deity. Listed below are the names and aspects of the Titans and Protogonoi that you will be working with, as well as the quarters and cross-quarters that each Titan and Protogonos will be representing.

Eastern Quarter, Chaos

Chaos was the very first Protogonos. Chaos was the void that came into being before anything else. Some say, however, that Chaos was born from Mist, and that Mist was the first to exist.

Southeastern Quarter, Nyx

Nyx (pronounced *nix*) is the Protogonos of night. She is the mantle of darkness that spreads itself across the sky. Nyx sprang from Chaos, the Protogonos of the void. Some say that Nyx had a pair of black wings; others say she appeared cloaked in a robe of darkness.

Southern Quarter, Hyperion

Hyperion is the Titan who is considered to be the bringer of light. He was also considered to be an early sun god and was said to be the first to understand the movement of the sun, moon, and stars. He is the son of Gaia and Uranus and was married to his sister, Theia. Their children were Helios (the sun), Selene (the moon), and Eos (the dawn).

Southwestern Quarter, Oceanus

Oceanus, another Titan, is the god of the unending river of water that encircles and binds the earth. It is from this river that all waters are said to flow. It is also believed that to reach the underworld that you must cross his river. Oceanus with his wife, Tethys, created the rivers, fresh water springs, and wells of earth. Their daughters are the ocean nymphs.

Western Quarter, Eros

Eros is the Protogonos of love. It is said that he overpowers the mind and tames the spirit of gods and mankind alike. Eros is dual natured and androgynous. When he mated with Chaos, it is said, the race of the birds came into being.

Northwestern Quarter, Eos

Daughter of the Titans Hyperion and Theia, Eos is the goddess of the dawn. She is perpetually in love. She is the saffron robed goddess who sits on a golden throne and announces the light to mortals and immortals

Northern Quarter, Gaia

Gaia is the Protogonos of the earth, the great mother goddess who is said to nourish all life. As the mother of the Titans, Gaia brought the ruler of the Titans, her son, Cronus, into power by having him revolt against and defeat her husband, Uranus, who was the father of Cronus.

Northeastern Quarter, Mnemosyne

Mnemosyne (pronounced *neh-MAHS-uh-nee*) is the Titan of memory. She is the goddess who is said to have owned all tales, and it was believed that tales could not exist without her power because without memory the words would vanish without a trace. If a person were deprived of the gift of memory, they would not know who or what they were. They would not be able to retain knowledge, for knowledge is inseparable from memory.

The God, Cronus

The Titan, Cronus, became the second ruler of the universe after dethroning his father, Uranus. Cronus and his wife, Rhea, parented all of the Olympic gods and goddesses. He was the ruler during the first stage of civilization, which was known as the Golden Age.

The Goddess, Rhea

The Titaness, Rhea, was the mother of the gods of Olympus. She hid her last son, Zeus, from her husband Cronus to keep Cronus from swallowing him whole, as he had done with all their other children. By hiding Zeus from Cronus, Rhea paved the way for the war between the Titans and the Olympians.

�֎ ✩ ✦

I have hopefully covered everything that you need to know about the initiation of self ritual. I hope that it is an interesting and spiritual experience for you. It is now time to respect the huge amount of work that you have undergone, and honor your completion of a cycle with a rite of passage, *the Initiation of self.*

Ritual for the Initiation of Self

Before you begin the ritual, carry out any preparations that you feel are necessary to assume your magickal mind, spirit, and persona. You will also need to prepare an area of sacred space. I have not included any instructions for setting up an altar or casting a circle in this ritual, so if you feel that they are necessary for this ritual, plan what you want to do well ahead of time. I don't feel that it's my place to tell you how to set up your altar or prepare your sacred space.

Other than yourself, the only things you must have for the initiation of self ritual are a container and a single candle (any color you like). The container is purely symbolic. It can be a bottle, a chalice, an envelope, or any other kind of container you care to use. During the first half of the initiation of self ritual, you will be symbolically shedding the spirit of the "old you," and you will need something in which to contain your old spirit for a time. In section four, "The Book of Shadow," you will be transforming the spirit of your old self into something new that will be highly beneficial as you embark on astral adventures with your shadow spirit. Again, the container is purely symbolic, so feel free to use anything you desire to contain the essence of your old spirit.

If you do not ordinarily use candles during ritual or you cannot afford to purchase one, simply imagine a soft glow of flickering magickal light in the palm of your hand as you begin the ritual and use that magickal light in place of a candle. If you like having lots of candles while you perform a ritual, you may want to consider placing eight candles on your altar to represent each of the four elemental quarters and the four cross quarters, as well as two candles for deity. You will also need a single candle that you can carry with you during the ritual. You will begin the first half of the initiation of self ritual in the northeastern (spirit) cross quarter and move widdershins to each compass-point until you reach the eastern (air) quarter. This will be the symbolic shedding of your old spirit and your old self. During the second half of the ritual, you will be moving deosil to each of the compass points while invoking the aid and favor of the Protogonoi. You will move to each compass point until you have returned to the starting point of the northeastern cross quarter. This will be the symbolic donning of your new spirit and your new self.

If you're ready, we will now begin your rite of passage...

If so desired, prepare your sacred space, light your altar candles, and cast your magickal circle. Place the spirit container in the center of the altar and have a single candle (or magickal light) in hand, but do not light the candle just yet. Move to the northeastern cross quarter, close your eyes, and reflect on all the steps you have taken in your magickal life that have brought you to this moment.

When you are ready, light the candle you are holding and speak aloud these words:

> *Guardian of the Northeastern Gateway, Spirit of the All, I have come before you this day to shed what has passed behind me. My spirit can no longer contain my magickal essence. It must be transformed. I ask that you watch over my spirit and guard and protect me while I undertake this rite of passage. By my vital spark and by my will, this work shall now be done!*

Place the candle in the northeastern quarter and feel your spirit enter into the candle's flame. Know that your spirit is safe with the Northeastern Guardian and that you will be well protected as you move from point to point.

Shed the lit candle in the northeastern quarter, move widdershins to the eastern quarter and speak aloud these words:

> *Guardian of the Northern Gateway, Spirit of the earth, I have come before you this day to shed what has passed behind me. My foundation can no longer support my strength. It must be transformed. I ask that you watch over that which I have used to brace myself and keep me steady as I undertake this rite of passage. By my vital roots and by my will, this work shall now be done!*

Know that the foundation of your past is safe in the care of the Northern Guardian. Feel the steadying energies of the northern gateway enter your feet and move throughout your entire body. Move widdershins to the northwestern quarter and speak aloud these words:

> *Guardian of the Northwestern Gateway, Spirit of the Scribe, I have come before you this day to shed what has passed behind me. The book of yesterday has been written. A new story must now begin. I ask you to add the book of my past to the Akashic Records so that the expression of my magick shall never be forgotten. By my vital words and by my will, this work shall now be done!*

Feel the book of your past being closed by the Northwestern Guardian. Know that your history is safe in the Guardian's hands, that the book of your past will be added to the Akashic Records. Move to the western quarter and speak aloud these words:

Guardian of the Western Gateway, Spirit of the Sea, I have come before you this day to shed what has passed behind me. The stream of my magick has grown into a mighty river. Its banks must be transformed before they overflow. I ask that you seal the floodgates and hold back the river while I undertake this rite of passage and until I have returned. By my vital blood and by my will, this work shall now be done!

Feel the ever-growing river of your magick as it swells within the western gateway. Feel the hand of the Western Guardian holding back the flood and keeping it safe. Move to the southwestern quarter and speak aloud these words:

Guardian of the Southwestern Gateway, Spirit of the Threshold Between the Worlds, I have come before you this day to shed what has passed behind me. The doorway of magick has become too easy for me to pass through. It must be transformed. I ask that you seal the doorway so that I may discover new and challenging ways to gain access to the magick that lies beyond the veil of the mundane world. By my vital steps and by my will, this work shall now be done!

Feel the doorway between the worlds being sealed by the Southwestern Guardian. Know that the Guardian will present you with a far greater challenge the next time you knock on the door of magick. Move to the southern quarter and speak aloud these words:

Guardian of the Southern Gateway, Spirit of Fire, I have come before you this day to shed what has passed behind me. The Witch that was can no longer contain the fire of my magick. I must be transformed. I ask you to burn away the facade that is the old me, so that like the phoenix I may rise from the ashes and be reborn. By my vital essence and by my will, this work shall now be done!

Feel the heat of purifying fires burning within the southern gateway. Feel the fiery hands of the Southern Guardian move over you burning away the old you, and transforming it into ash. Know that the Southern Guardian will guard the ashes of who you were until you return to be reborn from their glowing embers. Move to the southeastern quarter and speak aloud these words:

Guardian of the Southeastern Gateway, Spirit of the Lawgiver, I have come before you this day to shed what has passed behind me. The rules and laws of the past can no longer govern me. They must be transformed. I ask that you rewrite the rules and the laws by which I have lived so that I may never cease to question my motives or myself. I must now live by a higher code. I must now answer to the higher power that I am about to become. By my vital charter and by my will, this work shall now be done!

Feel the Southeastern Guardian taking the book of your own laws from your hands. Know that the Southeastern Guardian will rewrite the book of laws to meet the higher standards and ethics that you must now answer to. Move to the eastern quarter and speak aloud these words:

Guardian of the Eastern Gateway, Spirit of the Wind, I have come before you this day to shed what has passed behind me. My old spirit has reached the end of its journey. It must be transformed. I ask you to extinguish the flame of my old spirit so that a brighter flame may be ignited to guide me through the darkness. By my vital breath and by my will, this work shall now be done!

Pick up the candle that is burning in the northeastern quarter and hold it before the eastern gateway. Feel the hands of the Eastern Guardian folding over your own and holding the candle with you. Feel the breath of the Guardian mixing with your own and filling your chest. Take in a deep breath, close your eyes, and blow out the candle. Feel the spirit of the person and Witch that you were depart from the wick of the candle and enter into the container on the altar.

The first half of your journey through the quarters is now complete. It is now time to invoke the aid of the Titans and the Protogonoi and claim your new spirit. Move to the altar and speak aloud these words:

> *Great God Cronus, Father of the Olympians and ruler of the Titans, he who ruled during the Golden Age, I ask you to join in my rite of passage to give form to my new spirit. I ask you to bless my spirit with the gift of longevity.*

> *Great Goddess Rhea, Mother of the Olympic gods and goddesses, I ask you to join in my rite of passage to give form to my new spirit. I ask you to instill within it the spark of creation and the drive to grow ever stronger.*

Your new spirit has begun to take form and contains within it the spark of creation. Your new spirit is symbolically being held within the shaft of the extinguished candle. But the past journey of your old spirit must not be forgotten. Place your hand over the container that holds your old spirit and feel its essence entering your hand through your fingertips. Hold the essence of your old spirit tightly in your hand. Pick up the extinguished candle and hold it aloft in front of you. Speak aloud these words:

I add the essence of my old spirit to that of my new spirit. I combine the wisdom and experience of the old with the power and the promise of the new. In so doing, I will now breathe life into the spirit of what is to be.

Move to the eastern quarter, and holding the unlit candle aloft before the quarter, speak aloud these words:

Chaos, Protogonos who emerged at the beginning of existence, I ask you to join in my rite of passage. Part the mists and bring clarity to my new spirit. I bid you to combine your strength and skills with those of the Eastern Guardian and instill my new spirit with your gifts. By my will, the journey of my new spirit must now begin!

Feel the essence of your old spirit in your hand enter into the candle, combining with your new spirit and becoming whole. Feel the combined gifts of Chaos and the Eastern Guardian pouring into your new spirit. Move deosil to the southeastern quarter and speak aloud these words:

Nyx, Protogonos of night, of the dark mists that spread across the sky, I ask you to join in my rite of passage. Help to guide my new spirit through the darkness. I bid you to combine your strength and skills with those of the Southeastern Guardian and instill my new spirit with your gifts. By my will, my new spirit will accept the responsibilities to be laid out by the lawgiver!

See the Guardian of the Southeastern Gate returning the book of laws to you. Know that the laws have been rewritten to meet your higher standards. Feel the combined gifts of Nyx and the Southeastern Guardian pouring into your new spirit. Know that Nyx will be by your side to help guide you through the darkness. Move to the southern quarter and speak aloud these words:

> *Hyperion, Titan of the light and God of the sun, I ask you to join in my rite of passage. Add wonder and the fiery passion of life to my new spirit. I bid you to combine your strength and skills with those of the Southern Guardian and instill my new spirit with your gifts. By my will, the embers of my old spirit will ignite the ashes of creation and my spirit will be transformed!*

Relight the candle you hold in your hand. As you light the candle, feel the combined gifts of Hyperion and the Southern Guardian pouring into your spirit. Feel the fires of the sun God mixing with those of the Southern Guardian to create a pillar of flame and light in the southern gateway. Feel this pillar of flame enter into the flame of the candle. The fires of life have combined with the flame of the old and the flame of the new. Your spirit has now risen fully transformed! Move to the southwestern gateway and speak aloud these words:

> *Oceanus, first-born son of Uranus and Gaia, Protogonos of the great earth-encircling river from which sprang all springs and wells, I ask you to join in my rite of passage. When the time for me to leave the magickal circle has come, aid my transformed spirit to reopen the doorway to the mundane world. I bid you to combine your strength and skills with those of the Southwestern Guardian and instill my new spirit with your gifts. By my will, when the time has come, the doorway to the mundane world shall be reopened!*

Feel the combined gifts of Oceanus and the Southwestern Guardian pouring into your spirit. Feel Oceanus waiting by the sealed doorway to the mundane. Know that he will aid you in reopening the doorway when the time has come for you to leave. See that, according to your invocation, the Guardian of the Southwestern Gateway is standing steadfast at the doorway. Oceanus will assist in your leaving, but when you next return, the Guardian of the Southwestern Gateway will challenge and task your re-entry into the sacred space of your magickal circle. Move to the western quarter and speak aloud these words:

> *Eros, Protogonos of love, tamer of the spirit, I ask you to join in my rite of passage. Bless my new spirit with love and the ability to see the differences between what was, what is, and what must be. I bid you to combine your strength and skills with those of the Western Guardian and instill my new spirit with your gifts. By my will, my new spirit shall possess understanding and knowledge of all things!*

Feel the combined gifts of Eros and the Western Guardian pouring into your spirit. Feel the knowledge hidden within the sea of the universe swelling within your new spirit. Know that you can access this knowledge when needed. Feel the love and calming energies of Eros flowing through your spirit. Move to the northwestern quarter and speak aloud these words:

> *Eos, Titan of the dawn, announcer of the light that spreads across the sky and reaches the immortals, I ask you to join in my rite of passage. Bless my new spirit with the hope and promise of a brand new day and a bright new beginning. I bid you to combine your strength and skills with those of the Northwestern Guardian and instill my new spirit with your gifts. By my will, my spirit shall be filled with light!*

Feel the light of Eos washing over you. Feel the combined gifts of Eos and the Northwestern Guardian pouring into your spirit. See the Guardian of the Northwestern Gateway holding a book full of nothing but blank pages. Know that you are now beginning a new journey and that the Northwestern Guardian will record your experiences in the book of your life. Move to the northern quarter and speak aloud these words…

Gaia, Protogonos of earth, Great Mother Goddess who nourishes all life, I ask you to join in my rite of passage. Bless my new spirit with the ability to work in perfect harmony with every living creature and the elements of nature. I bid you to combine your strength and skills with those of the Northern Guardian and instill my new spirit with your gifts. By my will, my foundation grows stronger and I am one with all life!

Feel all life flowing around you in perfect harmony. Feel the grounding energies of the Guardian of the Northern Quarter anchoring your spirit and strengthening your foundation. Feel the combined gifts of Gaia and the Northern Guardian pouring into your spirit. Move to the northeastern quarter and speak aloud these words:

Mnemosyne, Titan of memory, I ask you to join in my rite of passage. Bestow on my new spirit a creative beginning, and help me hold the memories of all that I was. I bid you to combine your strength and skills with those of the Northeastern Guardian and instill my new spirit with your gifts. By my will, I impart the final breath of magick into my new spirit and it is born anew!

Feel the combined gifts of Mnemosyne and the Northeastern Guardian pouring into your spirit. Hold the candle aloft before the gateway of the Northeastern Quarter. Close your eyes and feel the energies and the gifts of the Guardians, the Titans, and the Protogonoi swirling within you and around you. Draw in a deep breath and blow out the candle. As the flame is extinguished, feel your new spirit being released from the flame and reentering your body. Move to the southwestern quarter and speak aloud these words:

> *Guardians of the Quarters and the Cross Quarters, Ancient and Powerful Gods and Goddesses who are the Titans and the Protogoni—I thank you for your presence and for your gifts. Know that I will use the blessings and the gifts that you have bestowed upon me to do good works to the best of my ability. My rite of passage has reached its end and I must now begin a new journey. Oceanus, I bid you to grant me your assistance in reopening the door to the mundane world.*

Feel the hand of Oceanus unsealing the doorway to the mundane world. Know that as you pass through the doorway the circle will be opened and the Guardians, the Titans, and the Protogonoi will return to their realms. Pass through the doorway, and as you do, speak aloud these final words:

> *Great and Powerful Ones, I bid you all a final thank you and a fond farewell. By the powers, gifts, and blessings of the mighty Guardians, the powerful Titans, and the ancient Protogonoi, by the spirit of all that I was, all that I am, and all that I am to become, I begin my new journey with joy in my heart, power in my spirit, and purpose in my mind. By my will, my new journey begins!*

Take some time to reflect upon your experiences and revel in your new beginning before cleaning up your ritual area. Place the container that holds the essence of your old spirit in a safe place. Relax for a time and enjoy yourself. You have earned it!

The Spirit Temples

Chapter
13

Deep in the Shadows, or the Thing at the Top of the Stairs

Have you ever seen the stranger things? People's private
hells, they've hidden well on closet shelves? Have you ever
felt there was something there, as you've climbed to bed up
a darkened stair? Or felt the presence and sensed the
gloom, behind bolted doors, in shuttered rooms? Stranger
things than this, I have seen, stranger places, I have been,
things that you don't want to know, places you don't want
to go.

—Anonymous

I am going to guess that there's a question you have been just dying to ask me since you read the first few paragraphs of this book. *Does the shadow spirit really exist?* Or did I just make the whole thing up to have something interesting to write about?

This is a loaded question. I could believe in the reality of your shadow spirit every day from now through the end of eternity, but if *you* do not believe in the reality of your shadow spirit, then, no, it could not possibly exist. To put an even finer point on it, if you don't believe in your shadow spirit, then *it doesn't matter if it exists.* To answer your question more directly, however, and put your mind at ease, no, I did not make up the shadow spirit, or anything else in this book.

You must realize, however, that what the shadow spirit means to *you,* and how *you* perceive it is a very personal experience that will differ greatly from one person to the next. Once our work in this book has been completed, the path of the shadow spirit becomes a journey you will walk alone without me as a guide. Each and every traveler who has dared to walk this path will have his or her own take on what the shadow spirit meant (and will mean) to him or her personally. Some will read this book through to the very last sentence, place the book on a shelf, and never again consider the shadow spirit or its implications. Others will implement the shadow spirit into their lives and use it as a symbol or a metaphor for their inner and/or outer power and strength, but nothing more. Other readers will consider their shadow spirit to be a magickal companion and guide that will remain by their side for the remainder of their life's journey.

None of these end results of walking the path of the shadow spirit should be viewed as being wrong, and one result should not be judged as being better than any other, only different. These end results are simply different levels of individual perceptions of reality that can be found in any given topic. Even if you merely read this book, you will have gone through an amazing journey. In the end, if you get nothing more out of it than a few new ideas and perspectives to consider, then I will call it a job well done. There will, however, be a few (just a few) who will follow the path of the shadow spirit through to its ultimate end. These individuals will not be satisfied until every last veil has been lifted, every mystery unraveled, every facet unmasked, and they have joined with the magick and power of the shadow spirit itself. From there, these individuals will probably go on to become the future teachers of, and guides on, the path of the shadow spirit. They will share their own personal experiences and insights with anyone who wishes to partake of the knowledge and mystery of the path that they have traveled.

The true magick of the shadow spirit lies in its utter simplicity. As with anything else, however, our perceptions, memories, and experiences can color the "truth" with the chosen shades of our liking. In its uncolored state, truth is an absolute that has not yet been broken down into individual versions of itself by the human mind. Simply put, if we view truth as black lines on white sheets of paper in the pages of a coloring book, we will see truth for what it really is, and not for what we would *like* for it to be. This, unfortunately, is much easier said than done. It is in our nature to pull out our crayons and fill in the empty spaces in the coloring book of truth. We enjoy using our imagination to envision what the pages might look like once all the pretty colors have been added to the pictures. The only problem with this way of looking at truth is that we all have our own favorite colors, and what one person may perceive as perfection, another person may see as an abomination.

The same can be said for the shadow spirit. Each person's "truth" of his or her shadow spirit will vary greatly from the next. Therefore, only *you* can answer the questions that pertain to who or what your shadow spirit really is. If I or anyone else were to add our favorite shade of the truth to your page of the coloring book, your shadow spirit might end up becoming something completely different from what you originally imagined, or even different from what you would have liked for it to become. This unintentional coloring of your shadow spirit by outside influences could easily end up altering your perceptions of it.

I want you to be mindful of this as we walk the path of the shadow spirit together. I will share many of my own personal experiences with you and relate my own observations about the shadow spirit so that you will be able to grasp some of its possibilities and complexities. Ultimately however, you should be able to make up your own mind, and decipher your own "truth" as it pertains to your experiences with the shadow spirit. Use your *own* crayons to color in the pictures. Mine are pretty much all used up anyway.

In Chapter 10, I told you how, during my first attainment of a harmonic trance, I was given the first part of the key that would eventually allow me to unlock the initial mystery of the shadow spirit. What I didn't tell you then is that the harmonic trance itself was also given to me at that very same moment, although it ultimately took quite some time before I was able to figure the whole thing out. I was not yet a Witch at that time, nor did I possess even a rudimentary understanding of magick. The events that I am about to share with you, therefore, come from my own personal experiences as I have perceived them to be true. Not one word is made up; not one experience has been manufactured or dramatized for shock value.

We will begin my personal story at day one of my travels into the mysterious unknown, when first contact with my shadow spirit was made. This is the day that I felt magick flowing through me for the very first time. I was in my early 20s at the time and, as do most kids at that age, I thought I had it all pretty much figured out. I thought that I knew all there was to know. Nothing could possibly surprise me. *Boy, was I wrong.* It was a typical summer day in the Midwest and, as I drove along a backcountry road in a $400 Camaro equipped with a set of five-dollar tires, I had no idea that my life was about to be changed forever. A good friend of mine was riding in the car with me that day, and as we drove along we were having our usual conversation on topics such as music, girls, partying, and other such juvenile nonsense. It was very warm that day, and the heat and the rough gravel eventually took their toll on the Camaro's cheap tires. The inevitable blowout came without warning. After pulling the car off to the side of the road, and then discovering that the spare was also flat, my friend and I set off on what promised to be a very long walk back to civilization.

It was about 10 minutes into our walk that the world started to become surreal to me. Everything started to look different than it ever had before. Everything *felt* different. Suddenly I was hearing a faint buzzing sound. Pretty soon, I discovered that I wasn't hearing the buzzing sound with my ears. It was inside of my mind. Then the trees along the side of the road grabbed my attention. I couldn't keep my eyes or my attention off them. The leaves of the trees seemed to churn and swirl with an energy force that I was somehow not only seeing, but *feeling*. This sensation was, of course, entirely new to me. I'd never had any psychic or mystical experiences. I started thinking I was sick, maybe having a heat stroke or something. I asked my friend to sit down with me at the side of the road for a few minutes.

My attention was inexplicably drawn to the leaves in one nearby tree. I don't even remember what kind of tree it was. As I sat there, thinking I was resting, the sensation of swirling energies overtook me to the point where I couldn't tell the difference between my own self and anything else. I seemed to be lost in space. Lost in time. And this was my first experience with lost time. My first experience with magick.

When I finally came back to something approaching ordinary awareness, I wasn't sitting on the side of the road anymore. I was in the basement of the house in which I was living in at the time! How could that be? I looked around. I found myself surrounded by the members of the rock-and-roll band I was playing with at that time. They all had very scared looks on their faces.

Then I noticed that I had a pencil and a piece of paper clenched tightly in my fist. When I unfolded the paper and read what was written on it, it made no sense at all. It looked to be four or five poems, very badly written poems, all mish-mashed together in some strange, deliberate fashion. I didn't even recognize the handwriting, so I held the paper aloft in front of my bandmates. "Who wrote this crap?" I asked. They were staring at me as if I was crazy, and almost in unison they raised their eyebrows and said, "You did!" "Bullshit!" I exclaimed. "Not me!" I went on to explain to them that I was a much better poet that this—and I waved the paper around in front of them again—and whoever wrote this garbage just sucked. They backed off, at least physically, and one after another assured me that not only had I written what was on the paper, but also that for the last hour and a half I had been repeating what I had written over and over, "like some kind of a chant," the drummer said. One of the other guys added that I had been going on and on about the "gray man" who had been walking with me on the trek back to the house. All four of the guys said that I had explained to them that he had told me what to write down on the sheet of paper.

I looked down at my watch. It was 3:33 in the afternoon.

I will explain to you the significance of time as it relates to my shadow spirit, but first let's take a closer look at what the automatic writing I had done while in the harmonic trance (a label I would not coin until many years later) had to do with this first contact. Let's look at where the words on the sheet of paper would eventually lead me. Although I would love to be able to share what was written in its entirety, I feel it would be a very bad idea so to do. I believe that what I wrote (or *was guided to write*) is a very powerful incantation that relates to *my* shadow spirit alone, and no one else's.

I can, however, share bits and pieces of it with you so that you can understand why it was given to me. Hopefully, you'll also understand the final outcome I experienced by following its directions. I use the word *directions* because that is what I discovered hidden within that god-awful poem. It turned out to be a roadmap to my shadow spirit. The following events that I will describe to you took place several weeks after I had unconsciously written the poem. My friend and I were the only people in house while these events were taking place.

I cannot recall if it was I or my friend (who, for reasons of privacy, I will not name here) who first noticed how the words of the first section of the poem seemed to relate to a specific area in my home. *Square by square,* I had written, *the cracks sleep there.* It was so obvious that we almost missed it, but yet there the squares were, right in front of us for anyone to see: the cracked square tiles in the foyer that led into the living room.

Our curiosity was piqued to the max at this point, so we decided to see where things would lead us next. The aforementioned gaps in the poem will probably leave you scratching your head, so bear with me here. The next part of the poem I will share with you is, *Don't fear for I will be here with us, the conquest conquers living sands.* We need to break this down into two sections. *Don't fear for I will be here with us* relates directly to the shadow spirit, myself, and the eventual union that was to take place between the two of us. I didn't figure this out until sometime after the events I am relating to you, but it is relevant to the entire process and therefore demands explanation at this point. *I* relates to the presence of the shadow spirit. *With us* relates to me and the shadow spirit combined into a single entity, wherein the shadow spirit speaks of itself as being an entity distinctly separate from itself, and yet is still a part of the whole that is the sum of the two of us combined. Feel free to read that sentence over a few times if you need to. I know *I* had to while I was writing it.

The second part of the poem was more relevant to the situation at that point in time, and the following line had us stumped for a few minutes: *The conquest conquers living sands.* "Living sands…" I thought to myself. "What the hell are 'living sands'?" I scanned the living room for clues. After through examination, I assured myself that there were no sands to be found, let alone *living* sands.

I was starting to think that we had been reading something into the poem that wasn't there, that the cracked tiles were just a coincidence. We were just about to give up the search when I saw it: the framed Winslow Homer print hanging on the wall over the landing at the bottom of the stairs. If you know anything about Winslow Homer, then you probably already know that this wonderful artist had a favorite theme that was the inspiration for most of his work: *the ocean.* There it was in the painting: *living sands.*

Things progressed quickly from there. *Forever time, time at hand* was the next line, and there it was—the third piece of the puzzle. The broken cuckoo clock hanging on the wall at the bottom of the stairs. *Forever time, time at hand.*

Where did the poem lead us next? *Strange spaces, traces, empty faces.* I looked up, and what I saw sent a chill down my spine. The "spaces" that made up the walls of the staircase were indeed very strange. They jutted off in weird angles and directions, but what was of even more interest (and responsible for the chill) were the two black-and-white profile silhouette drawings hung on the wall along the staircase. *Strange spaces, traces, empty faces.*

I had probably looked at all of these things a thousand times, but today they were taking on a whole new meaning. I looked down at my friend who was standing at the foot of the stairs. He looked very frightened. I held up the badly wrinkled piece of paper in my hand, and spoke aloud the last sentence of the poem. *Reach now for the gifts within my hand.* We both looked up at the top of the stairs, and if only for a split second, we both saw it: a gray figure. A shadowy outline of someone or something standing on the landing at the top of the staircase. I heard my friend yell, "NOOOO!" at the top of his lungs, but it was too late. I was making for the top of the stairs like a bullet.

What happened next is very difficult for me to relate with words, but I will try my best. When I reached the top of the staircase, there was absolutely nothing there. Well, at least nothing I could *see,* but the feeling of standing in the middle of a very powerful presence was unmistakable. I could feel some unseen energy force flowing around my feet and legs. It was so cold on the landing I could see my breath, even though my body felt very warm. I would not understand it until many years later, but I was standing at the edge of a portal to a place beyond this world. The feeling of intense energy was flowing freely through my body. I recall feeling very excited and thrilled about what I was experiencing.

However, I was not the only person standing on the staircase at that moment, and, unfortunately for my friend, his response was something less than pleasurable. I remember hearing him gasp, and, as I looked down at him, the look and feel of sheer terror on his face was somewhat unsettling. I had heard the expression "every hair on his head was standing up" many times, but for the first time I was actually *seeing* it. My friend's face had turned a ghostly shade of white and tears were streaming from his red eyes. He was literally shaking from head to toe. I remember that I started moving down the staircase towards him, but, as I did, he started screaming uncontrollably. Then he ran out of the house like a man in fear of losing his very soul.

I only saw my friend a few more times after this incident took place. He would not speak of the events of that day for a long time, and when he finally did it was very hesitantly. Here's what he finally told me. First, he claims that he saw *two* of me standing at the top of the staircase that day. Second, he said that both pairs of our eyes were pitch black. I have been told many times since my first encounter with my shadow spirit that whenever I am deep in the throes of intense magickal energy my eyes turn pitch black.

What ever became of my friend? Well, all I can say is that to this day he is a *very* religious man and that his religion is not of the pagan persuasion.

I suppose that if we eliminated the trance, the contents of the poem, and where that poem led me, the events that I have just related to you could easily be written off as having simply been an encounter with a poltergeist or a wayward spirit. I myself have been a skeptic all my life, and it takes quite a bit to convince me that supernatural encounters and events such as the one I've just described to you actually take place and that they do not solely exist inside of the mind of the person who *believes* that they have experienced these types of encounters and events. This is not to say that I do not believe that forces and powers beyond this world and beyond our understanding truly exist, just that I have known people who have wanted to experience the supernatural so badly that they have constructed elaborate stories and fantasies that eventually become so real to them that their fantasies took on a life of their own and grew beyond the control of their creator.

I only mention this here because I want you to do a reality check on yourself every once in a while as we travel the path of the shadow spirit together. Don't misunderstand me; there is nothing at all wrong with having a bit of fun with fantasy here and there. Believing in fairies is just fine. But if the fairies start telling you to do strange things in the middle of the night, then I would suggest that you make an appointment with a psychiatrist ASAP.

If I were to go on to describe to you each and every one of my personal experiences and encounters with my shadow spirit in great detail, this book could easily end up being a thousand pages long. For obvious reasons, therefore, I will not get into any more blow-by-blow descriptions of these encounters. I did promise you, however, that I would explain the significance of time (or, more specifically, numbers) as it relates to my shadow spirit. This information may or may not be pertinent to you should your own shadow spirit decide to materialize itself into our plane of existence and reveal itself to you.

From the time of my first encounter with my shadow spirit to this day, very specific numbers on the clock have marked every materialization, feeling of an unseen presence, or strange event or occurrence that I determined was directly related to my shadow spirit. You may recall that when I came out of my first harmonic trance I looked at my watch and noticed that the time was 3:33. I later discovered that this series of numbers (333) directly related to every physical manifestation of my shadow spirit and that different series of numbers coincided with lesser events. For example, every bona fide physical manifestation of my shadow spirit (with the exception of one) has occurred at precisely 3:33 a.m. or p.m., and only on the 11th or 22nd day of the month. The lesser incidents—doors opening or slamming shut on their own, things being moved across the room, unplugged clocks with no battery backup turning on while I was carrying them in my hands—always occurred at times such as 11:11, 12:34, 2:22, and so on. The physical manifestations also occurred only when a single light source was illuminating the room. If my shadow spirit decided it wanted to materialize itself, and more than one source of illumination was present in the room, it would extinguish all other sources of light before appearing. As to exactly why it was only happy with a single light on is a mystery that has never been revealed to me.

Above all else, however, the numbers and their possible significance were (and still are) one of the most intriguing facets of my shadow spirit. The stumbling block for me to be able to unlock the mystery of these numbers was that I never did like learning about mathematics or dealing with digits. (I dread the simple task of balancing my checkbook.) I never took it upon myself to further investigate what my shadow spirit may have been trying to relate to me by using numbers as signifiers. The presence of the numbers eventually became a comfort to me, so I just left well enough alone and unfortunately ended up taking them for granted. Lucky for us, however, I have two very good friends, Lord Sampsun and Lady Amber Morrigan, who have a passion for numerology. They were kind enough to take a look at the dominant sequences of numbers, evaluate them for me, and give me their opinions on what my shadow spirit could have possibly have been trying to tell me through numbers. After some deep and long conversations between the three of us, however, it became obvious that my shadow spirit's use of digits did not have as much to do with numerology as it did with communication. I was about to learn how to speak a whole new language: the language of my shadow spirit.

As investigation of the numerological aspect of my shadow began, intriguing phrases such as *master numbers* and *master builder* kept cropping up in our conversations. Notes on creativity, mysticism, and the possibility of unlearned lessons were frantically being scratched on blank sheets of paper for future reference. Everything seemed to be coming together very quickly. It was evident that the mystery of the numbers was beginning to be revealed to us, that it would simply be a matter of Lord Sampsun and Lady Amber formulating their thesis and tying all the loose numerological ends together and reaching a conclusion.

According to Lord Sampsun and Lady Amber, it was evident that my shadow spirit was speaking to me about major life lessons that were occurring and to which I needed to pay close attention. Because all of the numbers were time-oriented, the possibility was presented that perhaps my shadow spirit was using linear numbers to try and get me to think outside of the linear box. It was also possible that my shadow spirit was actually trying to show me that time meant absolutely nothing at all. It was at this point that our research into the numerological aspects took a dramatic turn, and we suddenly found ourselves working in an entirely different direction.

Was what my shadow spirit saying to me really relevant to my readers? Were the lessons being presented not of a highly personal nature that would have little or no impact on anyone other than me? It soon became apparent to us that it was not *what* my shadow spirit was saying to me that was of great importance to my readers, but instead *how* it was saying it. In conclusion, all the talk about numerology had brought us down to one thing: communication.

The pages of charts and numerological calculations were quickly swapped for blank sheets of paper as we realized that the most pertinent information that we needed to analyze and share had shifted from numerological messages to the shadow spirit voice itself. It was suggested that in very much the same way that we "speak" to our parents when we are babies, the shadow spirit speaks to each of us in a way that we can understand. Before we became self-aware and learned how to speak with words and sentences, we communicated our emotions, situations, and physical needs to our parents without the aid of the spoken word. It was further suggested that, because our shadow spirits do not possess a human voice to speak with, but rather a magickal voice, the shadow spirit chooses a symbolic "language" of sorts that it uses as a magickal voice.

I had already pointed out to my fellow analysts that I really don't like dealing with numbers, so I now told them that I felt it was very odd that my shadow spirit was using numbers to speak to me. That observation opened up a discussion of how other people's magickal selves spoke to them, and we discovered a common thread that ran through these lines of magickal communication. Everyone's magickal self that we were aware of, it seemed, had spoken to him or her in a "voice" they either didn't like or were unfamiliar or afraid of. Lady Amber's magickal self had first spoken to her by prompting her to draw an unusual symbol over and over again until it became familiar to her. At the time, Lady Amber loathed having to draw so much as a stick figure, and she didn't understand what it was that her magickal self was trying to tell her. She also mentioned that the magical self of a friend of hers "spoke" by using the mental image of a spider on a web. The spider would walk along a single thread of webbing until it arrived at what it was her magickal self wanted her to see or to learn. This person was deathly afraid of spiders!

As each person's story or recollection of others' experiences was told, it became clear to us that each person's shadow spirit (even though they may not have realized that it *was* their shadow spirit) used a voice to "speak" to them that was either unfamiliar or frightening to them in some way. It was deduced by Lady Amber that, by using a "voice" that was either unfamiliar or frightening, it made a much larger impact on the person than if their magickal self had tried to communicate with them in a way that was pleasant or familiar. In other words, each magickal voice rang louder simply because it was unfamiliar or frightening. This caused the listener to sit up and take notice.

It's possible that your shadow spirit has been "speaking" to you from the very beginning. You must now use your magickal eyes to see, your magickal ears to hear, and your magickal mind to interpret what your shadow spirit is trying to "say" to you. Your *other* will use its own unique "voice" to communicate with you. Its voice will symbolically manifest as something that means something to you and only you. Your shadow spirit might use numbers, colors, symbols, totem animals, or just about anything else as a language when it chooses to "speak" to you. Once you figure out how your shadow spirit has been communicating with you (or will communicate with you), then you can do your own research to find out how this language works. But do not take anyone else's approach or research as gospel when it comes to your shadow spirit. Use what you learn to discover your own truth and gain your own insights.

Your magickal self wants to talk to you. Are you ready to listen?

Let us now take some time to discuss some of the more obvious concerns and fears that you may have as they relate to your own shadow spirit. First is the very real possibility of your shadow spirit materializing itself into our plane of existence. You may already have experienced a physical encounter with your *other*. You may already know what to expect should this occur, but, for the sake of relaying information, I will assume that you have not yet had such a meeting with your shadow spirit.

It is likely that you have already been taught or have read in books on Witchcraft about the possibility of a spirit or unknown entity materializing itself either inside or outside of your magickal circle. The author or teacher probably explained to you that this is nothing to be afraid of, as these spirits or entities are usually not malevolent and your circle is protected sacred space where you make up all the rules. I can tell you from experience, however, that to even the bravest of Witches, materializations can be quite chilling and unsettling occurrences. Most Witches strive and thirst for contact with the unknown, but if you were to discover that the "unknown" was suddenly standing right next to you and staring you in the face, I don't think anyone could blame you for being a little creeped out by it.

To continue walking the path of the shadow spirit however, *you must be prepared for this to happen.* In the remaining chapters of this section of the book, you will begin to construct what you will come to know as the spirit temples. As with your shadow realm, these temples will be mental, physical, and astral places of power that you will use to make contact with your shadow spirit. In them you will learn to gather and focus intense and powerful magickal energies. As you build these temples, you will also undergo the final preparations of your mind, spirit, and body for what I call "the becoming." The becoming is the metaphysical "family reunion" where you will be aligning and joining your magickal energies with the powers of your shadow spirit.

Before you whip out your magickal tools and begin to hammer together your spirit temples, however, there are a few more concerns that we must address. I have said several times in this book that your shadow spirit is a mirror image of your magickal self. I've told you that what you fear it does not fear, that what you don't know it has stored in its memory. You may have already asked some important questions. "Does that mean that what I love and care about my shadow spirit will hate?" "Will my shadow spirit try to harm me or the people I love because of this?"

Of course not. Please also remember that I clearly pointed out that you are an earthbound entity and your shadow spirit is a magickal astral entity. Love and hate are *human* emotions. Vengeance and violence are *human* qualities. Your shadow spirit is your *magickal* counterpart and counterbalance. It could probably care less about such human nonsense. It exists *knowingly* within the balance of light and dark within itself and all magickal things. It is not beyond giving you a metaphysical slap on the wrist, however, if you were to try to use it as a channel for baneful and harmful magicks without a pretty damn good reason.

I could continue to hammer at this point, but doing so could undermine the main message that I am trying to relate here. That message is to *be prepared for anything*. Again, many of the instances that I have related to you in this chapter are my own personal experiences, and you may or may not experience anything even remotely similar to them.

We have now pretty much covered what you might expect to happen or experience with your shadow spirit on the *physical* plane. We should press on and discuss what you might expect to experience with your shadow spirit on the *astral* plane.

Above all else, your shadow spirit is your astral guide, and in so being it has probably already mapped out most, if not all, of the territory in the astral world. This is good news for you because it means you don't have to do the mapping on your own. Your shadow spirit can also steer you clear of astral pitfalls or unbalanced entities and pockets of energy that exist within its world. It has probably encountered, or even interacted with, many of the spirits and entities that exist there. Your *other* could easily serve as your ambassador should you desire to make contact with these astral spirits and entities yourself. Your shadow spirit is *not,* however, beyond giving you a little push in what it feels is the right direction for your magickal growth, and, as with any really good teacher, it might leave you all alone to get yourself out of a metaphysical jam you've gotten yourself into. Your *other* does not exist to coddle and baby you or kowtow to your every desire and demand. Don't expect it to be the magickal equivalent of a servant or a slave. Above all else, it is your shadow spirit's greatest need and desire for you to grow stronger as a person and a Witch. As your magickal power and skills increase, so does its own.

There is much more that you may come to expect on the inner, outer, and astral planes of existence by joining with your shadow spirit, and I will cover many more of these possibilities and eventualities as we begin construction of the spirit temples. For now, however, I want you to reflect and meditate on what we have discussed in this chapter. Consider my experiences with the shadow spirit. Make sure that you have a pretty good handle on everything before you continue with the work in this book.

The shadows on the path that still lie ahead will grow darker and darker before the light will once again make itself known to you.

Gateway to the Spirit Temples

It is now time to begin construction of the spirit temples. As I previously explained, the spirit temples are inner, outer, and astral points of power. Once construction of the three spirit temples has been completed, you will be able to connect the power of the spirit temples to the power of the shadow realm, and then ultimately directly to the power of the shadow spirit itself. Once you are able to focus the magickal energies of these five points of power together into a single force, you will have formed the *pentagram of power.*

Before we begin construction of the spirit temples, let's take a closer look at the pentagram of power so that you can gain a better understanding of how and why it works. To do this, we will break the pentagram of power down into its five individual points and examine the purpose and function of each point of power separately. The five points of the pentagram of power do not directly relate to the five points of a standard Witch's pentacle or pentagram, so do not confuse them as such.

Following on page 194 is a diagram of the pentacle of power. To follow this diagram, we will begin with the living temple (the "air" point on a standard Witch's pentagram) and move counterclockwise around the pentagram until we reach the point of the shadow spirit. For now, we will only discuss a brief synopsis of the function and purpose of each point on the pentagram of power. Each point will be examined in greater depth as you undergo construction of the spirit temples.

The Pentagram of Power

The Shadow Spirit

The Living
Temple

The Hidden
Temple

The Shadow Realm

The Eternal Temple

Point of Power Number 1: The Body, The Living Temple

The living temple is your foundation and source of strength. Do not confuse the word *strength*, however, with power. The strength of the living temple should be viewed as a grounding anchor. It is the point of stability and readiness on the pentagram of power. The living temple is where you will undergo your initial preparations for combining the power of all five spirit temples together. The living temple is where you will ground and center the energies around you, and the energies within yourself.

Point of Power Number 2: The Shadow Realm

You are already quite familiar with the shadow realm, so you already know that the shadow realm is your place of power. It is also the *point* of power on the pentagram of power. The point of the shadow realm as it pertains to the pentagram of power should be viewed as a kind of "collection cup" in which the magickal energies being transmitted by the third point on the pentagram of power (the eternal temple) will be gathered and intensified.

Point of Power Number 3: The Astral, The Eternal Temple

The eternal temple serves two separate yet interconnected functions on the pentagram of power. To understand these two functions, we will envision the eternal temple as a very powerful antenna on the astral plane. This antenna is capable of gathering magickal energies and then sending the collected energies to any desired location. As far as the pentagram of power is concerned, we will be using the antenna of the eternal temple to gather magickal energies from the astral plane and then use the eternal temple as a transmitter to transfer these magickal energies to the shadow realm, where their powers will be intensified. These beefed-up magickal energies will then be redirected back to the eternal temple by the fourth point on the pentagram of power, which is the hidden temple.

Point of Power Number 4: The Mind, The Hidden Temple

The hidden temple is the point of willpower, purpose, and (above all else) focus. The hidden temple is the point on the pentagram of power where the intent of the collected magickal energies will be clearly stated and where personal willpower will be added into the mix. The hidden

195

temple will then be used to focus the magickal energies back to the eternal temple where they will be transmitted directly to point number five, the shadow spirit.

Point of Power Number 5: The Shadow Spirit

The initial purpose of the pentagram of power is to make first contact with the shadow spirit. However, once this first contact has been made and the shadow spirit has accepted you, the pentagram of power will be used, as previously described, to gather, intensify, and focus magickal energies directly to the shadow spirit itself. At this point you will have established a direct mainline not only to the astral plane but also to your magickal counterpart itself. The shadow spirit is then capable of virtually doubling the power of the gathered and focused magickal energies and releasing them to manifest into the desired goal.

Once all five points of the pentagram of power have been constructed (or contact established) and you fire it up and use it for the very first time, I assure you that it will be an experience you will never forget. You will also have one of the most powerful magickal tools imaginable at your disposal. If you're half as excited about the thought of assembling the pentagram of power as I am by teaching it to you, then I'm sure you are quite eager to get the process underway. So...without further hesitation, we begin construction of the spirit temples.

Chapter 14

The Body: The Living Temple

We will now begin construction of the living temple. As the title of this chapter suggests, the living temple is the point of power that is established within your body. The two key elements of the living temple are your body and an earth altar, which is a physical altar that you will construct to gather and concentrate earthly energies and which will serve as the foundation for the living temple of your body. You will also begin the process of learning to master "lucid daydreaming."

As I explained in the previous chapter, the living temple is the first point on the pentagram of power. It is where the initial state of readiness to connect with the remaining four points of power will be attained. The living temple should thus be considered the anchor point on the pentagram of power. It is also the temple that will maintain stability within your self and within the energies that you will be collecting, ultimately transferring through all five points of power.

Because the creation of the earth altar will require you to do some forethought and gather physical materials, we should begin the work in this chapter by taking a close look at the earth altar's function and construction. We will next move on to discuss the role your body plays in the living temple, and we will then examine the art of lucid daydreaming.

Finally, we will tie everything together, and you will work through a step-by-step process to establish your body as the living temple on the pentagram of power.

The earth altar will be a physical representation of the foundation of the living temple. It will also be used to collect and focus earthly energies before transferring those earthly energies directly into your body. Besides being fun to construct, the earth altar will serve as a fantastic visual aid when you begin connecting together the five points of the pentagram of power. Before you begin gathering items for the earth altar, however, I have a few suggestions that you may find interesting. Let's take a look at some of the possibilities you may want to consider.

The earth altar of the living temple could be constructed by any means at your disposal. As we go along, keep in mind that you are under no obligation to go out and spend any of your hard-earned cash to purchase items for the earth altar of the living temple. You can easily make do with anything you may already have at home or in your yard. Taking into account the fact that you will be constructing an altar that represents the foundational aspect of earth, you will be better off using natural items in the construction of the earth altar. A large flat stone or a cross-section cut from a tree stump is perfect for the base of the earth altar, but a small table or even the floor will also work just fine. Once you have decided on the base for the earth altar, you can take either a traditional or non-traditional approach to what you add to the altar to give it your own personal feel and flair. Some of the more traditional items and symbols that Witches and other pagans use as representations of earth energy are copper, salt, soil, grains, stones, green candles, and pentacles or pentagrams. Representations of deity are not essential for the earth altar, but if you feel that they might be helpful in providing you with added strength, consider using representations of Gaia or the Green Man to keep the energies of the earth altar consistent with the aspect of earthly foundation you are trying to achieve. Keep in mind, however, that this is your earth altar. You should be using items that represent what you personally consider earth energies to be.

There are also many non-traditional approaches that you can take in assembling the earth altar. Again, have some fun with it and see what else you might be able to come up with. Being eclectic and inventing new approaches to the practice of Witchcraft can be one of the most powerful learning tools that you will ever find. As I said earlier, *you* must now take on the mantle of the pioneer and the explorer and later share what you have learned with those of us who walk the path with you. Sharing knowledge and insight is the only way that *any* of us will truly learn how to advance and grow stronger as we walk the path together.

Now that you understand the purpose and construction of the earth altar, we will move on and discuss the preparation of your physical body, and the role it plays as a living temple.

You have probably read many books that explain the importance of the Witch's preparing his or her magickal mind before undertaking any serious magickal workings. Taking a "luster" bath, purifying the body and mind by smudging with incense or an herbal smudge stick, assuming a magickal persona by donning robes and magickal jewelry—these and numerous other techniques have probably been presented to you as possibilities for magickal preparation. One of the most interesting purification techniques I recall from my own personal experience is being magickally purified by drumming. Nothing quite compares to standing naked under a full moon while two priestesses of the Craft purify you with primal beats pounded out on two large bodhrans!

There is nothing wrong with using any of these techniques to assume your magickal identity, but, for the purposes of establishing the living temple, I would like you to pay particular attention to your body itself and what it is telling you about its state of readiness to do magickal working. Because your body will be used as a living temple in the pentagram of power, if it is not in good order before you begin working with the spirit temples, your foundation may be weak and unstable.

Let's begin then with some initial observations you can make regarding the state of readiness your body should be in before you establish it as the living temple. If you are physically ill, it is probably not a good idea to push yourself, no matter how badly you may want to do the work. If you're hungry, eat something before you begin, but don't overdo it. If your belly is stuffed with food and drink, wait until you don't feel so full before working with the spirit temples. If your body is sore from overwork, take a long shower or a soak in a hot bath to ease the soreness and tension in your muscles. The point is that you need to be as *physically comfortable* as you can be before you establish your body as the living temple and begin working with the pentagram of power.

Once you have begun the process of establishing your body as the living temple, you will be concentrating on gathering as much strength and stability as possible into your body's central core. Once again, it is not the gathering of power or focusing of the mind that you should be concentrating on as you establish your body as the living temple. It is the heightening of your inner and outer strength, stability, and foundation that you will be attaining by gathering earthly energies and concentrating these energies within your body. Power and mental focus will come later as you continue to construct and connect the remaining spirit temples.

The final goal of this chapter is taking the first steps in learning how to master lucid daydreaming. Lucid daydreaming is much the same as lucid dreaming (that is, controlled dreaming at night), the main difference being that the lucid daydreamer is awake, not asleep. If you don't already understand what a lucid dream is, a lucid dream is a dream in which you are *aware* of the fact that you are dreaming *while* you are dreaming. This awareness by the lucid dreamer usually greatly increases the extent to which the dreamer can deliberately influence the course of events in his or her dream. When we daydream, we are usually already somewhat aware of the fact that we are daydreaming, so to some extent daydreaming is already lucid. What you are now going to learn to do is establish more control over what is being played out in your mind than the average daydreamer can.

Scientists and psychologists are finally realizing some of the benefits that can be reaped by daydreaming. Let's take a closer look at some of those benefits and examine how you can apply them to the practice of Witchcraft. The following observations about the benefits of daydreaming are extracted from work done by Erik T. Mueller and Michael G. Dyer in a research paper titled "Daydreaming in Humans and Computers." Mueller and Dyer believe that a relationship between creativity and daydreaming was suggested by Sigmund Freud. The attributes of daydreaming they discuss are "support for creativity," "relaxation of constraints," and "fortuitous analogy recognition." Daydreaming, they write, "explores possibilities which would normally not have been pursued. Some of these possibilities, while perhaps unlikely at first glance, may lead to a new and useful solution to a problem." They compare this finding of solutions to the process of brainstorming.

Recognizing "fortuitous analogies," they continue, happens because "it is possible to stumble into a solution to another problem" while we are daydreaming. "That is, daydreaming often includes the serendipitous recognition of analogies among problems. Daydreaming often consists of the exploration of hypothetical future scenarios. This allows the consequences of possible future actions in possible future situations to be considered in advance. In this way, advantageous actions may be employed over less advantageous ones."

Mueller and Dyer go on to say that daydreaming "aids not only in making life choices, but also in choosing among detailed alternative methods for carrying out a plan in the face of various contingencies." They give the example of when someone is facing a job interview. When we prepare for the interview, we anticipate questions and create good answers. When we rehearse in a daydreaming state, we can prepare better, possibly more creative, responses.

> The functions of daydreaming and a computational theory of daydreaming are being implemented and tested in the DAYDREAMER computer program. We have argued that, far from being a useless epiphenomenon, daydreaming serves an important cognitive role in supporting creativity, future planning and rehearsal, learning from failures and successes, and emotion modification and motivation. Truly intelligent computers should not be idle when left unemployed by their users, but daydreaming like ourselves.

Mueller and Dyer make a strong case for the many benefits that can be derived from daydreaming and the cognizant incorporation of daydreaming into our lives. The complete research paper, *Daydreaming in Humans and Computers,* can easily be accessed in its entirety on the Internet at *www.signiform.com/erik/pubs/ddijcai.htm.* Mueller and Dyer use two keywords that are important for our work: *relaxation* and *creativity.*

Before you can realize the benefits of lucid daydreaming for yourself and apply these benefits to your magick, you are going to have to do some more self-analysis and purge your subconscious of the negativity that you have probably come to associate with daydreaming. You have, I'm sure, been told more times than you can remember to "stop daydreaming" by your teachers, parents, and perhaps even by your friends. Because you've been told this so often, you've been taught to have negative associations with daydreaming. What you have probably *not* been taught about day-dreaming is that it's a potential gold mine of learning experiences and skill enhancements that are just waiting to be tapped.

At the end of this chapter I will provide you with an easy-to-follow, step-by-step process for establishing your body as the living temple. As you undertake this process, you will also be taking the first steps in learning how to attain a state of lucid daydreaming.

Before we move on, there are two more observations about lucid day-dreaming that I will present for consideration.

First, I'm sure that almost everyone who has worked with visualization techniques would agree that it's much easier to visualize an image or scenario in our mind with our eyes closed. When our eyes are closed, external visual distractions are eliminated. Without the extra visual clutter invading our mind, it's much easier to focus on what we're visualizing. If my observation about visualization being much easier when our eyes are closed is correct, then this leaves us with one major problem. How many Witches do you think perform ritual or spellcrafting with their eyes closed the entire time? Not many, I'm sure; I know that I certainly don't. So if most Witches do their magickal working with their eyes wide open, then we need to factor in the visual clutter our minds are absorbing into the equation of magick and determine what affect it's having on the effectiveness of our Craft. If we determine that visual clutter *is* having a direct impact on the effectiveness of our magick, how do we get around this problem without having to resort to practicing Witchcraft while wearing a blindfold? We do this when we learn how to meditate with our eyes open, learn how to remove or manipulate the visual clutter for our benefit by becoming masters of the art of lucid daydreaming.

The mastering of visualization and scenario development skills that you can acquire by learning how to use lucid daydreaming can also greatly enhance your magickal skills. Possessing the ability to mentally play out all of the possible scenarios of your energy and spell-work quickly and with little or no effort gives you a powerful advantage in being able to avoid magickal pitfalls and undesirable outcomes. The mastering of lucid daydreaming can up your odds of successful spell casting and give you yet another powerful tool to add to your ever-growing arsenal of magickal weapons.

Keeping everything we have discussed so far in this chapter in mind, let's sew up all of the loose ends and run through the entire process of establishing your body as the living temple.

To begin the work of establishing your body as the living temple, you first need to gather up the items for your earth altar and set up the altar in the spot you have chosen to do the work. Your body should already be in the best state of comfort and readiness that it possibly can be. The place you choose to do this work should also provide your body with as much comfort as possible. Any discomfort will become a distraction to you, so keep this in mind as you pick out a place to do the work, and get yourself into as comfortable a position as possible somewhere near the earth altar.

To begin the process of establishing your body as the living temple, you need to thoroughly relax your body and your mind. Unlike achieving a meditative state, however, you do not want to lose awareness of your surroundings. On the contrary, you are trying to connect with the energies of the world around you as much as possible so you can draw strength from the earthly energies. Earth energies are anything that you personally consider to be tied directly to the earth. They can be either physical or mental representations of earth energy. For example, what did you choose to place on the earth altar as your symbols of earthly energies? You may have things such as leaves, a pinecone, soil, seeds, stones, or a plethora of other items on you altar that you chose to represent earth energies. Place your hands on your earth altar or hold these items in your hands. How do they feel to you? Can you feel the grounding energies in them? Can you feel the strength of the earth within them? Around you? Now picture in your mind other things in nature that you consider to be either grounding or strong with earthly energies. Do you see a mountain or a great forest? Perhaps you see a huge bear on the side of the mountain or a powerful deer running through the forest. These physical and mental representations of grounding energies and earthly strength are what you want to focus on as you gather earth energies into yourself. You do not, however, want to over focus on your surroundings. This is not the time to be concerned by the thought of mundane tasks. Let the little things go for now, and open yourself up to experiencing how the world *feels* to you, not how it appears.

At this point you want to lightly focus your attention on the earth altar. Empty your mind of conscious thought, *but do not close your eyes at any point in this exercise.* You are basically learning how to meditate with your eyes open. Keep this instruction in the back of your mind as you go along. You now want to imagine that a symbol of strength (anything you consider to be strong with earth energies) is rising up from the earth altar and floating in the air directly above it. *Do not focus your attention on this symbol.* Instead, keep your focus on the altar itself. You should treat the symbol of strength as being within your field of vision but not your main focal point.

Without looking directly at the symbol, imagine that you can move it anywhere you want it to go. Try moving the strength symbol, but don't let it leave your field of vision. Once you are able to move the strength symbol at will, without looking directly at it, imagine that, one after another, different symbols of strength are rising up into the air from the earth altar. See them moving to where you want them to go. At the same time, keep your main focus on the earth altar at all times.

At this point you are simultaneously beginning the process of lucid daydreaming and gathering earthly energies in and around the earth altar. Without losing sight of the symbols of strength, take a few moments to further relax your body and your mind. Slip into your comfort zone as deeply as you can, but stay just above the point of where you feel that you want to close your eyes and drift away.

Now that your body is fully relaxed, and your mind is lightly focused on the earth altar and the strength symbols, it's time to let the creative juices of your mind flow freely. Drift along on their mental tides. In your mind, hear yourself saying the word *strength* and, without looking directly at them, see if you can notice any change in the symbols of strength. If you cannot see a change in the symbols after a few moments, don't give up. Repeat the word *strength* in your mind a bit more firmly, a bit louder than you did the first time. Keep repeating the word *strength* over and over again, making it firmer and louder each time you repeat it. You will know if you have attained a state of lucid daydreaming by what is happening in your mind and by what you can (or cannot) see happening around you.

At this point, the symbols of strength may change. They may transform into different shapes that represent the strength of the earth. They may also stay the same and simply grow stronger. These symbols are a combination of the earth energies and what your subconscious envisions these energies as being. The earth energies can take on any shape or form that you can imagine, and you may be surprised by what your subconscious thinks symbols of strength look like.

Once the earth energies have been brought up to full power, you will be drawing these energies into your body, thus establishing your body as the living temple. You should envision the earth altar as being the grounding and anchoring foundation for the living temple. Your body is the receptacle for the strength of the earthly energies.

What you see and experience will probably vary wildly from what another person may see and experience, so it is difficult to tell you what to expect. The process of establishing your body as the living temple can, in fact, be a bit confusing at first, as it involves following a series of steps that I have laid out for you. To simplify things for you, here is an easy-to-follow, step-by-step reference guide for the process of establishing your body as the world temple:

- Assemble and set up your earth altar.

- Prepare and purify your body so that you can attain a state of comfort, relaxation, and readiness.

- Get yourself situated comfortably near the earth altar. Relax your mind and body.

- Lightly focus your concentration on the earth altar. Empty your mind of conscious thought. Do *not* close your eyes.

- Imagine a symbol of strength rising from the center of the earth altar and floating in the air directly in front of you. Keep your vision focused on the earth altar and not on the symbol of strength.

- Imagine the symbol of strength moving to anywhere you want it to go within your field of vision. Keep your eyes fixed on the earth altar.

- Imagine many different symbols of strength rising one by one from the earth altar. Move these symbols to where you want them to be, but keep them around you and within your field of vision.

- Further relax your body and your mind. Allow the creative process of lucid daydreaming to begin. Allow the daydream to follow its natural process for a few moments without attempting to alter it with your will. Observe the scenarios being played out in your mind and take note of any changes that may be occurring with the symbols of strength.

➡ Say the word *strength* in your mind. Take note of any changes in the symbols. Keep your vision focused on the earth altar.

➡ If there is no change in the appearance or strength of the symbols, repeat the word *strength* over and over again in your mind until the symbols begin to change form or grow stronger. Once the symbols begin to grow stronger or change form, you will have established direct control over the symbols and their energies.

➡ Build the power of the symbols by imagining them growing stronger and stronger. Imagine the energies of the earth filling the strength symbols and that they are brimming with strong earthly energies.

➡ One by one, begin pulling the strength symbols and their energies into your body. As each symbol and its energy enter your body, see your body growing stronger. See a mighty foundation being laid all around the earth altar.

➡ Draw the last symbol and its energy into your body. Using the power of your mind and your will, visualize the earth energies are being compressed into a ball inside of your body. Once the earth energies are compressed and concentrated inside you, release the compressed energies. Allow them to fill your body with their strength. You have now established your body as the living temple.

At this point, if you have followed the step-by-step process of establishing your body as the living temple and have given it your best shot but nothing happened, it's probably a good idea to call it a day and try the process again tomorrow. We all progress at different rates of speed and in our own unique ways, so it may take a few more efforts before you are able to get the process of establishing your body as the living temple operating smoothly. Once you have mastered the art of lucid daydreaming, you can use it in any way you desire, but for the purpose of establishing your body as the living temple, you should precisely follow the prescribed process every time until you have mastered it and can add your own personal touches and preferences to the process.

You can easily implement the powerful tool of lucid daydreaming into your magickal workings. Imagine the ability to visualize magick to the point of actually being able to *see it* all around you. Combine this ability with a well-trained mind that will be hard at work developing creative avenues and magickal scenarios before you are even aware that it is happening. The possibilities are endless.

You have now successfully established the living temple and the first point on the pentagram of power. The second point on the pentagram, which is the shadow realm, has already been well established, so we will move past it for now and begin construction of the second spirit temple, which will be established on the astral plane. This is the eternal temple.

The Astral: The Eternal Temple

We now begin construction of the eternal temple. This will be a completely different experience from that of the living temple. You will not have to learn any new techniques or skills to construct the eternal temple, but your sending and receiving skills will be pushed to their limits once you have empowered the eternal temple and put it into use. Also, unlike the living temple, the eternal temple will be created while you're in a state of deep meditation. Creation of the eternal temple will not be a *guided* meditation, but rather one with *guidelines* for you to follow during its construction. You therefore must have the guidelines that I will lay out for you committed to memory and the goals of this chapter clearly fixed in your mind before you attempt to construct the eternal temple.

As you learned in the introductory "Gateway to the Spirit Temples," the eternal temple is the third point on the pentagram of power and serves two separate yet interconnected functions that directly relate to each other. The eternal temple is an "astral antenna" of sorts that, when completed, must have the ability to both send and receive magickal energies. The eternal temple must have the power to collect magickal energies from the astral plane and then transmit the collected energies to the shadow realm, where they will be gathered and intensified for further use.

In your third voyage into the shadow realm, you passed through the portal of the looking glass and entered the astral plane. You may recall that before you passed through the looking glass I explained that the two huge crystalline circles of power in the shadow realm exist in the astral world as well. I instructed you not to pass beyond the protective boundaries of the circles, but to observe the astral world from within the safety of their walls. That same area of protected sacred space on the astral plane is where you will be constructing the eternal temple. Before we discuss construction techniques for the eternal temple, let's do a little "groundbreaking" ceremony on the astral plane and gain a better understanding of the lay of the astral landscape. To do so, we will stir your memories of the astral world with a little creative visualization. The goal is not to go into a meditative state, but to access the deepest parts of your mind and do a quick memory flashback so that you can develop a clearer mental picture of the astral area that you will claim as a foundation for the eternal temple.

You will now begin your astral surveying task by envisioning yourself standing before the mirror in the shadow realm. In your mind, you now see the living waters of the looking glass as they begin to churn and separate, opening a gateway to the astral world. You are now stepping through the portal of the mirror, and you are entering the astral word. As you step through the portal of the mirror, your memories of the astral plane become very clear and vivid. The opposite side of the mirror is now directly behind you. The mirror is your exit from the astral plane back into the shadow realm.

You can see the two gigantic circles of power around you. The astral area contained within the twin circles of power is where you will be constructing the eternal temple. Survey this area carefully. Take a mental snapshot of it for future reference. Make sure that this mental picture is fully developed and completely in focus before you leave the astral world.

You are now returning to the mirror. Exit through the looking glass and reenter the shadow realm. You quickly grasp the key hanging over your heart and immediately return to the conscious world.

Okay, that was indeed a very brief trip into your memories of the astral world, but your mission was only to make a quick internal journey and to take a detailed mental photograph of the astral area in which you will be constructing the eternal temple. I'm sorry for not allowing you the opportunity to meditate and do some more astral traveling, but the time when you will be constructing the eternal temple is very close, and I would like for it to be as fresh an experience as possible for you. Also, I do not want you to be hanging out in the shadow realm right now. As I promised, I will relinquish all of the keys to the shadow realm to you very soon, but I haven't finished decorating the place for the family reunion with your shadow spirit. I don't want the little surprises I've cooked up to be prematurely revealed.

Now that you know precisely where you will be laying the foundation and constructing the eternal temple, let's discuss the temple's architecture and the various building materials you can use in its construction. As with the magickal mirror of the shadow realm, *you* will be the draftsman of the plans for the eternal temple, but this time you'll put a little more conscious effort into its design. Taking the area of space you have to work with on the astral plane into consideration, you need to get a very clear mental image of what you want the eternal temple to look like before you begin constructing it. As I stated earlier, the eternal temple will be of your own design. There are, however, three key elements that I insist that you include in its structure. (As I did for you in the previous chapter on creating the living temple, near the end of this chapter I will provide you with a step-by-step reference guide to help you through the entire process of constructing the eternal temple, so you don't have to worry about memorizing every little detail right now.)

First, because you will be entering and existing the astral plane and the eternal temple through the portal of the mirror, you will need to include in your mental blueprint some kind of hall or entryway that leads from the astral side of the mirror frame directly into the eternal temple. If you want your eternal temple to have an open concept design, then at the very least consider some sort of flooring or bridgework that leads from the mirror frame into the heart of the temple.

Next, the exterior of the temple will need to have a very tall steeple or obelisk that will serve as the eternal temple's energy sending and receiving antenna. You will be learning more about how the eternal temple's antenna operates a little later in this book, so for now concern yourself only with what you want the antenna to look like. Just make sure that the antenna's structure is taller than any other part of the temple. The height of the antenna really doesn't play a role in how well it functions, but your subconscious will be much happier with an antenna towering overhead. (I will explain this in more detail in the next chapter.)

Lastly, on or very near the edge of the eternal temple, you will need to build a dock that is large enough to harbor a massive sailing vessel. Why do I want you to build a ship dock on the astral plane? Let's just say that the dock will come in very handy later on as you continue to do the work in this book. You are just going to have to trust me on this one.

If you find that the area of space inside the twin circles on the astral plane is too small to accommodate the eternal temple and the ship dock, then when the time comes to construct the eternal temple, simply gather up a little magickal energy and push on the walls until they expand enough to allow you ample space in which to build what you need.

We have discussed the function, location, and appearance of the eternal temple, so let's finish up your building plans by deciding on the raw materials you will use in the temple's construction. Because you alone will be deciding what you want to use to build the eternal temple, when the time comes for you to begin construction, you are going to have to manifest the raw materials yourself. This is as simple as drawing in magickal energy from anywhere and in any form you desire and forming the raw energy into the needed shapes.

You should know (or be able to figure out) how to do this by now, so get that confused look off of your face. Envisioning what the raw construction materials look like and (even more importantly) where you get them from are two very important key roles in how you will ultimately use the power of the eternal temple. Just how appealing the eternal temple is to you will determine just how excited you will be to use it, which directly translates into the amount of energy the eternal temple will be able to send and receive. Simply put, you are the one who will have to be working in the eternal temple, not me, so if you're unhappy with it, the temple's effectiveness will be limited at best, and you will either have to live with its weakness or tear it down and start over from scratch.

Before you begin the process of gathering energies for creation of the raw materials, you will need an exact picture in your mind of what you want the temple to look like. The possibilities are as endless as your imagination, so be creative and have some fun with it. The eternal temple can appear ancient and mystical or modern and realistic. Its architecture can be Greek, Roman, Egyptian, Asian, or inspired by any known or mythological culture you might imagine. It can look similar to an English castle, a Buddhist temple, or the palace for Arabian royalty. It can be constructed of stone, marble, wood, or any combination of building materials you come up with. The eternal temple can be made entirely out of glass, or even stardust.

Once you have decided on the overall design and visual feel of the eternal temple, you can begin the process of gathering energies for creation of the raw building materials. Even though the eternal temple will be established on the astral plane, if the temple is to appear to have been constructed of natural materials, you should concentrate on gathering up earthly energies to give it a solid foundation. If the temple is to appear to have been constructed out of ethereal or mystical materials, you should gather up energies from the astral plane to give it a magickal foundation. Ultimately, the most important factor will be your mindset and how you feel about using the eternal temple. The temple's energies should be well suited to your own personal and magickal tastes.

Once you have considered all of these factors and reached your final decision as to the overall look and feel of the eternal temple, you will need to gather up the desired energies and manifest the building materials onto the astral plane. To do this you will need to clearly envision the type of energies (earthly, ethereal, and so forth) in your mind, and then draw the desired energies to you. You will next need to envision the building materials you have chosen to construct the eternal temple and impress the images of the building materials into the energies. Once you have done this, it is simply a matter of magickally willing the energies to materialize what you've envisioned on the astral plane. You will want to make sure that you manifest the building materials inside the twin circles on the astral plane, not outside them. The area of space within the circles represents your claimed astral land. This is where you currently have the most control in the astral world.

After you have magickally willed your raw building materials into existence, you will then begin constructing the eternal temple piece by piece using the mental blueprint you drew up. As you did during the creation of the magickal mirror in the shadow realm, if you are in need of some mortar or a little "magickal glue," you can easily draw energies directly from the sun and moon pool in the shadow realm. Pull their energies through the portal of the mirror and onto the astral plane and combine the energies of the sun and moon pools together and use them in any way you see fit.

Your main goal for right now is to get construction of the eternal temple completed and its presence established on the astral plane. You will not be learning how to use the antenna of the eternal temple for now. In Exercise 5, you will be connecting all five points of the pentagram of power together and establishing contact with your shadow spirit. During the final guided meditation, you will be using the skills and tools you already posses to activate the eternal temple and bring its antenna up to full power.

That pretty much sums up the goals for this chapter, so I will now provide you with an easy-to-follow, step-by-step reference guide for the process. Before you begin the process of establishing the eternal temple, make sure that you fully understand all of the goals and that you have created an exact mental blueprint of the eternal temples architecture.

- ➡ Assume a comfortable position, and prepare your mind and body to enter into a state of deep meditation. Do not meditate on any particular thing or place. Just achieve a deeply relaxed state of being.

- ➡ Once you have reached a deep meditative state, imagine that the necklace is around your throat and the key is hanging over your heart.

- ➡ Take the key into your hand. As you do, you are instantly transported into the portal of the mirror and deposited on the astral plane within the protective boundaries of the twin circles. Do not transport yourself directly into the shadow realm for any reason. If at any time you need to leave the astral world before your work is finished, grasp the key and will yourself directly back into a state of consciousness on the earthly plane.

➤ Once you are on the astral plane, survey the area while envisioning the eternal temple in its completed state. Make sure you have enough room inside of the twin circles to build your temple in. If the area within the twin circles is not large enough to accommodate the temple and the ship dock, magickally push the surfaces of the circles until they expand to the desired circumference.

➤ Keeping the vision of the temple and the dock in your mind, start gathering up energies that contain within them the appropriate signatures (earth, ethereal, and so forth) and draw these energies into the astral world.

➤ Clearly envision the raw building materials you want to use to construct the eternal temple. Now impress this mental vision into the gathered energies, and magickally will the energies to take on the shape of the desired raw materials.

➤ You are now free to lay the foundation and construct the eternal temple in any way you see fit. Keep in mind, however, that there are three important and necessary additions that you must include in the temple's architecture. These three additions are:

1. A hallway or bridgework that leads from the astral side of the mirror into the temple.

2. A towering steeple or obelisk that will serve as the eternal temple's antenna.

3. A dock large enough to accommodate a massive sailing vessel.

- Keep in mind that if you are in need of any kind of bonding materials you can draw the energies of the sun and moon pools through the portal of the mirror, combine their energies, and create anything you may need to complete construction of the eternal temple.

- After final construction of the eternal temple has been accomplished, you may dwell within your new temple for as long as you desire and bask in its power and beauty.

- When you decide that it is time for you to leave the eternal temple, keep in mind that you *do not want to exit directly into the shadow realm for any reason.* When you wish to leave the temple and the astral world, go to the portal of the mirror and grasp the key hanging over your heart. As you step through the portal of the mirror, will yourself directly back to the earthly plane and into a state of full consciousness.

As I stated earlier in this chapter, you will be learning how to use the eternal temple and its energy antenna as you undertake the fifth and final guided meditation (Exercise 5). There are still a few veils on the path of the shadow spirit that remain to be lifted, but for now take some time to relax and reflect on everything that you have accomplished. But don't get too comfy; there is still one more temple to establish before you can reunite with your shadow spirit.

Chapter 16

The Mind: The Hidden Temple

We will now begin construction of the third and final spirit temple, which we will call the hidden temple. The hidden temple will be created and will exist solely within your mind. As you discovered in the introductory "Gateway to the Spirit Temples," the hidden temple is the fourth point on the pentagram of power. It is the temple of willpower, purpose, and focus.

The hidden temple is the point on the pentagram of power where your intent will be impressed onto the magickal energies that you will be collecting while using the pentagram of power. It is also where your personal will power will be added to these energies. The hidden temple will then be used to focus the magickal energies back into the eternal temple, where the collected energies will be transmitted directly to the fifth and final point on the pentagram of power: your shadow spirit.

The hidden temple is a highly personal place of power where the most dominant parts of your mind—the light and the dark, the seen and the unseen, the conscious and the subconscious—will be focused for the goal of commanding and directing the magickal energies. Beyond the establishment of a mental temple, one of the main goals you will be facing in this chapter will be to bring order and direction to the many different facets of your mind that will be dwelling within the hidden temple. To do so, you will basically be learning how to perform mind control on your own mind.

What exactly is mind control, and how can using mind control on yourself be to your advantage? There are many different types of mind control, but the general definition of the type of mind control that we will be discussing and investigating in this chapter is as follows: *Mind control is the purposeful manipulation of the subconscious to control or redirect unconscious thought patterns to bring about a specific behavioral outcome.* If you were to get on the Internet and do a search for "mind control," you would find thousands of Websites, mostly fanatical sites, citing mind control as being everything from a government conspiracy to alien implants, plus pretty much anything else you could possibly dream up. I even found a Website that suggests using what is known as an AFDB (aluminum foil deflector beanie) as a practical solution for preventing mind control from outside influences. This Website is of course a joke, poking fun at the paranoid delusions of mind control. It's not necessary to run to the supermarket and stock up on Reynolds Wrap just now.

Although decades of fear and paranoia have overshadowed the legitimate work and serious scientific study in the area of mind control, the kind of mind control you will be attempting is not the standard conspiracy theory variety. By establishing the hidden temple, you will be learning how to take even more control over your mind and thought patterns than you probably already have. The main tool you will be using to accomplish this is known as *subliminal influencing.* In 1974, the United States government issued bans and restrictions on the use of subliminal influencing in radio and television advertising, but you've probably been subjected to subliminal influencing more times than you know. According to the 1957 book *The Hidden Persuaders* by Vance Packard, in 1954 advertising mogul

James Vicary supposedly ran a series of highly controversial tests on moviegoers using subliminal messaging. Vicary claims that he ran a six-week test at a movie theater in Fort Lee, New Jersey, and discovered that he was able to achieve dramatic increases in the sales of popcorn and soft drinks by subliminally flashing the phrases "eat popcorn" and "drink Coke" to the audience every five seconds during the screening of the feature film.

Beginning in the early 1970s, it was common for large department stores to use what was know as the "little black box" to send subliminal messages to their shoppers, usually as a deterrent to shoplifting. This was done with a device similar to a DJ mixer that combined background music with subliminal anti-theft messages such as "I am honest" and "I will not steal." These anti-theft messages would be repeated up to nine thousand times an hour over the store's loudspeakers, but at a barely audible level. Though the *conscious* mind of the shopper didn't register these subliminal messages, the *subconscious* absorbed them quite readily. Before the governmental bans were set into place, there were also television commercials selling a wide variety of products that used subliminal messages in their advertising. A prime example of subliminal influencing that you may recall was used in the Warner Bros. film *The Exorcist*. Several times during the movie, the image of a "death mask" was quickly flashed on the screen to give the theater audiences a little extra scare. Today, subliminal influencing is being widely used in a number of different ways to achieve more beneficial results. Self-empowerment, weight loss, the kicking of bad habits, and everything in between is being attempted by using subliminal influencing.

So exactly how does subliminal influencing work, and what does it have to do with Witchcraft and the hidden temple? Subliminal influencing is achieved by either flashing visual messages in front of a person at very high speeds or by subjecting a person to an audible message that is replayed over and over again at a low enough volume level where the conscious mind doesn't realize it is absorbing the subliminal message. Whereas your conscious mind seldom sees, hears, or understands these subtle messages, your subconscious picks up on them and reacts quickly. To put the power of subliminal influencing to work in the hidden temple, therefore, you are basically going to equip the hidden temple with the equivalent of an advanced mental movie theater and subliminal sound system for the enjoyment (and manipulation) of your subconscious mind.

Unless you have already studied self-hypnosis or personal mind control, your subconscious has probably been bossing you around for quite some time now. The time has come for you to consider turning the tables on your subconscious and evening out of your mental scales. Your subconscious will be dwelling within the walls of the hidden temple as much as, if not more than, your conscious mind will be, so you're going to want to take some steps to ensure that there's no mental monkey business going on in there while your conscious thoughts are somewhere else.

Before we go any further, I am going to guess that you probably have a major concern about using subliminal influencing on yourself. You want to know if subliminal influencing is safe. I will begin addressing this possible concern by pointing out that subliminal influencing is potentially as safe or as dangerous as anything else is. Ultimately, it's all in how you use something that makes it what it is. You can use a shovel to dig a hole or to bash someone's brains in. You can use a bottle of prescription drugs to cure an illness or to poison someone. You can use the power of subliminal influencing to build yourself up or tear yourself down. If you constantly tell yourself that you are a worthless person with no future, then you will probably end up being a worthless person with no future. If you repeatedly tell yourself that the world is full of possibilities and that you can achieve anything that you put your mind to, then you will probably accomplish many great things over the course of your lifetime. Whether you have realized it or not, you've been using the power of subliminal influencing on yourself all along.

Before we go any deeper into subliminal influencing and how you are going to be putting its power to work, we should probably take a closer look at the hidden temple itself so you can gain a better understanding of exactly how the construction of the hidden temple will be taking place in your mind. Unlike the living temple and the eternal temple, the hidden temple will exist solely within your mind. Does this mean that the hidden temple is strictly imaginary and that it really doesn't exist? Of course not. One of the fundamental laws of Witchcraft that you have been (or should have been) taught is that "thought equals form." Thought forms are basically how Witchcraft and magick begin to work. You use your imagination to visualize the goal of your workings as clearly as possible in your mind, and then "will" that goal into existence; this is the very essence of magick. Using the power of thought forms to manifest and manipulate energies and turn your magick into something tangible and real is thus the very essence of Witchcraft. The imagery and thought patterns you will use to construct and establish the hidden temple should be viewed as being as real as anything you can touch, see, and feel in the physical world. When you view and think about the hidden temple this way, you are using elements of your imagination as the hidden temple's primary building blocks. The transformation of your imagination into thought forms also makes the hidden temple the most magickal of all the temples. The hidden temple will be the only temple where your magickal imagination can work without inhibition. You must, however, never lose sight of the primary functions of the hidden temple: *intent, will,* and *focus.*

Because we have established that you will be using your imagination as the primary tool to construct and establish the hidden temple, you will want to use this precious tool to your full advantage. Don't be satisfied with the first image of the hidden temple that pops into your head. Dig deeper; go further with the process of your imagination. I guarantee that ever since your conscious mind discovered that you would be constructing a hidden temple your subconscious has been hard at work drawing up its own blueprint. If you accept this as fact, then you're going to have to do some serious meditation to discover exactly what your subconscious has been cooking up. If you don't make contact with your deeper self and establish a bone fide plan of collaboration with your subconscious mind, then you can easily end up with two separate and conflicting temples being built inside your mind. I want you to consider this point very carefully. It is one of the first things you will need to accomplish before you can begin serious work on the hidden temple. As I did with the previous spirit temples, at the end of this chapter I will provide you with a step-by-step outline to help guide you through the entire process of constructing and establishing the hidden temple of the mind.

We have now pretty much covered the where, how, and why of the hidden temple, but let's lay these three steps out more clearly before we move on to the temple's appearance and possible sub-function. *Where* is in your mind. *How* is with your imagination. And *why* is to establish will, intent, and focus within the energies of the pentagram of power. Now that these three primary concerns have been properly addressed, let's move on to the hidden temple's appearance and sub-function.

What the hidden temple looks like and the thought patterns of your imagination that you use to construct it are entirely of your own choosing. I am still your guide on this adventure, however, so let's just make sure you have all of the bases covered and that you have considered the appearance of the hidden temple from as many different angles as possible. Have you considered that the hidden temple doesn't have to be a building or a structure? Why can't the hidden temple be a stream or a forest? Why can't it be a robe, or even a ring that you don in your imagination? Have you taken into account that the primary functions (will, intent, and focus) of the hidden temple may not be found as easily in a building as they could be in a special place or an imaginary object? Is it easier for you to find focus in the halls of a great library or in a peaceful meadow? These are some of the questions you need to ask yourself before you decide how to build and decorate the hidden temple.

When you have decided what the hidden temple is going to look like, you may want to consider the possibility of setting up the mental movie theater I mentioned earlier in this chapter. Use the mental movie theater to establish subliminal influencing over your subconscious. The conditioning and influencing of your subconscious mind is the sub-function of the hidden temple. Although the subliminal influencing of the subconscious is not absolutely necessary for the hidden temple to be able to function correctly, it can be a valuable tool for the unification of the conscious and the subconscious to attain the desired goals of will, intent, and focus in the hidden temple and throughout the energies you will be using in the pentagram of power. However, because the use of subliminal influencing is somewhat controversial, I am not going to make it a requirement in the establishment of the hidden temple, merely a suggestion. Keeping this in mind, let's take a closer look at the mental movie theater of the subconscious.

Your subconscious mind already knows what your conscious self is up to, so you will need to make the mental movie theater as appealing to your subconscious as you possibly can. Your imagination has already seen how the mental movie theater will look and operate. Earlier in this chapter when you read the phrase *mental movie theater* for the very first time, your imagination undoubtedly manufactured an image of it. Now all you have to do is recall this image, which is stored somewhere in your short-term memory. This stored image of the mental movie theatre has already been presented to your subconscious as being an absolute. In other words, don't get tricky. If you try to change your original visual image of the mental movie theater, your subconscious will probably reject the new image; you'll probably have a hard time convincing your subconscious to accept the new image. Manipulation of your subconscious is one of the possible goals of this chapter, however, so if you're up to the challenge, feel free to tear down the old theater and build a new one. You still have a lot of work ahead of you in this book, so keep this in mind before you decide to pile on any more of your own making.

If you're having a hard time recalling the original image of the mental movie theater, do some meditation work to refresh your memory. Once you have the original image of the mental movie theater set firmly in your mind, you can begin production of your very first feature-length subliminal film. The script is simplicity in itself. To write your subliminal screenplay, all you need are the three keywords that I have used repeatedly in this chapter: *will, intent,* and *focus.* Once you have mastered the art of being able to subliminally influence your subconscious mind, you can put its power to work in any number of ways, from increasing the amount of aid your subconscious can lend to your magickal workings to the way your conscious mind operates in the mundane world. For right now, you need to focus your attention on the task at hand and create your first subliminal film.

Before you begin production of your first subliminal film, let's use a little creative visualization to get your artistic juices flowing in the right direction and hopefully spark your imagination. Although you will be the writer, producer, and director of the subliminal films that will be screened within the confines of the hidden temple, just for today, allow me to purchase a ticket for you and guide you to your seat for a matinee screening of a sample subliminal film.

I want you to imagine yourself walking through a swinging door that leads into a dimly lit movie theater. Other than you, the theater is completely empty. There are no other moviegoers or theater employees selling tickets or popcorn. The entire theater is silent and still. You imagine yourself walking down a gently sloping aisle and choosing a seat. When you sit in this seat, you find it unusually comfortable for a movie theater. You relax your body and empty your mind. Any concerns or thoughts of anything beyond the walls of the theater melt away and vanish. The lights in the theater grow dimmer and dimmer.

The movie is about to begin. The screen flickers for a moment, and suddenly the image of an ancient winding path leading through a forest appears on the screen. The camera begins to move forward on the path, and suddenly it seems as if you are actually walking along the path and seeing it through your own eyes. As you continue to follow the path, you come across a small pond of blue-green water. The water of the pond is very still, and you notice a frog sitting on a lily pad near the edge of the pond. You take a step or two closer to the pond, but as you do the frog is startled by your approach and jumps into the middle of the pond. Waves ripple across the pond's surface, and for just a moment you see a word (*WILL*) reflected on the surface of the water. A leaf lets go from the branch of a tree high above you. You catch the falling leaf out of the corner of your eye, and, as you look up, you see a wisp of clouds in the sky. The wisp of clouds seems to be forming a word (*INTENT*) as it slowly drifts through the sky. As you walk back to the path, you see a grouping of small gray pebbles that seem to spell out a word (*FOCUS*) as they lie scattered across the path. You start walking back down the path, returning to where it began. Everywhere you look, you seem to see (*will*) words (*intent*) forming (*focus*) all around you. When you reach the end of the path, you think about the dimness of the movie theater when you first walked in through the swinging door. You think about walking down the aisle and choosing a seat. You think about just how comfortable the seat was, and suddenly you can feel the seat beneath you. You are back inside the movie theater. The screen is dark. You see three words quickly flash across the screen. Will. Intent. Focus. The movie has ended. You stand up, walk up the aisle, and exit the theater.

Let's take a closer look at what you have just experienced. The first thing you may have noticed was that I didn't provide a soundtrack with my subliminal film. Did you hear anything on your own? As you were walking up the path, did your imagination or your subconscious supply you with the sounds of chirping birds? Did you hear gravel on the path gently crunching beneath your feet? Did you hear a soft splashing sound as the frog jumped into the pond? If you did, then your subconscious was playing along with the film quite nicely. It is susceptible to subliminal influencing. If you heard no sounds, then your subconscious was probably on its guard. This most likely occurred because you were over-thinking the process instead of just letting everything flow along smoothly. If you were over thinking, then you will need to work on being able to relax and not be overly concerned about everything.

As I did for you in my sample subliminal film, your main goal when creating your own movie is to sneak in the words *will, intent,* and *focus* in as many strategic locations as possible. You don't want to overdo it, but you don't want to fall short, either.

If you decide to incorporate subliminal influencing while working with the hidden temple, you will have to get your subconscious all nice and comfy in a chair in your mental movie theater before you begin your workings. You will have to let the subliminal movie play on its own without your conscious mind concentrating on it. Believe me, you will have plenty of other things to be concentrating on once you begin to connect the five points of the pentagram of power together. All of the steps involved in connecting the five points may seem a bit overwhelming right now, but keep in mind that a great deal of what we have covered in the chapters on the spirit temples has had to do with preliminary setup work. Don't worry, I'm still your guide on this journey. I promise that you will make it through the entire process with very few hitches.

As with most of the work in this book, the possibilities for putting the power of subliminal influencing to work for your own benefit are nearly endless. We should, however, press on and get all of the loose ends of the hidden temple tied up. The time of "the becoming" is almost at hand, and you have been very patient with all of the work I have put you through, so let's not dawdle any longer. As I did in the previous chapters on the spirit temples, I will now lay the entire process of creating and establishing the hidden temple out for you as clearly as possible in a step-by-step format: (These steps are quite involved, however, so you may want to read through all of them several times before you begin actual construction of the hidden temple.)

➡ Before you begin the process of constructing the hidden temple, you need to meditate on all the possibilities for the hidden temple to discover how your subconscious mind sees the temple's function and appearance. To keep your subconscious from constructing its own separate temple, you will need to incorporate at least some of what is revealed to you during this meditation. While you're meditating on the hidden temple, you can also discover how your subconscious sees the mental movie theater.

➡ Next, use your imagination to draw up the blueprint for the hidden temple. Your mental blueprint should encompass all aspects of the hidden temple, including location, appearance, and surroundings. Do not forget to include some of what you learned about your subconscious's interpretation of the hidden temple in the blueprint. While you're drawing up the plans, remember that the hidden temple doesn't necessarily have to be a building or a structure. It can simply be a place or a thing.

➡ If you have decided to incorporate the use of subliminal influencing in the hidden temple, you need to establish a mental movie theater in your plans. Where you decide to screen your subliminal films is entirely up to you and your subconscious. Your movie screen can be the sky, a wall, a pool of water, an actual movie screen, or anything else you can imagine. *Your imagination is key in establishing a successful hidden temple.*

➡ Keeping in mind that the main objectives of the hidden temple are to establish *will, intent,* and, above all else, *focus,* go into a state of deep meditation and construct the hidden temple of the mind in any way you see fit. Just make sure that you are well prepared and that your mental blueprint is in order before you begin the process. You will discover that your blueprint will end up only being a guideline for how the temple appears in its completed state. You may be surprised by how much your imagination will alter the final outcome.

➡ Finally, if you decide to put the power of subliminal influencing to work for you in the hidden temple, you will need to produce at least one subliminal film. Incorporate the words *will, intent,* and *focus,* used in some degree of frequency, in the film.

That sums up everything you need to know at this point about the hidden temple's construction, appearance, function, and sub-function. You will learn how to operate the hidden temple as you connect all five points of the pentagram of power in the fifth and final guided meditation (Exercise 5) in this book.

If you wish to study subliminal influencing beyond the introductory information in this chapter, there is a wealth of information to be found in books and on the Internet on the subject. What appeals to you about subliminal influencing will probably be very different from what appeals to me or anyone else, so for that reason I will not recommend any specific books or Websites for you to check out. I will recommend, however, that your steer clear of any information that seems overly fanatical or that contains the word *alien* or the phrase *government conspiracy* in its title or text.

Closing the Temple Gates

If you have successfully completed construction of all three spirit temples, congratulations are in order. You have now established a total of four realms of power that exist on four entirely different planes of existence. The living temple is on the earthly plane. The eternal temple is on the astral plane. The hidden temple is on the mental plane. As for the shadow realm, it was constructed within a void, so technically it exists nowhere and everywhere at the same time. To put a finer point on it, the shadow realm exists somewhere between the living temple and the astral temple, and your mind (the hidden temple) is the vehicle that delivers you to the shadow realm's boarders. Though it is true that you have yet to empower the spirit temples and put them to use, you will soon do so. At that point, you will have tapped an endless well of resources from which you can draw magickal energy to use in any way you desire.

The initial goal that you will hopefully realize by combining the power of the shadow realm and the spirit temples is to make contact with your shadow spirit. Once you have done this, your shadow spirit will (with its permission and your own acceptance) become the fifth and final point on the pentagram of power, at which time the extent and capability of your magickal skills will effectively be doubled.

Now that the spirit temples are built and ready for operation, they will serve as an enticement for your shadow spirit to make first contact with you. If you have done a sloppy job or put a half-hearted effort into the construction of the spirit temples, you may find yourself all alone in the final meditation wondering what went wrong. As with anything else, mundane or magickal, you will only get out of this work what you put into it. You will only reap what you sow. Neither your shadow spirit nor I are going to whip up everything you desire and hand it to you on a silver platter.

As are the temples of the gods and goddesses of old and the ancient places of power that lie abandoned and unused by modern civilization, the silent and darkened halls of the spirit temples are awaiting the moment that you will illuminate them with the light of magick. At long last, the time has come for you to breathe life into the spirit temples and claim the whole of your power and your potential.

The time of the becoming is at hand.

First Contact

Chapter 17

The Becoming

A good traveler has no fixed plans, and is not intent on arriving.

—Lao Tzu

We will begin Section 3 by making final preparations for first contact with your shadow spirit. Then you will undertake the fifth and final guided meditation in this book, Exercise 5: The Avatar: And Then There Were Two. After alignment with your shadow spirit has taken place, I will offer some possible adventures upon which you can embark with your magickal twin in Section 4. These adventures will not be presented as guided meditations, but as outlines for possible astral experiences.

Once you have made first contact and aligned with your *other,* it will be virtually impossible for me to be able to predict what will happen between the two of you, so to a large extent my ability to guide you will be compromised. This is not to say that any further teachings and suggestions in this book will be ineffective or insignificant, just that the new paths that will open up before you after alignment has taken place will be unpredictable at best. You should therefore consider any work in this book that takes place after first contact to be a possibility, and not an absolute necessity, to continue walking the path of the shadow spirit. For you, the shadow spirit is about to become the ultimate astral and magickal guide. It will open doors that it alone can lead you through and to places in which you alone may travel.

Before your alignment takes place, however, we must first delve a bit deeper into the world of the shadow spirit and take a closer look at what you might expect to happen by aligning with your *other*. Above all else, after alignment with your *other* has taken place, you must be prepared to accept the possibility that, in one form or another, your shadow spirit will be constantly watching over you. This is not to say that your shadow spirit will materialize on the earthly plane and hang out with you as a new best friend, tagging along with you everywhere you go, but rather that your shadow spirit will be keeping a close eye on you and that your mundane life may very well become as interesting to your shadow spirit as your magickal life.

This can be both a good thing and a bad thing, and you need to strongly consider this possibility before you make the final decision to align yourself with your *other*. It is also highly possible that your shadow spirit can or will become an earthly (and astral) interloper if it decides its involvement is necessary in any given mundane or magickal situation. For example, if you (or even someone you know and care about) were in a dangerous situation, your *other* might take powerful and possibly drastic steps to protect you or your loved ones. Again, this can be a good thing and a bad thing—good for you and your loved ones, yes, but potentially bad for the person who is trying to do you harm. Where your safety is concerned, your shadow spirit will probably feel no need to use discretion in its actions. Your *other* is potentially a *very* powerful magickal entity, which is a direct reflection of you; so, depending on how strong you have (or will) become, it may be capable of doing just about anything it wants to do on the earthly or astral planes of existence. Once your shadow spirit has become strong enough, it will have the ability to punch a hole between the worlds and manipulate earthly forces as it sees fit. You don't believe me? On many occasions I have witnessed a very powerful unseen force at work that most people would consider unexplainable phenomena. *Every single one* of these events was heralded by my shadow spirit's hallmark of numerological signifiers.

There have been many instances where my shadow spirit has championed me and those that I care about. It has protected me and my loved ones by using intense displays of physical force. Though you may or may not experience anything even remotely similar to the incidents I've experienced, when you align with your shadow spirit and develop a close relationship with it, *you must be prepared to accept any and all earthly responsibility for its actions.* After everything is said and done, *you* are the one who created your shadow spirit. As Dr. Frankenstein did with the life that he created, you alone must take responsibility for your creation. In Chapter 13, we discussed the possibility that your shadow spirit might materialize itself on the earthly plane, thus revealing itself to you in what seems to be a physical form. What I didn't tell you in Chapter 13 is that when and if your shadow spirit decides to materialize and reveal itself to you or to anyone else, it is possible that your shadow spirit will look exactly like you—not only as you do in the present, but also as you did at any point in the past or will at any point in the future. My own shadow spirit has displayed this ability on many different occasions, so it is possible that your shadow spirit may possess this same skill. My shadow spirit's ability to mimic my physical appearance in the here and now is one thing, but its ability to look as I did in the past or as I will in the future presents the fascinating possibility that my shadow spirit is capable of traveling through time. Perhaps not in an H. G. Wells's *Time Machine* sort of way, where a person or a thing is physically transported backward or forward through time, but instead using a mental or metaphysical vehicle to voyage to any location within the spiral of time that it desires.

If you think about this, your shadow spirit's ability to travel in time is not really such a far-fetched concept. After all, as human beings, we are constantly using our minds to travel backward or forward in time, aren't we? The average human probably spends as much (if not more) of their mental time in either the past or the future as he or she does in the present. I want you to think about this seriously and consider the point I'm trying to get you to understand here.

Think about what you're doing at this very moment. You're reading— and hopefully comprehending—the words on this page of this book, correct? But isn't part of your mind also considering future scenarios and envisioning things that haven't happened yet? Are you not using your experience and imagination to develop a mental image of what may or may not happen next? As you near the end of this page, will your memory and experience of the past not remind you that to continue reading this book you will have to turn the page? At the same time, will you not be anticipating turning the page before you actually do it? Of course you will. Not only are you experiencing the present, but also, at the very same moment, you are mentally traveling both forward and backward through time. Without realizing it, you have been a time traveler of sorts all along!

So what does all this mental time-travel stuff have to do with your shadow spirit? For starters, I just planted a few mental seeds that may possibly take root and grow, but, more than anything else, it has to do with your *awareness*. If you weren't aware of the fact that you're a mental traveler in time before I told you that you were, you're aware of it now. This awareness will transfer over to your shadow spirit. Once it has been transferred, awareness of any kind can be developed into knowledge, experience, and (eventually) skill by you and your shadow spirit, giving the two of you another powerful tool to add to your mental and meta-physical arsenal. The larger your bubble of awareness becomes, the larger your magickal cabinet of resources becomes. Be mindful of this as you walk the path of the shadow spirit. Learn all you can about as many dif-ferent subjects, theories, and concepts as possible.

Before we move on to the role your magickal counterpart plays in the astral world, I want to share one more thing with you about my personal experiences with the shadow spirit in the physical world. Almost every-thing I know about my shadow spirit's physical appearance had to be relayed to me by other people who saw the apparition of my shadow spirit on the earthly plane. Why? Because my shadow spirit has never allowed me to look at it directly for an extended period of time after it has mate-rialized in our world. Exactly why is anyone's guess, but my experience and intuition tell me that it's the metaphysical equivalent of the theory that the same patterns of energy cannot occupy the same space in the physical world without canceling each other out. In other words, because my shadow spirit and I basically share the same "magickal DNA," if I were to look directly at my shadow spirit with my physical eyes, my mun-dane mind would disrupt the magick and erase the apparition of my shadow spirit from the physical world.

After all is said and done, however, this is just a theory of mine that pertains to one of the mysteries of the shadow spirit that has never been revealed to me. As you are, I am still a traveler on the path of the shadow spirit. I have merely traveled a little bit further up the road than you have.

Whereas I have caught glimpses of my shadow spirit many times, my *other* has induced everything from episodes of intense vertigo to tempo-rary blindness and everything in between to prevent me from looking directly at it in the physical world. Others who have been allowed to look directly at my shadow spirit all ended up the way my unfortunate friend at the bottom of the stairs on the day of first contact did: They've had red eyes and tears streaming down their ghostly white cheeks. Their bodies were covered with gooseflesh and every single hair on their head was standing at attention. The only exception is my wife, who has become so jaded by the numerous materializations of my shadow spirit that she barely pays attention to it anymore. She pretty much just ignores its presence.

As we wrap up our examination of the possible physical attributes that your shadow spirit may exhibit on the earthly plane, keep in mind that the incidents I have related come from my own experience. You may or may not expect your own encounters with the shadow spirit to be similar to mine. It is possible that your shadow spirit has already made contact with you, and I may be preaching to the enlightened choir. We will, therefore, move on to a deeper investigation of the shadow spirit as it pertains to the astral world.

As we discussed earlier in Chapter 13, you shadow spirit is probably already a pretty familiar presence in the astral world. Your *other* has undoubtedly already mapped out most, if not all, of the astral terrain. It has probably already established its own territory. Exactly how your shadow spirit rules in its ethereal domain will greatly depend on your own magickal personality. Do not confuse your magickal personality with your mundane personality. Although these two facets of yourself may be very similar, you will discover that there are many subtle differences.

If you want to discern these differences, imagine a scenario in your mind, then first play it out from a mundane point of view, and then repeat it from a magickal point of view. Observe the differences in the way your magickal and mundane personalities handled the scenario. For example, is your magickal personality more or less aggressive than your mundane personality? Was one of your personalities less inhibited than the other while the scenario was playing itself out in your mind? Was one more confident than the other? To be able to get a glimpse into the magickal inner workings of both yourself and your shadow spirit, you will need to ask yourself these questions and dig up the answers. Though your shadow spirit does not possess a mundane personality, it most certainly has a magickal one, and the magickal personality of your shadow spirit will be an exact copy of your own magickal personality instead of being an exact opposite. Why is it not an opposite? Your *other's* magickal personality is not an opposite of your own because you gave birth to your shadow spirit and imprinted a magickal personality onto it *before* your own magickal personality was fully realized. Your shadow spirit basically became the source from which you would one day draw your own magickal powers and personality. In other words, at the exact moment that you felt magick flowing through you for the very first time, everything came together into a neat little package that we call your shadow spirit, but at that time you didn't possess full (or possibly any) understanding of your magickal self. Your shadow spirit thus, in essence, became a magickal chalice that you filled with the hopes, dreams, and desires of a brand new Witch. It also became the sum of what would one day become the extent of your magickal skills. But back then you had not yet fully drunk of the magick within the chalice of your shadow spirit. At the moment it sprang into being, your shadow spirit was already the epitome of the Witch that you would one day become. This is why I refer to aligning with the shadow spirit as "the becoming." Very soon now, you will become the Witch that you were always meant to be.

Flying back to the astral plane, we find your shadow spirit awaiting you. You now have a clearer vision and definition of your *other* than you had before. In your mind, picture your shadow spirit floating in its territory in the astral world. It behaves and uses magick exactly as you do.

Imagine yourself in the astral world. What would you be doing if you were actually there? What would you have done in the astral world in the past? How would you treat other nice or not-so-nice astral entities? How would you rule your astral territory?

Now, with these visions in your mind, imagine how it would be different if you knew no limitations and possessed the knowledge of everything that you don't already know. Imagine that your magickal intuitions and skills were at the height of their power and that you could travel to anywhere in space or time you wanted to go. Imagine that all the realms and dimensions of this and any other universe were all the same to you. Imagine that you could see, feel, and experience these realms and dimensions without effort. Imagine that you are the absolute whole and the absolute nothingness of magick at the same time. Imagine being, seeing, and feeling all of these things at the same time. Now you know what it is to be your shadow spirit.

The time of the becoming is now at hand. Every step you have ever taken, every second of this or any other life has led you to this moment. For the very first time in your existence, you will know the real truth of who and what you are. Now you know what it is that you are to become. The final veil between you and your *other* is about to be lifted. The magickal mirror of self is about to be exposed. As you walk through the final veil, keep in mind that it was *you* who had the courage to do it. As you ascend the final staircase to your true magickal self, do so with grace and with confidence. As you knock on the door of the shadow spirit and cross over the threshold, remember that it is only yourself that waits on the other side of the doorway.

Exercise 5

The Avatar:
And Then There Were Two

Avatar. n. A temporary manifestation or aspect of a
continuing entity.

—American Heritage Dictionary

You will now undertake the fifth and final exercise on the path of the shadow spirit. Unlike the previous four exercises, you will need to do a bit more setup work before you begin the final meditation.

Your first consideration is the spirit temples. It is absolutely vital that you have completed the construction of and established all three spirit temples before you begin this exercise. If you have not properly constructed and established the spirit temples, you need to stop reading this exercise right now and go back and finish the job. The spirit temples and the pentagram of power were carefully devised and developed as a safe, practical way to make contact and practice magick with the shadow spirit. I will not hold any karmic responsibility for what might happen if you have not done the required work in this book. The work in this book is in no way a joke and, if you have a take-it-or-leave-it attitude toward it, I suggest that you leave it all behind you right now and shelve this book. If I sound overly serious about this, then you have my apologies, but

Exercise 5 is a very serious step in your magickal evolution. It *must* be approached with the proper attitude and state of mind. If you are not serious about your intent, your shadow spirit will probably not make contact with you and you will only be wasting your time.

If your shadow spirit does decide to make contact with you, it could choose to do so in a number of different ways. Physical materialization, mental contact, astral contact, or entering directly into the shadow realm are all possibilities. You will basically be linking the shadow realm and the three spirit temples together, thus establishing the first four points on the pentagram of power. By doing this you will be making the equivalent of a "metaphysical phone call" to your shadow spirit. Once your call has been answered and contact with your shadow spirit has been made, your shadow spirit will become the fifth and final point on the pentagram of power. If you don't actually *see* your shadow spirit, however, don't assume that it hasn't made contact with you.

The first steps in Exercise 5 take place outside of meditation and require you to prepare your body and set up the earth altar. In Chapter 14, I stressed the importance of having your body in good condition before you establish yourself as the living temple, so you will want to be sure to do whatever you feel is necessary to adequately prepare your body before you begin this exercise. Keep in mind that attaining a state of comfort is key to establishing your body as the living temple.

Preparation of your body and the setting up of the earth altar will thus be the first steps in Exercise 5. Make sure you have your earth altar set up and ready to go before you begin this exercise. If you would like to do an invocation to your deities, be prepared to do so before you begin Exercise 5. Because Exercise 5 is a very long and complicated process, I have omitted any steps that are not absolutely necessary to successfully complete first contact.

I should also quickly introduce you to what you will come to know as your "shade-self." Your shade-self is the part of you that will remain fixed in the shadow realm as you go about the process of empowering the spirit temples and establishing the five points on the pentagram of power. Your spirit and consciousness will be moving around quite a bit as you go about this process, so your shade-self should be viewed as the part of you that is tied directly to the shadow realm, where it will maintain the shadow realm's stability as your spirit and consciousness move between the spirit temples. Note that it could easily be argued that your spirit and your consciousness are in fact the same thing, but for the sake of this exercise your spirit should be viewed as the magickal "life force" inside you and your consciousness as your awareness of self and the power of your mind.

You have now, in effect, reached the point of no return. If you proceed from here, it means that your magickal and mundane lives will be changed forever. There will be no turning back after this exercise has taken place. What you are about to do cannot be undone by any physical device or magickal means.

You have, of course, already made your decision. Now you are going to have to step over the line all by yourself. I will not prime you with a little pep talk or soothe you by telling that that everything is going to be okay. There is no way I can be certain that everything *will* be okay. Nor can I live your life for you. As always, the choice is yours and yours alone to make.

What's that you say? Well all right, if you're sure, then … I'm ready if you are.

Alignment will now commence. First contact with your shadow spirit will be made. You will begin the process by establishing your body as the living temple. In so doing, you will become the first point on the pentagram of power. Establishment of the living temple will take place while you are in a state of lucid daydreaming, so be careful not slip into a state of meditation until you are instructed to do so.

Assume a comfortable position by your earth altar. Relax your body and your mind, but do not close your eyes. Lightly focus your concentration on the earth altar and empty your mind of all concern or conscious thought.

Imagine that a symbol of strength is rising up from the earth altar and floating in the air directly in front of you. Do not focus your vision on this symbol, however, but keep your focus on the earth altar.

Imagine now that you are moving the strength symbol to anywhere you want it to be, but keep the symbol within your field of vision. Keep your eyes fixed on the earth altar at all times. Do not look directly at the symbol.

Now imagine that many different symbols of strength are rising up from the earth altar. Keeping the strength symbols within your field of vision, move them to wherever you would like for them to be.

Further relax your body and your mind. Allow your mind to drift and begin the process of lucid daydreaming. Let everything play out as it will. Do not over-concentrate or interfere with what is happening around you. As you observe the scenarios being played out in your mind, take note of any changes that are occurring to the strength symbols.

Now you hear yourself saying the word *strength* in your mind. Take notice of any changes in the strength symbols, but keep your vision focused on the earth altar at all times.

Say the word *strength* over and over again in your mind until the strength symbols begin to change form or grow stronger.

Build the power of the symbols by imagining them growing stronger and stronger. Imagine the energies of the earth filling the strength symbols. See them brimming with strong earthly energies.

One by one, begin pulling the strength symbols and their energies into your body. As each symbol enters your body with its energy, see your body growing stronger. See a mighty foundation being laid all around the earth altar.

You are now drawing the last of the strength symbols into your body. Using the power of your mind and your will, visualize the earth energies being compressed into a ball inside the area of your body that you feel is your center.

Now that the earth energies are compressed and concentrated inside you, release the compressed energies from the ball and allow them to expand and fill your entire body with their strength.

You have now laid the foundation and established your body as the living temple. You have become the first point on the pentagram of power, and your strength and stability are unshakable. You can feel the grounding and anchoring energies of the living temple flowing through you and all around you.

Now that you have established your body as the first point on the pentagram of power, it is time to attain a state of deep meditation and enter into the second point on the pentagram of power. *This is the shadow realm.*

Close your eyes and empty your mind. You feel the living temple of your body remaining firm and anchored on the earthly plane, but your mind and spirit are now slowly drifting away from the waking world. You feel the necklace around your throat, the key hanging over your heart. You reach for the key and hold it in your hand. You can feel the energies within the key pulling you toward the shadow realm.

You are now nearing the borders of the shadow realm. You cross over the border, and, as you do, you can feel that your domain is quiet and still. It feels as if the entire realm were waiting in silent anticipation for the arrival of something or someone.

As you drift deeper into the shadow realm, you pass through the twin circles of power. Even the crystalline circles seem to be silent and waiting. You float down into the center of your domain and come to rest on the white marble circle in front of the great mirror of promise and magick.

You can sense that the earthly energies of the living temple have followed you into the shadow realm. You feel as though a rope of grounding and anchoring energy is looped around your waist and that the other end of the energy rope is tied to the foundation of the living temple on the earthly plane.

When you gaze upon the living waters of the looking glass of the mirror, you see that they are as still and silent as the rest of the shadow realm has become. You can clearly see your own refection in the looking glass of the mirror. It is crisp and vivid on the mirrored surface of the still and silent waters.

As you gaze upon your own reflection, you suddenly begin to feel a very strange sensation. You feel as if you were somehow in two different places at the same time. This sensation washes over your entire being. You feel as though your spirit and consciousness were floating away from your body. You feel as if your spirit and consciousness are slowly drifting toward your reflection in the looking glass of the mirror.

Suddenly you find yourself on other side of the looking glass of the mirror! You are gazing back at yourself in the shadow realm. The part of you that has remained in the shadow realm is your shade-self. You are now in your true astral body on the astral plane.

You can feel the magick of the astral world all around you. You turn away from the mirror, and the beauty of the eternal temple greets you.

The interior of the eternal temple is still and silent. You begin to move into the interior of the eternal temple, and as you do, you feel the magickal energies of the astral world gathering around you. The magickal energies envelop you. Suddenly you feel as though you are wearing the magickal energies like an invisible astral cloak.

As you move deeper into the interior of the eternal temple, the magickal energies around you are growing stronger and stronger. The magickal energies are instilling life and power into the eternal temple.

Each part of the temple you pass through is now glowing with intense magickal energy. Each part of the temple you pass through is now vibrating and humming with power. You move into the center of the eternal temple. Here you stop and wait.

You can feel that the cloak of magickal energy around you is now growing longer. Its magickal fabric is flowing and spreading through every part of the eternal temple. The entire temple is now glowing with its magick and vibrating with its power. The eternal temple has become the most enchanting and mystical place you have ever seen or experienced.

You now move toward the antenna of the eternal temple. The cloak of magickal energies flows along with you. As you approach the antenna, you can feel an immense wave of magickal energy building in the astral world just beyond the protective barrier of the twin circles of power. The wave of energy is being drawn and gathered by the increasing power and magick of the eternal temple.

As you reach the antenna of the eternal temple, you can feel that the flowing energies of the magickal cloak are growing even longer. The long flowing ends of the cloak begin to wrap themselves around the base of the antenna. You can see and feel the magickal energies of the cloak charging the antenna and bringing it to life.

The wave of magickal energy outside of the twin circles is growing stronger and more intense, building into a churning storm of astral power and magick. As the strength of the astral storm grows, the antenna of the eternal temple begins to hum and pulse with energy.

You open your arms and extend them toward the astral storm. You open yourself completely to its power. Your openness dramatically increases both the energy and the strength of the astral storm. Flashes of magickal lightning begin to appear deep within the clouds of the energy storm. Bolts of magickal lightning begin to bombard the outer walls of the twin circles.

The walls of the twin circles are now heavily charged with magickal astral energy. Waves of astral energy begin to pulse and flow along their inner walls. Fingerlike streams of magickal electricity suddenly fill the inside of the circles like a gigantic plasma ball.

The streams of magickal electricity are being drawn toward the antenna of the eternal temple like iron filings toward a magnet. A stream of magickal electricity hits the antenna, and its powerful current flows up and down along antenna's surface.

The antenna of the eternal temple has been empowered. It is now fully activated.

You must now return to the shadow realm and empower the hidden temple. Return to the portal of the mirror now, but do not pass through it just yet.

At the portal of the mirror, you can feel the powerful magickal energies of the eternal temple building all around you. When you look beyond the portal of the mirror, you can see your shade-self waiting in the shadow realm on the other side.

You are still wearing the invisible cloak of magickal energy. You can feel the long flowing fabric of the cloak extending throughout the eternal temple. You feel a sudden rush of power as the magickal electricity being collected by the antenna of the eternal temple begins flowing to you through the cloak.

The magickal electricity flowing through the cloak is concentrating and building around the astral side of the mirror frame.

The purpose of the eternal temple, to gather magickal energies from the astral plane, has been fulfilled. It has been established as the third point on the pentagram of power.

It is now time for you to return your consciousness to your shade-self in the shadow realm and empower the hidden temple. Your spirit will remain in the eternal temple by the portal of the mirror until it is time to transfer the astral energies into the shadow realm.

You look beyond the portal of the mirror and directly into the eyes of your shade-self in the shadow realm. You feel that your consciousness is now passing through the portal of the mirror, leaving your spirit behind and entering into the eyes of your shade-self. As you enter into the eyes of your shade-self, you feel as though your spirit and your consciousness are separating.

You can feel your spirit in the astral world, but your thoughts and awareness are now entering into the mind of your shade-self in the shadow realm.

Your consciousness begins to travel deep into the recesses of your mind. It is moving closer and closer to the hidden temple. Your consciousness moves deeper and deeper into your mind until you can clearly see the hidden temple before you. Your consciousness is now moving inside the hidden temple.

You are now inside the hidden temple of the mind. The hidden temple is a secret and mysterious place. Only *you* know the true shape and form of the hidden temple. If you have created a subliminal film for your subconscious mind, ready the movie theater of hidden temple and begin to screen the film.

It is now time to empower the hidden temple and establish it as the fourth point on the pentagram of power.

You hear yourself softly saying the word *will* in your mind, and as you do you can feel a small pulse of power pervade the hidden temple like a faint heartbeat.

You hear yourself saying the word *intent* a little bit louder in your mind, and as you do you can feel an even stronger pulse of power moving through the hidden temple.

You hear yourself saying the word *focus* even louder in your mind, and as you do you feel the hidden temple beginning to come to life.

You hear yourself repeating the words *will, intent,* and *focus* over and over again in your mind. Each time these three words are repeated they grow stronger, louder, and more purposeful. The hidden temple is quickly becoming empowered by the strength and intensity of these words. *Will. Intent. Focus.* Over and over, louder and louder, stronger and stronger, they resound and echo in the hidden temple of your mind. The hidden temple is quickly reaching the height of its power.

Will!   You can feel your spirit in the eternal temple and the powerful astral energies all around it.

Intent!   You can feel the magickal energies flowing through the invisible cloak and growing more and more powerful.

Focus! The long, flowing ends of the cloak begin reaching toward the portal of the mirror frame like long, fluid fingers of invisible energy.

Will! The ends of the cloak enter into the portal of the mirror and are whipping about as if caught up in a mighty storm.

Intent! You feel the energies of the eternal temple swelling behind your spirit in an immense wave of astral power and magick.

Focus! The cloak is drawn through the portal of the mirror and your spirit is pulled through with it.

Will! Your spirit enters into the body of your shade-self and the cloak of energy wraps itself around you.

Intent! The energies of the cloak are attracting the growing wave of astral power and magick in the eternal temple.

Focus! The wave of astral power and magick crests in the eternal temple and washes through the portal of the mirror in a flood of energy.

Will! The flood of astral energy washes all around you and begins to encircle you like a flowing river of power and magick.

Intent! The flowing river of power and magick rises up like a waterspout and spins around you.

Focus! The spinning waterspout of energy fills with magickal electricity and boils over into your spirit.

Will! Your spirit is filled with the powerful magickal electricity of the eternal temple.

Intent! You feel your entire being calling out to your shadow spirit. You see the union in your mind.

Focus!   You compress the magickal electricity that is being conducted into your spirit into a ball of power inside you.

Will!   You *will* make contact with your shadow spirit. You know this without question.

Intent!   You feel the power in yourself and in the spirit temples. You feel the pentagram of power forming around you. You stand fearlessly at the center of these powers.

Focus!   You focus the sum of your will and intent on the ball of energy compressed within you. You will the ball of energy to rise up out of you. Using your magickal hands, you hold the ball in the air above you.

Will!   You feel the anchoring energies of the living temple.

Intent!   You feel the power in the shadow realm.

Focus!   You feel the magickal energies of the eternal temple.

Will!   You feel the commanding energies of the hidden temple.

Intent!   You feel the first four points of the pentagram connect together.

Focus!   You release your hold on the ball of compressed energy and the ball flies through the portal of the mirror.

The ball of energy strikes the antenna of the eternal temple and countless rays of astral light and energy are beamed deep into the astral world.

An astral beacon has been created and empowered. The call to your shadow spirit has been made.

Relax your spirit and empty your mind. Open yourself to first contact. Open yourself to the becoming. Open yourself to the avatar. Open yourself to your *other*.

Open yourself to your shadow spirit as you would your arms to someone you love with all of your heart….

First contact with your shadow spirit has now been made. Your shadow spirit has responded to your call. A new world of possibilities has opened up before you, and very soon you will be taking your first steps onto the path that leads into this new world. But this new path will have to wait for you awhile longer. You have done much work this day and you need time to rest and to reflect upon your experiences before you begin your new adventures. Only you can know how and where your *other* has made first contact and if it has revealed its true form to you. Only you can know if your shadow spirit is at your side.

The time has now come for you to power down the spirit temples and return to your earthly existence. As you go about the process of powering down the spirit temples, be observant of everything around you. Look for any signs that your shadow spirit may have left for you to discover. Take note of how the shadow realm and the spirit temples look and feel. They may look and feel very different than they did before. This day will forever be recorded in your memory and branded upon your spirit as the day that you met your true magickal self. You must now power down the spirit temples and return to the waking world.

You are now moving into in the hidden temple of the mind. The movie screen of the hidden temple flickers and fades to black. The will, intent, and focus of the hidden temple are still present, but they are now only an afterthought. The work here has been done. The goal has been achieved and realized. You acknowledge this fact, and your consciousness is now moving away from the hidden temple of the mind. As you move further and further away from the hidden temple, you can feel the temple becoming dormant and still. The hidden temple is now silent and empty. It will remain this way until you return to awaken it once again.

You are now moving deep within your own spirit. Your spirit still tingles with the intense energies of the eternal temple. The invisible cloak of magickal energy is still wrapped around your spirit. You feel the cloak gently lifting your spirit into the air and you are now floating towards the portal of the mirror.

You pass through the portal of the mirror and enter into the eternal temple of the astral world. You are now moving toward the antenna of the eternal temple.

As you reach the antenna of the eternal temple, you can feel the invisible cloak of energy lifting away from your spirit and rising up toward the beaming ball of energy at the top of the antenna. The cloak blankets the ball of energy, and the rays of light beaming from the ball become muted and vague. The light softens to a faint glow, then disappears completely. The ball of energy will remain dormant at the top of the antenna of the eternal temple until you are in need of it once again.

You are now moving away from the antenna of the eternal temple toward the portal of the mirror.

As you move through the eternal temple, it grows silent and still behind you. The magickal energies of the eternal temple will sleep until you return and awaken them.

As you reach the portal of the mirror, the last of the magickal energies of the eternal temple grow quiet and begin to slumber. It almost feels as if the temple itself were somehow dreaming.

You pass beyond the portal of the mirror and enter into the shadow realm.

As you return to the shadow realm, you are greeted by a gently blowing ethereal wind. The unspoken voice of magick itself seems to loft and swirl around you. Your entire domain seems to be speaking to you with this magickal voice.

The shadow realm has been changed forever. *You* have been changed forever. You look down at the circle of white marble at your feet, and you see that a large pentagram of black onyx has been inlaid into its surface. The soul sword is imbedded in the exact center of the pentagram.

The smooth black pentagram shines with the mystical twilight of your world. You sit down next to the soul sword in the middle of the pentagram and you wrap your hand around its hilt. You can feel the dormant magick of the spirit temples sleeping deep within the pentagram's shiny black surface. The sleeping magick relaxes you, and you can feel your mind and your spirit beginning to drift.

You feel yourself gently rising up and floating away from the shadow realm. You are returning to the waking world.

Higher and higher you float, further and further you drift away from your domain.

As you near the border between the shadow realm and the waking world, without expectation you look down for one last glimpse of your domain.

You see the twin circles of power slowly spinning in opposing directions, protecting the center of the shadow realm.

You see the shimmering pools of the sun and of the moon being watched over by the statues of the Goddess and the God.

You see the sleeping griffon encased within a bed of stone atop the great mirror of promise and magick.

The shadow realm is growing distant and vague. You are crossing over the borders of your domain.

You are returning to your earthly reality and the waking world. You open your eyes to your earthly existence.

You are not alone....

Before you put away the earth altar and close down your sacred space, you may want to spend some time reflecting upon what you have just experienced. You may also want to consider writing down everything you felt and saw during the meditation. Remember: Even if you did not actually see your shadow spirit during the meditation, it has probably made contact with you in some way and will probably continue to make contact with you frequently for some time. As you go about your day-to-day life, take note of anything that seems peculiar or different from what you normally see, feel, and experience. Your *other* may decide to "speak" to you in any number of ways, so do your best to make sure that your eyes, ears, and spirit are as open as they can be so you don't overlook the signs.

Your shadow spirit is ready to speak to you. Are you ready to listen?

Chapter 18

After Worlds

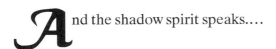nd the shadow spirit speaks....

You are now standing on the perimeter between the worlds. Between two realities and two understandings. The space between what was and what will be. Let us make the most of this opportunity that we have been given and do a perimeter walk together, you and I. Let us take a moment to retrace the times that you and I have been here before, standing on the perimeter's edge.

There is a presence here.... Can you feel it? No, it is not me. It is something more than me, something more than you. It is the presence of the Witch that you were, of the worlds that you have left behind, of the shades of the past and the calling of an unwritten future. In a way, by choosing to make contact with me, you have been initiated. For what is an initiation, if not a new beginning? What are initiates, if not people who have taken their first step across a new threshold? What is a threshold, if not a doorway to change?

We have been here before, you and I. This place should not seem unfamiliar to you. A bit uncertain, perhaps, but not entirely unwelcome. This is the place of reflection and anticipation. This is a time of rest and preparation. We are in an empty waiting room at the point of transition.

But we are quite a bit further out than we were the last time we were here, are we not? The perimeter that you and I now walk is larger than the ones we have walked together in the past. Yes, I have been with you all along. You were just not ready to see me before now.

Look deep inside the perimeter of what was and what you have left behind…. Like rings within rings, each perimeter grows smaller and smaller, the deeper you look into your magickal past. Do you see the empty spaces between the rings? Each space is the threshold between the stages of your magickal evolution. Each is a doorway that led you to a new world, a new beginning. Each doorway led you closer to me. Each perimeter you have walked has brought you more and more experience and understanding.

Now look beyond the perimeter and into the world of what has yet to be…. Yes, it is still shadowy, still veiled. But the shadows do not seem nearly as dark and deep as they did the last time we were here, do they? The veils have thinned to the point of almost being transparent, have they not? You have drunk deeply from the chalice of your true magickal self and even the perimeter between the world you have left behind and the one you are about to enter has grown vague, hasn't it? The day will come when you have tasted the last drop of your magickal self and you and I will become one.

The perimeters between the old and new worlds will meld together and vanish altogether. Yes, that day will come. I see that for now, however, our perimeter walk has nearly reached its end. The perimeter is large and the threshold between your worlds is deep, but they are not yet endless. Ah, yes, there it is…. We have reached the edge of the threshold. The doorway to your next stage of magickal evolution is upon you at last. I will see you on the other side….

There you are…. What kept you? Now that you're here, we can get back to business. The first order of business is to distinguish between first contact with your shadow spirit, which is what you (hopefully) accomplished in Exercise 5, and an actual joining or merging with your shadow spirit. The possibility of an actual joining with your shadow spirit is simply that: a possibility. An actual joining is something that is entirely between you and your shadow spirit, and, for reasons of personal ethics, I cannot and will not instruct you on how to go about this process. A joining could very easily involve the premature absorption of your magickal skills in their entirety, and, if you are not fully prepared for such a sudden and dramatic change, the mental and magickal consequences to you could be devastating. The only reason that I am even discussing this with you is because I feel that it is important for you to understand that there is huge difference between first contact and an actual joining with your shadow spirit before we go any further with the work in this book. Simply put, at this point you have only made preliminary contact with your shadow spirit, so you should take this preliminary contact for what it is and not read into it more than what is actually there. What you have felt and experienced with your shadow spirit thus far is nowhere close to what you would feel and experience from an actual joining with your *other*. Keep this in mind as you continue with the work in this book.

The second reason that I decided to omit the process for an actual joining with the shadow spirit was to protect all of the inexperienced "newbie" Witches who will inevitably pick up and read this book from attempting something that could potentially be very dangerous to them. If you are truly an advanced Witch, then I am sure that you will understand this decision, and advanced readers will be able to figure out how to accomplish a joining with their shadow spirit without my help anyway. That being said, let's move on and take a closer look at the current state of things.

As I said earlier in this book, my ability to guide you became somewhat compromised when you made first contact with your shadow spirit. It was at this point that your shadow spirit in essence replaced me as your guide on this particular path. This was, however, an inevitability and not unexpected, so I will do the best I can to try and make the most of our remaining time together. I still have a few magickal tricks up my sleeve to show you.

The next thing we should probably take a look at is how you might be feeling, both mentally and spiritually, after having made first contact with your shadow spirit. How you are feeling is of course highly relative at this point. It depends on a number of things. It depends on how intense your experience of connecting the five points of the pentagram of power together was for you. It depends on how strong the contact your shadow spirit made with you was. It depends on just how ready you *really* were to make contact with the whole of your true magickal self, and not how ready you *thought* you were.

If you have ever undergone a formal initiation by an established coven, then what you may currently be feeling and experiencing is probably familiar. You may be experiencing mental highs and lows, spiritual ups and downs. One moment confident and powerful, the next moment shy and unsure of yourself and your abilities. This is completely natural. It is also highly dependant on how intense first contact with your shadow spirit was, and how competent and magickally powerful the members of the coven that initiated you were. It is dependant on how big the impact the formal initiation had on you mentally and spiritually.

For quite a few years, I refused the offer of formal initiation from various covens and temples because I felt that a formal initiation would have little or no impact on me. This was not because I felt that these covens and temples were incompetent. It was because I had already felt magick flowing through me and had been in constant contact with my shadow spirit well before I even knew that I was a Witch. This was well before I knew that there were others of "my kind" out there in the world. I felt that no initiation could compare to what I had learned by working and communing with my shadow spirit, and that none of these covens or temples could truly understand that. When I finally accepted the offer to be formally initiated, the initiation ritual was performed by a coven that knew me inside and out. The priest and priestess tailored an initiation ritual specifically for my needs to create a deep spiritual impact on me.

I am only telling you this because, as you begin to work intimately with your shadow spirit and begin to absorb more and more of your true magickal self, your personal and magickal expectations from yourself and from other people and groups will become higher. Just be sure to keep yourself in check at all times. Just because you are becoming an advanced and evolved practitioner of the magickal arts does not give you the right to be spiritually pompous and magickally arrogant. If you become pompous and arrogant, your shadow spirit and I will have some pretty strong words (not to mention magick) to share with you on the subject. You are a Witch who has made contact with your true magickal self. Your strength must be tempered by kindness and gentleness, your magickal power instilled with fairness and responsibility. Your shadow spirit and I will accept nothing less from you, and you should accept no less from yourself. As I have said to you repeatedly, it is now you who must lead the way and teach and guide those who would follow in your footsteps. Just make sure that the footprints you leave behind are not so deep that those who follow you fall into them.

We should now take a deeper look into what you may have experienced in the shadow realm and in the spirit temples (and also possibly on the earthly plane) while you were undertaking Exercise 5. Only you can know if your shadow spirit made contact with you during Exercise 5. Only you can know just how strong and intimate that contact was. If the contact was obvious and revealing, then you already have a good idea as to how, where, and when your shadow spirit will be making contact with you in the future.

If you did not actually *see* your shadow spirit, however, do not assume that your *other* has not made contact with you. The signs of contact from your shadow spirit as you went through the process of empowering the spirit temples and the connecting together the five points on the pentagram of power may have been very subtle. You may need to do some deep reflecting on your experience to discover and unlock the mystery of these subtle signs of contact. This will also help to stir the memories of your first experience of working with the spirit temples and the pentagram of power to see if there were any signs of contact that you may have missed or overlooked. For example, as you moved through the spirit temples, did anything strike you as being peculiar or out of place? Was there anything about the spirit temples that looked or even felt different than they did after you constructed them? Was there anything in the spirit temples, such as strange symbols or unusual items, that you did not actually place in the spirit temples yourself or include in the spirit temple's architecture?

Did you feel a presence other than your own while you were working with the spirit temples? You may need to ponder these questions and do some meditating on your first experience with the spirit temples to discover any subtle or hidden signs of first contact.

It is also possible that your shadow spirit materialized onto the earthly plane while you were in deep meditation and that you missed actually seeing it with your own two eyes. You may therefore want to look for any physical signs of first contact from your shadow spirit. As I said earlier, my shadow spirit has never allowed me to look directly at it for an extended period of time on the earthly plane. This idiosyncrasy of the shadow spirit may be exclusive to mine, but it is still worth consideration if your shadow spirit displays this same characteristic. If you do not see any obvious physical signs of contact from your shadow spirit right away, keep your eyes, mind, and spirit open to contact from your *other,* and look for any repeated occurrences that seem strange or are subtly different from the norm. For example, my shadow spirit speaks to me by using numbers, and it's not unusual for my shadow spirit to wake me up four or five times a week in the middle of the night at exactly 12:34, 3:33, 4:44, and so forth. Over the years I have learned to take advantage of being awakened in the middle of the night. I go into the living room, where I won't disturb my wife, and open myself up to what my shadow spirit is trying to get me to see. Some of my most productive ideas came at theses times, so I learned not to be unhappy with my shadow spirit for waking me up in the middle of the night and sharing information with me. Given patience, openness, and time, your shadow spirit may make obvious contact and share its secrets and teachings with you, too.

Once strong and frequent contact with your *other* begins, you will be learning more and more about your true magickal self and your potential. If you have truly made contact with your shadow spirit, you will undergo some significant changes in the next few months, so keep a close eye on yourself to see how these changes are manifesting in your physical and magickal lives.

As I warned you at the very beginning of this book, *not all of these changes will be good or for the better.* But you and you alone have made the decision to make contact with your shadow spirit, and you and you alone must now accept the responsibility of this contact and the changes that will inevitably occur within you and around you. Your shadow spirit cannot bring out anything in you physically, mentally, or magickally that is not already inside you. Your shadow spirit cannot tell you anything that you don't already intuitively know. The depths of your knowledge and your magickal abilities have so far only been as deep as you have believed and allowed them to be. Your own hands have placed the chains of limitation about you, and only you can remove the chains. Your shadow spirit contains all you have denied yourself. Your shadow spirit embodies all of the magick you have refused to see.

Drink from the chalice of magick that is your shadow spirit, but do not drink too much too quickly, or you will become intoxicated by your own spiritual essence and your own magickal power. You wouldn't want your power to grow beyond your control. One sip at a time will do nicely.

Chapter 19

Impossible Magick

Impossible. adj. not capable of being accomplished: *an
impossible goal*

> —*American Heritage Dictionary*

*Like everyone else you were born into bondage. Born into
a prison that you cannot smell or taste or touch. A prison,
for your mind.*

> —Morpheous to Neo, in *The Matrix*

In the next section of this book ("The Book of Shadow"), I will be offering up some possible adventures for you to embark upon with your shadow spirit. Before you begin adventuring with your shadow spirit, however, it's important that we take a close look at how you can implement some of the new techniques you have learned into your magick, as well as the spirit temples and the pentagram of power. Before we do so, we need to discuss the relevance of the title of this chapter, which is "impossible" magick.

If impossible magick is simply that—*impossible*—then what is the point of even discussing it, you may be asking. Once again, it all comes down to *what you believe.* If you believe that a given goal is impossible to achieve, then you'll never be able to achieve that goal. If you believe that your magick and the practice of Witchcraft have limitations or that some things are just plain impossible to accomplish, then you'll never be able to accomplish those things.

But if you believe that *absolutely nothing is impossible,* then, although you may be let down from time to time, your magickal potential will far exceed that of the garden-variety practitioner of the magickal arts.

As with everything else we've covered in this book, you're going to have to take the concept of "impossible" to the next level. Before any of the new techniques you've learned and the spirit temples and pentagram of power will do you any real good, you're going to have to develop distaste for the word and a strong dislike for the concept of "impossible." You're going to have to view the spirit temples and the pentagram of power, not to mention your shadow spirit, as being limitless in their power before their potential can fully be realized. Before you can drink fully of the magick of your shadow spirit, you are going to have to truly believe that *absolutely nothing is impossible.*

Let's take a look at how you can make the most out of your new skills and places of power by learning how to practice "impossible magick."

Simply put, impossible magick is allowing yourself the freedom to use magick and Witchcraft as you see fit by removing the chains of dogma and restriction you have allowed to be placed on your Craft.

I'm reading your mind yet again. I can hear your protesting. "Dogma? Restrictions? He's kidding, right? Those things are for those *other* religions, not for Wicca or Witchcraft! Wicca and Witchcraft don't have a bible or a pope or one all-powerful god! Nobody tells *me* what to do with my beliefs and my magick!"

Really, I reply. Are you *sure* about that? I'm about to do some serious cage rattling, so hang onto your broomstick.

You would be correct in saying that Wicca and Witchcraft do not have a bible, a pope, or even one all-powerful god to answer to, but you would be very wrong in saying that you have not allowed restrictions to be placed on you and your magick. Although all Wiccans and Witches obviously do not follow the same traditions, pantheons, or belief systems, as a general rule, most Wiccans and Witches *do* believe in karma, in the Wiccan Rede, and in the law of threefold return. Though I understand that these beliefs have been instilled into the magickal community as moral and ethical guidelines, and I fully understand why they are a necessary system of checks and balances, they are still restrictions. I have had many debates and discussions on the topics of karma, the Wiccan Rede, and the law of threefold return, and it seems that everyone has their own particular take on what these things mean to them personally and how they affect the magickal and the mundane community as a whole.

It is my belief that my own personal karma is my purpose or "what I am here to do" in my current incarnation. I understand and accept that from time to time I am the "tool" through which karma works and brings balance to both the physical and spiritual planes of existence.

Because this is my belief, I have therefore interpreted the Wiccan Rede and the threefold law to match this belief. There have been a few Wiccan authors such as Phyllis Currott who believe that the threefold law is the same as the Christian threat to behave yourself or go to hell. I personally agree wholeheartedly with Ms. Currott on this particular subject, and I have neither used nor taught the law of threefold return to my students for many years now.

As for the Wiccan Rede, first, I do not consider myself to be Wiccan. I am a Witch, and I could write an entire chapter on what I believe the differences are between the two, but basically, as I see it, Wiccans follow the traditional English paths of Gerald Gardner and others, whereas Witches are more eclectic. But because the two are obviously interrelated, I will tell you that I have changed my personal rede to state what I believe to be the more realistic "I will do as I will."

So am I saying that morals and ethics should have absolutely no part to play in my or anyone else's practice of magick and Witchcraft or that it's okay to do harm and bad things just because you feel like it? Of course not. But, as I've pointed out several times, morals and ethics are highly personal points of view that rule and guide each of us individually. For me or anyone else to push our personal morals or ethics on an individual or society is, plain and simply, wrong. In Chapter 1 of this book I stated the following: *Only you can truly understand your concept of right and wrong, and it is not my purpose to change that.* This is what it all comes down to: *your* concept of right and wrong—not mine or anyone else's.

As have most of the modern Witches I've become acquainted with, I came to the practice of magick through Wicca. As a result, I developed a very idealistic and ultimately impractical view as to how magick, karma, and ethics should work. Because of the Wiccan Rede (or my inability to decipher it correctly), I would feel ashamed and distressed if I were to inadvertently harm a bug or a plant, let alone another human being. I would see bad things happening to good people physically, magickally, and spiritually, and I would assure myself that eventually karma would work its magick and make everything as right as rain. I would hold back and not use my mental, physical, or magickal powers to correct situations I knew were wrong because of four little words: "an it harm none."

But I eventually grew up and got smart and recognized those four words for what they really are: chains. Chains that were written to govern someone else's beliefs about life and magick. Chains that in one way or another were a form of control. Chains that *I allowed* to be clasped about my magick. Chains that now were there for only one reason: to be broken.

Once the chains were removed, I had to reassure myself that I was a good man and a good Witch. I had to remind myself that a lack of chains does not translate into a lack of self-discipline or self-control. I had to throw out the book of laws that was written by someone else to control and govern me and write a new book of laws that matched my personal beliefs. I had to learn to decide for myself how much ugliness I was going to stomach before I got off my magickal ass and did something about it. I had to learn that from time to time I was the tool through which karma would work its magick and that sometimes it wouldn't be pretty.

The reason I'm telling you this is because I feel it's important for you to recognize the fact that things are not always what they appear to be. As I said earlier in this book, "recognition is half the battle," so even if my observations about karma, the Wiccan Rede, and the law of threefold return hold no sway over you, at the very least you now have a new opinion and fresh perspective to consider. In one way or another, we all wear our own chains, but as long as we recognize that we're wearing them we may find a way to remove them one day. Just as the heavily chained ghost of Jacob Marley did with Ebenezer Scrooge, I am only trying to get you to see your possible fate. Perhaps I've grown more cynical over the years. Perhaps I've grown wiser. I'll leave that up to you to decide.

Getting back to business, we find the spirit temples, the shadow realm, the pentagram of power, and a plethora of newfound magickal skills and tools awaiting you. So what can you do with all these wonderfully magickal places, skills, and things now that you have made contact with your shadow spirit? The short answer would be, *Anything you can imagine, my friend, anything you can imagine.*

But that's really not a satisfactory answer now, is it? As far as the pentagram of power is concerned, you've already gotten a pretty good taste of the possibilities, but thus far you have only used it to make first contact with your shadow spirit. Once you and your shadow spirit begin working together more intently, however, the pentagram of power can be used to generate a magickal force far beyond anything you have probably ever imagined as being possible. Your *other* has the capability of establishing itself as the fifth point on the pentagram of power, and in so doing can literally double the power and effectiveness of your magick.

Picture it in this way. Imagine a powerful ray of sunlight being gathered and focused through a magnifying glass (the spirit temples) and then being collected by an immense solar energy cell (the shadow realm). Now imagine what would happen to this powerful, collected solar energy if it were released in a single, focused beam into a highly polished mirrored surface (your shadow spirit) and directed at something. Let it suffice to say that it probably wouldn't be a good idea to step into its path! Now imagine that the solar energy is magickal energy instead…. Kind of gives you a case of the magickal chills, doesn't it? Now imagine casting a spell or sending healing or protective energies using the pentagram of power. I'm going to guess that the word *impossible* just became somewhat less significant to you.

The process of empowering the spirit temples and connecting the five points of the pentagram of power together that I showed to you is a considerable undertaking. It will prove impractical for anything less than a major working until you have become extremely comfortable and adept at using it. The more you work with the spirit temples and the pentagram of power, however, the easier it will become for you to use them. With intensive work and study, you can expound on the methods I've shown you and develop your own unique approach to how you use the pentagram of power and connect each of the five points together. Given time, practice, patience, and the aid of your shadow spirit, I have little doubt that you will develop a quick and easy way to incorporate the pentagram of power into all of your magickal workings.

Let us now take a look at each of the spirit temples individually and see how they can be of service to you in your magickal and mundane lives and situations. We will forego any further discussions about the shadow realm because, if you are not already well aware of its power and potential, then you simply have not been paying attention.

The Body: The Living Temple

I have already sufficiently driven home the importance of preparing your physical body to be the best it can be for magickal workings, so I will not repeat myself here. What we will concentrate our attention on is the great service that using the power of the living temple can offer you in your mundane life and how lucid daydreaming can aid you in your use of magick.

If you envision yourself going through the process of establishing your body as the living temple, the physical benefits that you reap become quite clear. The entire process is nothing more than infusing your physical body with strength and grounding earthly energies. It is easy to imagine how you could benefit from these energies if your body were run down or if you were physically ill. Going through the process of establishing your body as the living temple could be the boost your body needs to get you through a tough work week or to start healing an illness. It is obviously not a good idea to overexert yourself if you are ill, but a slightly watered-down version of the process could give you enough of a bump to get over the sickness hurdle. If you are the type of person who enjoys sports and physical competition—and what Witch doesn't (sorry, I couldn't resist)—then using the power of the living temple could give you an extra edge over your competition. I will leave the moral and ethical ponderings of that one to you.

Moving along, we see the power of lucid daydreaming just waiting to be tapped. The mundane benefits of lucid daydreaming, such as scenario development, life choices, and alternative methods, were already covered in Chapter 14, so now we can focus on the magickal benefits that can be derived from lucid daydreaming. During the process of establishing your body as the living temple, you use the power of lucid daydreaming to "see" symbols of strength rising up from the earth altar and entering into your body. Though this is not an actual visual phenomenon, and the strength symbols are not images being projected into your mind but rather vice-versa, the power of lucid daydreaming makes the symbols much more real than they would be if you were only thinking about them.

We have already covered the fact that for most of us it is much easier to see an image in our minds with our eyes closed. But through the power of lucid daydreaming you are learning how to see these images with your eyes wide open. To master the art of lucid daydreaming and apply its power to your magick, the next time you are doing a ritual or a magickal working, use your knowledge of lucid daydreaming to try and "see" the magickal energies all around you and to take note of how different energies look and behave. Then use your knowledge of lucid daydreaming to "see" how many different outcomes you could bring about by using these energies in different ways.

Once you have become a master of the art of lucid daydreaming, you will have the ability to not only feel but also see magick all around you. You will be able to quickly determine the different outcomes that you can achieve with your magick and to avoid any possible interference or pitfalls that could have a profound affect on your workings. With a lot of practice and a little effort, you can bring a whole new dimension to your visualization skills by pulling images out of your mind and making them "real" all around you.

The Spirit: The Eternal Temple

If the mundane world becomes taxing and is getting you down, the eternal temple is a wonderful place to visit if you need a spiritual recharge or if you just want to "feel more magickal."

Because the eternal temple is the only spirit temple that was constructed using nothing but magickal energies, it can be a very refreshing and inspirational place in which to dwell. Because the eternal temple exists on the astral plane and is protected by the twin circles, it is also the perfect place to safely observe the astral world and its inhabitants. The eternal temple will also serve as the "launching point" when you begin adventuring with your shadow spirit.

Let us now take a closer look at the antenna of the eternal temple and investigate some of its further uses. In Exercise 5, you used the antenna to place the equivalent of a metaphysical phone call to your shadow spirit. Just as you did with your *other,* you can use the antenna to attempt to make contact with just about any astral being or ethereal spirit or force you can imagine. When you made first contact with your shadow spirit, you used the antenna of the eternal temple to gather magickal energies from the astral plane and to send the collected energies back into the astral world. You can use the antenna in the very same way to cast spells and do magickal workings.

Just as the eternal temple itself does, the power of the antenna lies dormant and asleep under a cloak of magickal energy. It is up to you and your shadow spirit to awaken the power and magick of the antenna and discover for yourselves its infinite number of uses and possibilities.

The Mind: The Hidden Temple

The power that the hidden temple is capable of infusing into your magick became apparent during Exercise 5, but you can also easily incorporate its power into your mundane life and mundane situations. Just imagine what you could do in the mundane world with the concentrated power of will, intent, and focus at your fingertips. The power of the hidden temple can give you a big edge in the areas of school, work, and competition by allowing you to focus in on the task at hand much more intently then without it.

Putting the power of the hidden temple to work for you in the mundane world is as simple as taking a few moments to relax and travel deep into your mind and empower it. Once you feel the hidden temple of the mind has been fully empowered, clearly view the objective (doing great on a test, giving a killer presentation, and so forth) in your mind and allow the power of the hidden temple to zero in on the objective and infuse it with the desired will, intent, and focus. Once this is accomplished, you will have much more focus and control over your thoughts, fears, and goals than you would have without incorporating the power of the hidden temple into your objective. Given enough advanced notice, you could also easily prepare a subliminal film to screen during the task and add the power of your subconscious into the mix.

The hidden temple is a very powerful mundane and magickal tool that, when used properly, allows you to excel far beyond anything you have ever know or experienced. As with any power, however, use the power of the hidden temple responsibly and discover ways to use it that will not only aid and benefit yourself, but everyone around you.

A world of possibilities and investigation has opened up before you. With your newfound skills, the spirit temples, and the pentagram of power in hand, invite your *other* to join you in discovering the full potential of these new skills and places of power. The greatest guide imaginable is now by your side. The whole of your true magickal self is waiting to be tapped. Walk proudly and unafraid into this new world and discover your destiny. Break the chains and learn the ways of impossible magick.

The Book of Shadow

Here There Be Monsters

Map. n. A representation, usually on a plane surface, of
a region of the earth or heavens.

—*American Heritage Dictionary*

It was not an uncommon practice for mapmakers of old to mark uncharted oceans on their maps where ships had disappeared without a trace with phrases such as "Here There Be Monsters" or "Here There Be Dragons." As are the deep and captivating oceans of the earth, the astral plane is an endless sea of mystery just waiting to be explored. I have read many books and Websites that warn of all the nasty creatures and entities floating around out there on the astral plane. Such books and Websites paint the astral plane as being a very dark and dangerous place full of pitfalls awaiting the unwary and unprepared astral traveler. When I read this kind of nonsense, I question whether or not the authors of these books and Websites have ever even been on the astral plane. If they have, I'm sure their astral maps must be covered with warnings of "Here There Be Monsters."

Scared and paranoid is no way to travel on the astral plane, or through any other plane of existence. Are there nasty creatures and entities on the astral plane? Of course there are, but, in my experience, your odds of having a face-to-face encounter and being harmed by one of is about the same as your odds are of being attacked and killed by a shark here on mundane earth. The odds are four times higher that you will be struck by lightning than attacked by a shark, and the odds are one in three hundred million that you will die during a shark attack.

Even though the chances are remote that you will ever have a close encounter with a nasty astral entity intent on doing you harm, and even more remote that you would actually be injured by the encounter, it never hurts to be prepared for that possibility. So exactly how are we going to prepare you for an encounter with a nasty astral entity? Perhaps you will remember this infamous saying: "As I walk through the valley of the shadow of death I shall fear no evil, for I am the meanest SOB in the valley!" We're going to turn you into the scariest thing on the astral plane.

If I've done my job correctly, your confidence in yourself and your magick has probably increased without measure through doing the work in this book. Factor in the power and skills of your shadow spirit, and you have effectively doubled your magickal prowess. See? You're pretty scary already. But we can even do better than that! To give you some formidable and impressive magickal astral tools to use and to set you up for some wonderful astral adventures with your shadow spirit, I have taken the liberty of adding the first few entries into what you will come to know as your "Book of Shadow." Unlike a standard Book of Shadows, where a Witch writes down his or her spells, rituals, and secret magickal workings, the Book of Shadow is where you will document the adventures that you will have by working with your shadow spirit. The Book of Shadow I've started for you will be laid out in an easy-to-read, "how-to" format, just as I would outline a spell or a ritual. The goal of each chapter in the Book of Shadow will be clearly stated and any items you need to complete the working will be listed. I will then provide a step-by-step process to meet the chapter's main objective. As I have already stated, however, my ability to guide you has become somewhat compromised by your first contact with your shadow spirit. Your *other* will probably have its own opinion as to how (and if) the two of you should proceed with each of the workings I have laid out for you in the Book of Shadow.

So, once again, consider my initial entries into your Book of Shadow as suggestions and guidelines rather than absolutes. You and your *other* should tailor my first few entries to fit your needs and expectations. Because it would be impossible for me to create entries in the Book of Shadow that would fill the needs of everyone who reads and does the work in this book, I'll keep my entries as generic as possible without being boring. It will be up to you and your shadow spirit to add your own favorite blend of seasonings to the pot and complete the recipes.

The adventures I'll lay out in the Book of Shadow will all be undertaken while you are in a state of deep meditation, but any further adventures with your shadow spirit could easily happen in any number of ways. Beyond meditation and physical materialization, your *other* may speak to you through your dreams or by using your subconscious as its "voice." Most of the contact between you and your shadow spirit is likely to be spontaneous and unpredictable, so you will need to let go of any preconceived notions you may be harboring. There's nothing at all wrong with initiating adventures or invoking the aid of your shadow spirit in magickal and mundane situations, but you must be prepared for the fact that anything can and will happen. You probably already know what is said about "the best laid plans of mice and men."

Before you begin adventuring with your shadow spirit, there's one last thing we should take a quick look at. Any "items needed" that I list in my entries in the Book of Shadow that do not already exist in the shadow realm or the spirit temples will have to be created by you or your shadow spirit. You can create the items you do not already possess by using the same process you used to create the mirror frame and the looking glass in the very first exercise of this book. Simply draw equal parts of energy from the sun and moon pools, visualize the item you need clearly in your mind, combine the energies together, and will the needed item into existence. Piece o' cake!

You are a wise and powerful Witch. You have the gods and goddesses of old watching over you. You have a mighty companion to aid in your quests and travel with you on your journeys. An infinite number of doors and pathways have opened up before you. All you need to do now is decide on which door to open first....

Book of Shadow Working Number 1
The Spirit Armor and the Soul Sword

Objective and Explanation

The goals of the first working are to forge what is known as "spirit armor" and to instill your soul sword with the power and magick of your shadow spirit. The spirit armor will protect your astral body as you embark on adventures with your shadow spirit and enter into unexplored areas of the astral world and different realms and dimensions. Once your shadow spirit has added its own power and magick to the already formidable soul sword, it will become a most fearsome magickal weapon, one that few astral, magickal, or elemental entities would dare to stand up against. The ultimate goal of Working Number 1, therefore, is to equip you with advanced magickal protection and the ability to defend your astral body should the need arise. You will be doing this in an old-fashioned manner, as if you were a blacksmith in ancient times.

Items Needed

1. The container that holds the essence of your old spirit that you shed during the initiation of self ritual.

    Note: *If you decided not to undertake the initiation of self ritual, to carry on with this first working you will need to either undertake the ritual or read it through and perform a similar ritual of your own making in which you symbolically shed the* *spirit of your "old self" and capture and hold the essence of your old spirit in some sort of vessel or container.*

2. A magickal fire or forge in which you can heat and purify the essence of your old spirit and the soul sword to prepare them for transformation.

3. A pool of magickal water with which to cool the heated spirit armor and soul sword.

4. An anvil, a pair of metal tongs, and a blacksmith's hammer.

The Process

Get out the container that symbolically holds the essence of your old spirit and hold it in your hands. Open the container and feel the essence of your old spirit leave the container and enter into the key to the shadow realm. Grasp the key in your hand. Using your normal method, attain a state of deep meditation and enter into the shadow realm. Once you are in the shadow realm, you will need to make contact with your *other* and extend the invitation to work with you in forging the spirit armor and instilling the soul sword with additional power and magick.

Making contact with your shadow spirit is a highly personal experience, but if you have not yet established an easy method with which to call your shadow spirit to your side, now is as good a time as any to begin working it out. In time, your shadow spirit will join in most, if not all, of your magickal workings automatically, without having to be called. It is possible that your shadow spirit does this already, but only you can know this for sure.

Assuming that your shadow spirit does not yet automatically join in your magickal workings, it is important that you establish a quick and easy method of making contact with your *other*. To do so, you may want to consider using a particular stance, a chant, a call, or a combination of all three to make contact with your shadow spirit. You want to be mentally, spiritually, and psychically open to your shadow spirit at all times, but during a calling you should put a little more "oomph" into it. If *you* are not excited about doing magickal workings with your shadow spirit, your shadow spirit certainly won't be excited about working with you, either. Now is the time to start figuring out a method of contacting your shadow spirit that works well for both of you.

Once contact has been made and an agreement to assist you in this working has been reached, you will need to create the items needed to forge the spirit armor. To do so, you and/or your shadow spirit will need to draw equal parts of energy from the sun and moon pools, combine the energies together while envisioning the needed items clearly in your minds, and, one by one, magickally will the items into existence. For this working you will need to create a magickal fire or forge, a pool of magickal water, an anvil, a pair of tongs, and a blacksmith's hammer.

You will now need to stoke the magickal fires of the forge. Next, draw the soul sword from the marble disc, draw the essence of your old spirit from the key, and place both of them in the fire. While the soul sword and the essence of your old spirit are heating in the forge, you need to decide on how you would like the spirit armor to look and feel. This is a very important part of this working and should be strongly considered before you begin creating the spirit armor. If you are unhappy with the overall look and feel of the spirit armor once it has been completed, your confidence and belief in the armor's ability to protect you will be compromised.

Once the soul sword and the essence of your old spirit have been thoroughly heated, use the tongs to remove the essence of your old spirit from the forge and place it on the anvil. You are now at the most critical phase in this working, which is the actual forming of the spirit armor. To do so, you will want to take the blacksmith's hammer in hand and, taking turns with your shadow spirit, hammer the armor into shape while infusing the armor with powerful, protective magickal energies. You should be very serious and focused as you go about your work, and with each fall of the hammer you should magickally will the armor to be filled with magick, protection, and strength. Once the spirit armor has been fully formed, use the tongs to lay the armor into the pool of magickal water to cool and harden.

Now that your spirit armor has been created, it is time to further strengthen and empower your soul sword with the magickal energies of your shadow spirit. If your shadow spirit agrees to do this for you, use the tongs to remove the soul sword from the forge and place it on the anvil. Watch your shadow spirit closely as it goes to work on the blade. Watching your shadow spirit work magick can be a very satisfying experience, and you may just learn a thing or two in the process. Deity created the soul sword from a piece of your own soul, and it already contains all of your own magickal power and essence that is necessary. If, however, you feel that the sword would benefit from further empowerment by you, feel free to hammer a little more power and magick into the blade once your shadow spirit has completed its work on the sword.

Once work on the sword has been completed to the satisfaction of both you and your shadow spirit, use the tongs to lay the sword into the pool of magickal water to cool and harden. After sufficient cooling, remove the spirit armor and the soul sword from the pool and allow them to dry. Try on your new spirit armor and brandish your fully empowered soul sword. I am confident that putting on the spirit armor and holding your fully empowered soul sword for the first time will be a feeling that you won't soon forget.

Step-by-Step Instructions

1. Get out the container that holds the essence of your old spirit and transfer the essence into the key for the shadow realm.

2. Attain a state of deep meditation and enter into the shadow realm.

3. Call out to your shadow spirit and ask for assistance in forging the spirit armor and instilling the soul sword with additional power and magick.

4. Draw equal parts of energy from the sun and moon pools. Combine the energies together while envisioning the items you need to complete the goal of this working as clearly as possible in your mind. One by one, will the items you need for this working into existence. These items are a magickal fire or forge, a pool of magickal water, an anvil, a pair of tongs, and a blacksmith's hammer.

    Note: *You can ask your shadow spirit to assist you in creating the needed items if you so desire.*

5. Once all of the needed items have been created, stoke the magickal fires of the forge and place the soul sword and the essence of your old spirit into the fire.

6. Envision the look, feel, and protective power of the completed spirit armor as clearly as possible in your mind.

7. Once the essence of your old spirit is thoroughly heated, use the pair of metal tongs to remove it from the fires of the forge and place it onto the anvil.

8. Taking turns with your shadow spirit, use the blacksmith's hammer to transform the essence of your old spirit into the spirit armor.

Note: *As you go about the process of creating the spirit armor, it is important to magickally will the armor to be filled with powerful protective energies with each fall of the hammer. The spirit armor will only be as strong as you will it to be, so muster up as much magickal power and intent as possible while you are creating it.*

9. Once the essence of your old spirit has been fully transformed, place the spirit armor into the pool of magickal waters to cool and harden.

10. Using the tongs, remove the soul sword from the fires of the forge and place it onto the anvil. Ask your shadow spirit to use the blacksmith's hammer to instill the soul sword with its own power and magick.

    Note: *Deity created the soul sword from a piece of your own soul, so further forging by you is unnecessary. If, however, you feel you need to add even more of your own personal power and magick into the sword, feel free to pick up the hammer yourself and go to work further empowering the blade.*

11. Once the soul sword has been empowered to the satisfaction of both you and your shadow spirit, place the sword into the pool of magickal water to be cooled.

12. Once they have cooled completely, remove the spirit armor and the soul sword from the pool of magickal water and allow them to dry.

Slip on the spirit armor and feel its powerful protective energies all around you. Brandish the soul sword and feel its powerful magick flowing through you. You are now one of the most formidable and well-protected magickal beings that have ever existed. *Know this without question.* You can now safely travel in the astral plane and into unexplored realms and dimensions without fear of being harmed. Use your new magickal tools wisely and practice becoming adept at using them. Take care of them and keep them in good order. Be confident, but don't get cocky. Be strong when you need to be, but remain humble in the light of deity and in the presence of the ancient ones.

Final Note

You may want to consider keeping the forge, the pool, and the blacksmith's tools that you created for this working as permanent additions to the shadow realm. The possibilities for their further use are as endless as your imagination, and I am sure that, given some thought, you can come up with some wonderful new magickal items and tools to create with the aid of your shadow spirit. Even if you cannot imagine any further uses for them right now, as you begin adventuring with your *other* I have little doubt that new magickal tools will become desirable and perhaps even necessary as you embark on new quests with your shadow spirit.

You will need to safely store the spirit armor when not in use. During Exercise 4 in your realignment with balance, the Goddess left a large wooden trunk in the shadow realm that contains a few items that will come in very handy in Working Number 2 in the Book of Shadow. Once you have undertaken the second working, the trunk will be empty and will therefore be an ideal place to store the spirit armor. As always, however, that choice is up to you alone to make.

Book of Shadow Working Number 2
The Starship

Objective and Explanation

The goal of the second working is to create a starship that you and your shadow spirit can use to travel anywhere you desire in the astral world or even through space and time. The construction of the starship will be a completely different experience from the creation of the spirit armor, and most of this working will take place at the edge of the eternal temple on the astral plane.

You may recall that, during the construction of the eternal temple, I required you to include a ship dock large enough to accommodate a massive sailing vessel into the eternal temple's architecture. Now is when that little bit of extra work on your part is going to pay off. I am a poet and a hopeless romantic, so once again I'm going to take an old-fashioned approach to the construction of the starship and suggest that your ship have a very old maritime look and feel to it, similar to that of a schooner or a Spanish galleon. This is *your* starship, however, so if you insist on using a more modern or futuristic (*Star Trek*) look, I will not be too disappointed in you.

You may also recall that, during Exercise 4, in your realignment with balance, the Goddess left a large wooden trunk in the shadow realm for you to investigate at a later time. When you look in this trunk, you will find that the Goddess has placed a set of sails that she has sewn for you by using all the symbolic veils that you have lifted while doing the work in this book. If you decide to build an old-fashioned sailing ship as your starship, you can use these sails to collect astral winds as the ship's source of power. If you decide to play Captain Kirk and equip your starship with warp drive, you will use the sails as a symbolic energy source for your warp engines. No matter what your starship looks like—ancient, modern, or futuristic—you will be using the same material to build the starship. This material is, of course, *stardust.*

Items Needed

1. The set of sails the Goddess left for you in the wooden trunk in the shadow realm.

2. Large ropes with which to moor the starship to the dock beside the eternal temple.

3. Any accessory items that you desire that will not be incorporated into the body of the starship itself. These might include any items that you feel would be comforting or beneficial in helping you navigate and sail the astral seas. Do not, however, concern yourself with creating a compass. An advanced magickal compass will be created in Working Number 3 in the Book of Shadow by using a tool that you already possess: the vision stone.

The Process

The design and creation of an astral starship was one of my all-time favorite magickal workings, and I hope that the experience is as fun and exciting for you as it was for me. Just as with the construction of the eternal temple, the design and construction process of the astral starship will allow you the freedom to be very creative and to let your imagination run wild. You should therefore take some time to consider all of your options before you actually build your starship.

As before, use your normal method to attain a state of deep meditation and enter into the shadow realm. Call your shadow spirit and extend an invitation to it to assist you in designing and constructing the starship. If your shadow spirit agrees to assist you, consult with it on the starship's appearance and any special items you may want or need to fully equip the starship. Again, do not concern yourself with creating a compass.

Draw equal parts of energy from the sun and moon pools and combine the energies together while envisioning the mooring ropes and any other items you need to equip your ship. One by one, magickally will the items you need into existence. Don't forget that you can also ask your shadow spirit to do this with or for you.

Once the mooring ropes and any other items have been created, remove the sails the Goddess has sewn for you from the wooden trunk. You and your shadow spirit now need to transport yourselves and the items you have created through the portal of the looking glass and into the eternal temple. You will transport yourself and all of the other items through the portal by using magick and your will alone.

Once you have entered into the eternal temple, you need to move everything to the ship's dock. This is where construction of the starship will take place. After everything is safely at the dock, go over every inch of your mental plans for the starship and make sure that you're satisfied with the design. If you want to make any changes or refinements to your plans, this is the time to do it. If you decide to make changes to the plans, be sure to relay this information to your shadow spirit. Once everything is acceptable, develop a strong, crisp picture of the completed starship in your mind.

Now establish a strong magickal link between you and your shadow spirit. If you're unsure about how to go about this, ask your shadow spirit to show you how. There is no point in having a magickally powerful guide if you don't take the time to learn anything from them. Once a strong link between you and your shadow spirit has been established, open your spirit and mind to the energies of the cosmos. Raise your magickal arms and hands to the heavens. Focus your magickal will and, using magickal energies (in any form you care to envision), begin gathering up stardust.

After you and your shadow spirit have gathered up a sufficient amount of stardust (you will be able to sense when you have enough to do the job), work with your shadow spirit to magickally pull the stardust to you and concentrate the stardust near the edge of the ship's dock inside the protective walls of the twin circles.

Now it's time to perform some very intense magick with your shadow spirit. You are going to combine your magickal skills and powers with those of your shadow spirit and will the starship into creation. Feel the magickal link between you and your shadow spirit growing even stronger. Feel the power of your magick and will combining with the magick and will of your *other*. Feel a powerful wall of magickal energies building all around you. Picture the starship clearly in your mind. Picture every inch and every detail of the starship in your mind. Feel the wall of magickal energy rising up and building into an enormous cone of power. Build the cone of magickal energy until it becomes too strong for you and your shadow spirit to hold back any longer. Release the magickal energy directly into the concentrated stardust and will the starship into creation.

The starship has now been magickally willed into creation. Take a moment to rest and recharge if you need to. When you are ready, secure the starship to the dock using the mooring ropes you created and equip the masts of the starship (or symbolically power up your warp engines) with the sails. Gather up any other items you have created and place them in the starship. Last but not least, give your new starship a name.

Before you do any major exploring with your new starship, I recommend that you do Working Number 3 in the Book of Shadow, in which you will learn how to equip your starship with an advanced magickal compass and guidance system.

Step-by-Step Instructions

1. Attain a state of deep meditation and enter into the shadow realm.

2. Make contact and invite your shadow spirit to assist you in construction of the starship.

3. Consult with your shadow spirit as to the overall look and feel of the starship.

4. Consult with your shadow spirit as to any extra items that may be needed that are not a part of the main body of the starship.

    Note: *You can always create any further items for the starship at a later date if you need to.*

5. Draw equal parts of energy from the sun and moon pools. Combine the energies together while envisioning the mooring ropes and any other items you need to equip the starship. One by one, will the items you need into existence.

    Note: *You can ask your shadow spirit to do this with you or for you.*

6. Remove the sails from the wooden trunk and place them with the other items you have created.

7. Using magick and your will alone, transport yourself, the mooring ropes, the sails, and any other items that you have created through the portal of the looking glass. Enter into the eternal temple and move the sails and the created items to the edge of the ship dock.

8. Before you continue, make sure that the image of the completed starship is crisp and clear in your mind. If there are any changes or refinements that you wish to make, decide on them now and relay the changes to your shadow spirit.

9. Together with your shadow spirit, open yourself to the energies of the cosmos. Raise your magickal arms and hands to the heavens, open your magickal spirit and mind, and begin gathering up stardust.

10. Working in concert with your shadow spirit, pull the gathered stardust inside the protective twin circles and concentrate the stardust near the dock of the eternal temple.

11. Feel the magickal link between you and your shadow spirit. See the completed starship clearly in your mind. Feel a wall of magickal energy building all around you into a cone of power. Build the cone of power until it becomes too strong to hold back. Release the energies directly into the concentrated stardust. Magickally will the starship into creation.

12. Secure the starship to the dock with the mooring ropes.

13. Equip the masts of the starship with the sails the Goddess has sewn for you or use the sails as a symbolic energy source for your engines.

14. Equip the starship with any extra items that you have created.

15. Give your starship a name.

Final Note

You now have a very powerful—and, I am going to guess, very beautiful—vessel to transport you and your shadow spirit to anywhere you wish to travel. You will, of course, need to learn how to pilot your new vessel, so when time allows, you and your shadow spirit should begin a series of practice runs to get a feel for how the starship maneuvers and handles. I advise you to not travel too far into the astral world, however, until you get a good feel for your new starship and learn how to captain her properly.

To do any extensive traveling with the starship you will need to learn how to plot a course. To help get you on your way, Working Number 3 of the Book of Shadow will show you how to plot a course to anywhere you wish to travel in the astral world and even through space and time.

Book of Shadow Working Number 3
The Wormhole

Objective and Explanation

The goal of this final working is to learn how to safely plot a course and navigate your star ship to wherever you wish to travel with your shadow spirit. You will be using the vision stone that is embedded in the shaft of the key to the shadow realm to plot a course and open up what is know as a wormhole.

If you're unfamiliar with exactly what a wormhole is, a wormhole (also know as Einstein-Rosen Bridge) is a hypothetical feature of space that is basically a "short-cut" from one point in the universe to another point in the universe that allows for much faster travel between these two points than it would take to travel between them through normal space. I will try to keep the scientific mumbo-jumbo to a minimum, as the wormholes you'll be using are magickal wormholes, not physical ones. But a little further study into how a wormhole works in theory is necessary so that you can grasp the concept of how you will be using wormholes to travel through space, time, and the astral plane.

First, think of a section of the universe as being a square of cloth laid out on a flat table. To create a wormhole, simply fold the square of cloth in half. This brings the two ends of the fabric that were furthest apart together. Now if you take a pair of scissors and cut a hole in the top piece of cloth near the edge, you are essentially creating a passage through which you can quickly get to the area of cloth directly beneath the hole. This is an oversimplified explanation of what a wormhole is and how it works, but it's decidedly easier to understand than if I were to go into long and dense descriptions of black and white holes in space and complex mathematical calculations. For the sake of this working, therefore, we will consider a wormhole to be a tunnel that provides a quick way of traveling through space, time, and the astral plane.

As I stated at the beginning of this chapter, you will be using your vision stone as a metaphysical compass to plot a course and help you open up your magickal wormholes, so you will want to be sure to bring your key to the shadow realm with you when you go into a state of deep meditation. Also, if you simply glanced over my explanation on how to use your vision stone and did not make a few decent attempts at using it, you will need to go back and reread Chapter 12. You will need quite a bit of practice using your vision stone before you can continue with this working.

Item Needed

The key to the shadow realm with the vision stone attached. You do not need to create any other special items to complete this working.

The Process

With key in hand, begin your migration into a state of deep meditation and enter into the shadow realm. Call out to your shadow spirit and extend the invitation to it to join you in an adventure. Ask your shadow spirit to assist you in opening up a wormhole. If your shadow spirit agrees, pass through the portal of the looking glass, enter into the eternal temple, and move to the dock where your starship is moored. Board the starship with your shadow spirit and make all of the preparations necessary to get the starship underway. You want to be sure that the starship is ready to depart at a moment's notice.

Using the technique you learned in Chapter 12, grasp the key to the shadow realm and focus your concentration on the vision stone imbedded in the shaft of the key. Clearly state your intention—that you will be using the vision stone to plot a course and help in opening up a wormhole—either mentally or aloud. The vision stone is now activated and awaits your further commands.

Now it's time to consult with your shadow spirit and decide where you would like to travel. You can travel to an alternate universe, an alternate dimension, or just about anywhere in time, space, or the astral plane that you can imagine. At this point in time, however, your choices for possible destinations may be limited by your degree of proficiency at using the vision stone. If you haven't done much work with your vision stone and haven't become adept at using it, it will be very difficult for you to travel to alternate dimensions or through time. Practice makes perfect, however, so if your skills with the vision stone are currently limited, there's nothing wrong with starting small and working your way up to bigger and more intense travels and adventures at a later time.

Once you and your shadow spirit have agreed on a destination, you can now use the vision stone as you were taught, to locate and project a three-dimensional holographic image of the destination you have chosen. Once the image appears, take a good look at what is being projected by the vision stone. You want to be reasonably sure that the destination is safe and that you won't have any nasty surprises awaiting upon your arrival. At this point, if you and your shadow spirit are satisfied with your travel plans and you have thoroughly scoped out the lay of the land, you can begin the process of opening up an astral rift that will become the mouth of the wormhole.

To begin opening up the astral rift, use the same technique you used while learning how to switch your magickal battery cables. In the first part of this technique, you switched around your sending and receiving hands and learned how to read energy patterns in a whole new way. To get the process going, you pushed with your normal sending hand on the stream of flow energy that naturally moves towards you, and in so doing you placed a dam in the stream's path and disrupted the energy flow. You will basically be doing the same thing to begin opening up the astral rift, but you will be doing it on a much larger scale. If you're foggy on this technique, I suggest that you go back and reread Chapter 3 before continuing with this working.

Once you're ready, use your normal sending hand to push on the stream-of-flow energy that is naturally moving towards you and begin deflecting the stream. When you can feel a disruption occurring in the stream, work in concert with your shadow spirit to begin opening up an astral rift. Keep your magickal energy focused on the rift and widen it until it grows large enough to safely sail the starship through. You have now successfully opened up the mouth, or point of entry, of the wormhole.

You will now once again need to focus your attention and concentration on the vision stone to cause it to project a second three-dimensional holographic image. This image should be of the point of origin, or the area of space that is currently being occupied by you and your shadow spirit. Once accomplished, the vision stone will be projecting the all-important images of both your point of origin and your point of destination. The vision stone has now effectively become a magickal compass that will navigate the starship back and forth through the wormhole.

Before you can sail into the wormhole, however, you will need to send the image of your destination into the mouth of the wormhole and transport the image to the point of destination. This will create a link between where you are and where you want to go, effectively creating a "fold" in the fabric of the universe.

Once you have successfully caused the vision stone to project an image of your point of origin, mentally command the image of your *point of destination* to move into the mouth of the wormhole. The image of your point of destination should instantly be transported to the other end of the wormhole. Your magickal wormhole is now complete and ready to be navigated. When you are ready, launch the starship and begin adventuring with your *other*.

Step-by-Step Instructions

Attain a state of deep meditation and enter into the shadow realm with your key in hand.

Call to your shadow spirit and extend an invitation to join you on an adventure.

Pass through the portal of the looking glass with your shadow spirit and move through the eternal temple until you have arrived at the dock where your starship is moored.

Board the starship and make any preparations necessary to the starship for departure.

Once the starship is prepared, grasp the key hanging over your heart and focus your concentration on the vision stone embedded in the shaft of the key.

Clearly state your intention to use the vision stone to plot a course and open up a wormhole. You can do this aloud, mentally, or both.

Consult with your shadow spirit as to an interesting or educational place that the two of you might set sail to.

Note: *This can be any place you can imagine in space, time, an alternate universe, or a different dimension or on the astral plane.*

Once you and your shadow spirit have decided on a destination, use the vision stone as you have been taught to project a three-dimensional holographic image of the place that you and your shadow spirit have decided to travel to.

Note: *Be sure to take your time and have a good look around at your point of destination. As well as being interesting, this is also a precautionary measure that will help assure that you don't end up in the middle of a bad or undesirable situation upon arriving at your destination.*

Once you and your shadow spirit are satisfied with your travel plans and you are reasonably sure that the coast will be clear when you arrive on the other end, you can begin the process of creating an astral rift that will open up and become the "mouth" that is the wormhole's point of entry.

To begin creating the rift that will open up the entry point of the wormhole, use the first part of the technique that you learned by switching your magickal battery cables to push on the stream-of-flow energy that naturally moves toward you.

Note: *If you do not remember how to do this, go back and reread Chapter 3 to refresh your memory.*

Once you can feel a disruption in the stream of flow energy, work with your shadow spirit to begin widening the rift to create a hole large enough to safely sail the starship through.

Concentrate on the vision stone and mentally command it to project a second image. This second image should be the point of origin. The point of origin is where you and your shadow spirit currently are.

Mentally command the image of your destination that is being projected by the vision stone (the first image) to move into the mouth of the wormhole.

> **Note:** *Once inside the wormhole, the image will instantly be transported to the point of destination.*

You have now established a direct link between the point of origin and the point of destination, thus completing your magickal wormhole.

Sail the starship into the mouth of the wormhole and begin your adventure.

Final Note

Your adeptness at using the vision stone is paramount to successful traveling using wormholes, so practice using the vision stone as often as you can. If used to its potential, your vision stone can be one of the most powerful magickal tools that you will ever possess.

Epilogue

Pages in Time

Regret. v. To remember with a feeling of loss or sorrow.

—American Heritage Dictionary

I truly hope that you have enjoyed my humble entries into your Book of Shadow and that, if nothing else, the adventures I laid out for you helped to open up a few doors and spark your imagination. The entries were based on some of my own personal adventures and experiences with my shadow spirit, and I hope that they were as delightful and thought-provoking for you as they were for me. The adventures themselves were undoubtedly much more fun and interesting than my explanations of them, but I felt that it was more important to present them to you in an easy-to-understand, step-by-step format than to fill them with flashy visions and million-dollar words. It is now up to you and your shadow spirit to author the rest of the book and complete the story. I feel that it is important for you to keep a record of your adventures and encounters with your shadow spirit, so if it is feasible, you should purchase or put together a book or folder for just this purpose. Beyond being fun to record, journaling your experiences with your *other* can be a very powerful learning tool that you may one day decide to share with a student or a fellow traveler. Even if your Book of Shadow is forever kept a secret, it can still be of great personal value to you from the standpoint of reflection and recollection. When I get out my own Book of Shadow and read some of the earlier entries, I am constantly amazed by how much I had forgotten and how much that didn't seem to make sense at the time now had profound relevance to my current magickal life and situations.

One of the biggest regrets that I have heard expressed time and time again by the magickal community is that there is very little if no written information available to the modern practitioner about the original ancient rites of magick and Witchcraft. It is now up to us to do all we can to make sure that future generations of magicians never have to know that same feeling of regret.

The Conclusion

The Sum of One

$\mathcal{I}$n the Preface, I talked about how each of us has added our own unique face and form to the cauldron of magick. I also talked about looking into the magickal spirit of the Witch. I'm going to guess that your face and form have changed quite a bit since you began doing the work in this book. I'm going to guess that your spirit glows with a brighter light now that you've made contact with your true magickal self. Now that you've walked the path of the shadow spirit, I am also going to guess that your reflection in the mirror looks quite a bit different than it did before you began walking this path.

As you advance on this path, your face and form will continue to change. The light of your magickal spirit will continue to grow brighter and brighter. You have taken your first footsteps into a larger world, and an infinite number of possibilities are now yours for the choosing. Doors along an endless hallway are waiting to be unlocked. You have become much more than you were before you stepped onto this path, and now you must accept who and what you have become. You are now the pioneer, the leader, the teacher, and the guide on the path of the shadow spirit. You must now be an example of how all intelligent magickal life should behave. You must now evolve into a higher, more responsible practitioner of the magickal arts.

True magick is not the "secret world" that you have been taught that it is. True magick is not for the privileged few to know and explore. True magick is within each and every one of us, and each and every person on the face of this planet deserves to see the reflection of his or her true magickal self, even if only for a fleeting moment. Even if he or she denies the reflection and turns away.

Keep your spirit fixed in the world of magick, but do not close your eyes and mind to the mundane. Do not turn your back on the non-magickal world. One day, someone who has never seen magick before may see it in your eyes and wonder. One day, someone may feel the light of your magickal spirit and be enticed to find the magick hidden within him or herself.

The mirror of your true magickal self hangs on the wall before you as an old friend. Look deeply into the eyes of your reflection in the looking glass…and what do you see? Do you see your own face and form in the cauldron of magick? Do you see your spiritual light illuminating the world? Because of you, the cauldron has grown larger. Because of you, what is in the cauldron has changed. Because of you, those who taste of the magick in the cauldron will grow stronger. Because of you, magick will live on.

Chapter 21

The Final Passage

It is widely (and arguably) believed that the ending of a book weighs in as having even more importance than the book's beginning. I am somewhat in agreement with this statement, and I must admit to you that, as I am writing this final chapter, I have quite the smile on my face. Is this because I have a killer ending in store for you? Sorry, but no. I am wearing a big smile because I don't *have* to write a killer ending for this book. I suppose that I could come up with a clever or intriguing way to end this book if I really wanted to, but it really isn't necessary. Life, as they say, is stranger than fiction, and besides the fact that life (or *supernatural* life, to be more specific) has already written the perfect ending for this book for me, the real beauty of it is that for you and me this story has just begun. The path of the shadow spirit still lies before both of us. Its promise of unknowable power and magick stretches out into the shadows before us similar to a black highway at night. The story of the shadow spirit has not ended, and perhaps it never will. But does anything ever *really* end? Do not all endings bring us to new beginnings? And if so, then aren't these new beginnings simply extensions of the supposed endings? If I have tried to teach you one thing above all else, it is that, where magick is concerned, there is no such thing as an ending. There is no such thing where magick is concerned as a room without a door or a no-win situation.

That there is no extent that you cannot reach with your magick if you *truly believe in yourself and you truly believe in your magickal skills.*

No matter how you slice it up, the undeniable fact remains that everything that you and I have ever done has led us both to this very moment in our lives, and I believe that we have both arrived here together for a reason. The full extent of that reason may or may not ever be revealed to us, but here we are nonetheless. And exactly where is here? Sadly, "here" is where I must say my goodbyes to you. I have taken you as far down the path of the shadow spirit as I am able, and now the rest is up to you and your *other.* Our journey together has been a long and good one, and I am comforted by the fact that I have learned as much along the way as you have. I will leave you now with the following statement and, if you care to partake of it, the true and somewhat interesting story about the night before I mailed off the manuscript for this work, my very first book to be considered for publication. Before I go, however, I did promise to give you *all* of the keys to the shadow realm, and I suppose I won't need mine anymore. I left my key in the shadow realm along with a small gift, a token of my esteem. You will know it when you see it.

At long last, the time has come for me to say goodbye, my friend. I will see you again, of that I have little doubt. I thank you for allowing me to accompany you on this part of your journey through the mysteries of the great unknown. I thank you for allowing me the opportunity to share with you my humble teachings. May you never be satisfied with the concept of "impossible," may you always aspire to be more than you are. I leave you now with these words....

We all receive our call to the Craft in our own time and in our own way. Only we can decide if we will answer the call or not. The roads that we must walk are not easy ones. The maps have been all but thrown away. We are writing a religion as we walk. We're cutting a path into tomorrow.

We who are the children of the gods and the goddesses are the teachers and the students of magick and of Witchcraft. Two thousand years from now, what will our kind make of us? How will they view what we taught and how we lived our lives? Here in this time, and in this place, we must create something worth living for. And something worth remembering...

It was the night before I was going to mail the proposal for this book to New Page Books, and I was in the final stages of getting everything for the proposal package organized and in the box. Being the artist that I am, I was excited about the creative proposal package that I had put together, and I was hopeful that it would get me noticed. I was, however, at that time an unknown author, so I wanted everything to be as perfect and professional as it could be. I was confident that I had a well-written manuscript and that I had paid attention to the details, but there was one aspect of my book that was missing and that had me deeply troubled. My shadow spirit was nowhere to be found. My *other* had been unusually silent for a long time now, and as the weeks went by without contact I became very concerned that my shadow spirit was unhappy with me for sharing our story. I was worried that his silence was his way of letting me know that he was not too pleased with me about the prospect of writing a book on this particular subject. Even with my shadow spirits apparent displeasure or lack of interest, I felt pretty good about sharing the secrets of the shadow spirit with the rest of the world. But the one thing that would put me at ease and give my confidence a huge boost was still missing: my shadow spirit's blessing.

Everything was ready to go except for printing out the sample chapters of the manuscript, so I opened a ream of fresh white paper and loaded my printer. My printer had seen better days, and I knew that it was going to take quite a bit of time to print out the manuscript. I set the printer to high resolution, hit the "Enter" button on my keyboard, and watched as the first few sheets of paper slowly came to life with my words. "This is going to take awhile," I thought to myself, so I lit a few candles, called up a little magick, and went out into the living room to watch a movie with my wife. I had gone to check on the printer several times during the movie, and each time my wife told me to "stop being so antsy." She assured me that the print job would get along just fine without me lording over my desk. I reluctantly agreed and rejoined her on the couch to finish watching the film. We were watching *The Lord of the Rings,* as I recall, and about halfway through the film I started getting a very odd feeling. Something was going to happen. Something big. I could feel it with every part of my being. Not wanting to be scolded again by my wife, I sat on the couch fidgeting and fussing until she finally looked me in the eye and asked me what was wrong. "Nothing's wrong," I stated. It wasn't a lie; nothing was really *wrong,* but the feeling of an impending supernatural event was overwhelming.

I sat on the couch waiting for whatever was going to happen to happen, and suddenly, as it has done so many times in the past, the feeling of realization washed over me like a warm bath. I picked the remote control up from the table and paused the movie. My wife looked over at me and asked, "*Now* what?" I held out my hand to her and said, "Come with me…. You've got to see this." I led her into our bedroom, where my computer desk is, and, as we stood in the soft light of the flickering candles and the computer screen, I looked at her and whispered, "Watch." It was at that very moment that the printer spit out the last page of the manuscript, clicked and whirred loudly, and came to a stop. The unmistakable feeling of a powerful unseen presence filled the room. A familiar shadow grew from nowhere and moved along the wall. We looked at the glowing red numbers on the face of the digital clock next to our bed, and a big smile came over both of our faces. It was 12:34.

The blessing of my shadow spirit had come at last….

Bibliography

Hesiod. *The Homeric Hymns and Homerica*, translated by H. G. Evelyn-White. Loeb Classical Library, No. 57. Boston: Harvard University Press, 1981.

Mueller, Erik T. and Michael G. Dyer. *Daydreaming in Humans and Computers. Proceedings of the Ninth International Joint Conference on Artificial Intelligence.* Los Altos, Calif.: University of California, Los Angeles, August 18–24, 1985, 278–280.

Packard, Vance. *The Hidden Persuaders.* New York: Random House, 1957.

Parada, Carlos. *Genealogical Guide to Greek Mythology. Studies in Mediterranean Archaeology, Vol. 107.* Philadelphia, Pa.: Coronet Books, Inc., 1993.

Rosenberg, Donna. *World Mythology: An Anthology of the Great Myths and Epics.* Lincolnwood, Ill.: NTC Publishing Group, 1994.

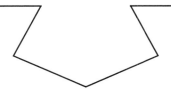

Index

About the Author

L ord Foxglove is one of today's leading pioneers in the fields of advanced Witchcraft and eclectic magick. An ordained priest and co-founder of the Live Oak Experiential Church and the Temple of Aradia, he is a well-known pagan artist and musician and has produced many beautiful works in these areas. He has studied with, and taught for, a wide variety of covens and temples, but for reasons of personal conviction he does not feel that it is appropriate to list his degrees of initiation in his credentials. Foxglove believes that the most important initiation is that of the self, and this is one of the main points he wishes to express to his readers. Lord Foxglove lives in northern Indiana with his wife and children in an enchanted home located on their sanctuary and covenstead, which is known as Nevermore Gardens.

About the Artist

From an early age, Carol Rosinski would pick up a pencil and turn paper and graphite into a living scene with depth and texture. Throughout her high school and college years she tried her hand at a variety of media, including sculpting and jewelry, but since 1990 she has worked almost exclusively with graphite pencil drawing.

Carol has developed a substantial portfolio, which can be viewed at *www.toadhollowstudio.com*. In addition, she has chosen to share her gift of art through a series of self-paced drawing lessons, also available at her Website.

Carol Rosinski lives with her husband and four cats in the wilds of Michigan, where she finds inspiration and enchantment amongst the trees.

About the Audio CD

Included with this book is an audio CD with recordings of the first three exercises, which are guided meditations. The folks at New Page Books were kind enough to honor my request to include the audio CD with this book, but, although there are a total of six guided meditations, only three would fit on a single CD. To keep costs down for you, the reader, and considering the fact that not everyone who does the work in this book will use the audio CD, we decided that it would be best to include only a single CD with the book. However, we also decided that not having the other three guided meditations available to you was a bad idea and that charging extra money for the additional recordings was an even worse idea.

Therefore, New Page Books decided it would be helpful to offer the remaining recordings of the guided meditations via free download from a Website. I agreed that this was a marvelous idea, so that's what we have done. Recordings of the last three guided meditations are available for free download at my official author's Website, *www.lordfoxglove.com,* or at *www.advancingthewitchescraft.com.*

The recordings are in a standard MP3 format and should be able to be played on any modern computer. Feel free to use the recordings in any way you wish, such as transferring them to an MP3 player or burning them onto a CD-R. I will also be offering a bare-bones audio CD for sale on my Website at an equally bare-bones price for any reader who wishes to own the additional recordings but doesn't want to mess around with having to download them.

The background music on the audio CD was written, performed, and recorded by Lord Foxglove and Lady Becca. The voice of the narrator is that of Lord Foxglove.

We truly hope you enjoy the audio CD!